Objective

Food Science and Safety Standards

Prabodh & Sanjeev

2025

JAIN BROTHERS **(New Delhi)**

16/873, East Park Road, Near Dr. N. C. Joshi Hospital,
Karol Bagh, New Delhi -110 005
Phones : 011-23618426, 45097398
E-mail : jain_bros@hotmail.com
Website : www.thejainbrothers.com

AF646495

Published by :

Shri Sunil Kumar Jain
for
Jain Brothers (New Delhi)
16/873, East Park Road, Karol Bagh, New Delhi-110 005
Phones : 011-23618426, 45097398

Branch Office at :

1. **M/s Sunil Book Service**
   Fatima Nagar, Opp. Andhra Bank,
   KAZIPET-506004 (A.P.)
   Ph. : 0870-2459617, Mob. : 9390115435
   E-mail : kpkulshrestha@yahoo.com
2. **M/s Jain Brothers**
   Vidya Vihar, Pilani (Rajasthan)
   Phone : 01596-242144

© All rights reserved. No part of this book should be produced or translated in any form without written permission from publisher and authors.

First edition	: 2015
Reprinted	: Nov., 2015
Second edition	: July, 2017
Reprinted	: Aug., 2018
Reprinted	: April, 2019
Reprinted with corrections	: July, 2019
Reprinted	: Feb,, 2020
Reprinted with corrections	: Oct., 2021
Third revised edition	: April., 2025

***Price :* ₹ 275.00**

ISBN: 978-81-8360-217-4

Laser Typesetting by :

Niyati *Graphics*
754/23, Khajoor Road,
Karol Bagh, New Delhi

Dedicated to

The Professionals from Processed Food Fraternity

सत्यमेव जयते

Dr. AJIT KUMAR, I.A.S. (Retd.)
Ph.D.IIT-D
Vice-Chancellor

NIFTEM
KNOWLEDGE • INNOVATION • OUTREACH

National Institute of Food Technology Entrepreneurship and Management
(A Deemed to be University Under De-Novo Category)
MINISTRY OF FOOD PROCESSING INDUSTRIES, GOVERNMENT OF INDIA

FOREWORD

Today, the world of processed food is expanding and so is the demand for qualified and competent food professionals. There are many educational institutions in India which are contributing towards building these qualified professionals. But, to make them competent they need guidance from all spheres of food technology, may it be the academicians from colleges, the professionals from food industries or the scientists from research centers. Students need to take the responsibility of not only as food technologists/scientists from research centers. Students need to take the responsibility of not only as food technologists/scientists but also as ambassador of quality and food safety. Whether they want to make a career in food industries or want to be the governing and monitoring bodies in government, they need to equip themselves with both the fundamentals of food science and principles of food safety. If they can get a proper guidance from experienced professionals to further build on the foundations laid by the educational institutions, they will surely be confident enough to face any kind of challenges in the real professional world.

The book **"Objective Food Science and Safety Standards"** is one such guide which is the result of perfect amalgamation of experience of food industry and food safety and experience of guiding and coaching the students. Mr. Prabodh Halde has almost two decades of experience in food industry in the field of quality and food safety. Mr. Sanjeev Kumar Sharma, for last eight years is not only involved in research and development in food industry but also involved in guiding and coaching students to crack different competitive entrance exams. These two professionals, envisioned to come out with an overall guide for those who want to make career in the food safety and finally they wrote this book.

I am happy to see the format and content of the book which not only covers the topics prescribed under different syllabuses but also questions are framed to judge the basics of food science and food safety. The conscious efforts are made to judge the width of knowledge rather than the depth of knowledge so that this book can be a quick guide for those who are even from the non-food science background. The quick reference table is so well crafted that it covers major topics and will be a ready to refer section for all the exam aspirants.

I congratulate Probodh and Sanjeev for this wonderful initiative and wish them success.

(Ajit Kumar)

Date: 18.10.2014
Place: Kundli

Plot No. 97, Sector-56, HSIIDC Industrial Estate, Kundli-131028, Distt. Sonepat (Haryana)
Phone: 0130-2281001,4,5 & 6 2219750-51 Fax: 2219749
Email: ajitji@niftem.ac.in Website: www.niftem.ac.in

Preface

Objective Food Science and Safety Standards is an initiative to guide the students and professionals who are aspiring to pursue their career in government jobs like food inspector, food safety officer, and assistant commissioner of FDA etc. Different states conduct such exams at certain interval. The aspirants are either students or working professionals. Students are still in academics and connected to the subject, library, professors and books. But, the working professionals need some guidance and ready study material for their preparation. Syllabus of these entrance exams are different but have many similarities. So, this is our effort to present both Food Science and Food Safety in a comprehensive way so that the exam aspirants can prepare for most of these exams in short time. The questions are framed in such a way that it covers the fundamental principle of food science and food safety standards.

As a complete guide, we have provided syllabus of different entrance exams and more than thousand multiple choice questions. To cover most of the topics mentioned in the syllabus of exams, we have divided questions in 8 chapters. The chapter classification is also done such that the exam aspirants should move forward from basics to science, from science to application and finally into the food safety standards. The most interesting part of this book is the "tables for quick reference." This section at the end of this book covers important aspects of entire food science and technology in tabular form. Exam aspirants can use this table for quick revision of those topics which are frequently asked in the entrance exams. There are four chapters dedicated to food safety and standards. This is the uniqueness of this book. The questions asked in these chapters will teach students entire aspects of food safety and standards and prepare them to face any competitive exams.

This is small endeavor from our side to share our experiences to guide students while preparing for the entrance exam and to contribute in the skill development of professionals from food fraternity. We will be more than happy to take your feedback and learn from your experience and further improve this book.

Wish you a good luck for great success in the exams you are aspiring for.

Prabodh & Sanjeev
15th July 2017

Preface

[illegible]

Acknowledgement

It all started with a telephonic discussion on "can we write a book which will guide exam aspirants to crack entrance exam". The journey from that discussion to this framing of book was not alone. First of all, big thanks to faculty of College of Food Technology, Parbhani where we became food technologist, learned fundamentals there and then further built our professional experience on top of it.

We would like to express our gratitude to few people whose fruitful guidance were crucial in creating this book. Dr Ajit Kumar, Vice Chancellor, NIFTEM through his encouraging words added fuel for driving this project till completion. We are thankful to Mr Ganesh Parlikar, Asst. Commissioner, FDA, Maharashtra, Shri Syed Imran Hashmi, Senior Research Assistant, College of Food Technology Parbhani, Ms. Sonal Nair, AFST for contributing in the chapters.

We are also thankful to AFST(I) team for encouraging us during entire book making process.

We would like to thank Mr Sunil Jain, Jain Brothers Publications and his entire team for showing faith on our work and helping in framing our work into a book. It is their hard work which will finally take the book to the exam aspirants.

We would like to thank to our family members whose patience was appreciable during the process of writing this book. We would like to acknowledge the encouraging words and good wishes from friends and students across India.

Prabodh & Sanjeev

15th July 2017

Contents

Syllabus of Different Entrance Exams

Maharashtra:
Assistant Commissioner (Food) cum Designated officer,
Gr.-A Food & Drugs Administration

Exam pattern:

General Knowledge and Core subject:

- 200 marks,
- 100 questions
- 1 hr

1. Chemistry

i. Periodic Table/Concepts of qualitative Analysis. *ii.* Bonding & structure of organic compound & their nomenclature. *iii.* Mechanism of organic Reactions Alkanel & Cycloalkanes. *iv.* Chemical calculations -Introduction to Molecular Spectroscopy. *v.* Chemical Thermodynamics. *vi.* Industrial organic chemistry. *vii.* Aromatic Hydrocarbon - Haloarenes, Phenols, Ether and Epoxides. *viii.* Source of organic compounds chemical industry.

2. Introduction to Food

i. Carbohydrates, Protein, Fat, Fiber, Vitamins, Minerals, ME etc. *ii.* Effect of food processing on food nutrition. *iii.* Basics of Food Safety. *iv.* Food Contaminants (Microbial, Chemical, Physical). *v.* Food Adulteration (Common adulterants, simple tests for detection ofadulteration). *vi.* Food Additives (Classification, Functional role, Safety issues. *vii.* Food Packaging & labeling (Packaging types, Understanding labeling rules & Regulations, Nutritional labeling, Labeling requirements for pre-packaged foodas per CODEX)

3. Introduction of Food Processing and Technology

i. F & VP, Milk, Meat, Oil, Grain milling, Tea-Coffee, Spices & Condimentsprocessing. *ii.* Food processing techniques (Minimal processing technologies, Photochemicalprocesses, Pulsed electric field, Hurdle technology). *iii.* Food Preservation Techniques (Pickling, Drying, Smoking, Curing, Caning, Bottling, Jellying, Modified atmosphere, Pasteurization etc.)

4. Codex Alimentarius Commission (CODEX)

i. Introduction. *ii.* Standards. Codex of practice, Guidelines and Recommendations. *iii.* Applying Codex Standards. *iv.* Codex India – Role of Codex Contact point, National Codex Contact Point (NCCP). *v.* Core functions of NCCP-India. *vi.* National Codex Committee of India–TOR, Functions, Shadow Committees etc

5. Emerging Issues in Food Processing

i. Organic food. *ii.* Identifying organic foods, Advantages, The Organic Certification Process, Organic food labeling. *iii.* GM food. *iv.* Why are GM food produced. Main issues of concern for Human Health, How areGM Food regulated Internationally, Regulation in India. *v.* Role of WHO to improve evaluation of GM food. *vi.* Benefits & Controversies. *vii.* Irradiated Food. *viii.* How is food Irradiated, Sources of radiation used. *ix.* Potential uses of Food Irradiation. *x.* Labeling of Irradiated Food. *xi.* Freeze dried food. *xii.* Definition, Principle of Freeze-drying, Process. *xiii.* The Benefits of Freeze-Drying. *xiv.* Functional Foods & Nutraceuticals. *xv.* Functional foods from plant sources, Animal sources. *xvi.* Nutraceuticals, Dietary supplements, Regulation. *xvii.* Nano-tech in food processing. *xviii.* What is Nanotechnology, use in food products and processing. *xix.* Food Fortification & Modification.

6. FSSAI Act 2006

i. Food Safety & Standards Act, 2006. *ii.* Major aspects of the act.

7. Advances in Food Safety & Quality

i. Prerequisite Programme – Good Hygienic Practices (GHP). *ii.* Objective, Scope & Use, Key aspects of Hygiene Control Systems etc. *iii.* Prerequisite Programme–Good Manufacturing Practices (GMP). *iv.* What is GMP, GMP in Food Industry etc. *v.* Food Safety Management Systems–HACCP. *vi.* HACCP seven principles, HACCP applications. *vii.* HACCP based SOPs by USDA. *viii.* Food Safety Management Systems–ISO 22000. *ix.* Key elements of ISO 22000. *x.* What does ISO 22000 bring to the HACCP Method. *xi.* Why to use ISO 22000. *xii.* Quality Management Systems–ISO 9001. *xiii.* Introduction, Clauses of ISO 9001: 2000. *xiv.* Documentation structure of ISO 9001:2000. *xv.* Quality Manual, Mandatory Procedures, SOPs, Formats and Records etc.

8.Other related acts

i. B.I.S. *ii.* C.R.P.C/I.P.C. *iii.* EC (Essential Commodities Act). *iv.* Consumer Protection Act

Uttar Pradesh: Food Safety Officer Exam

Exam pattern:

There are two Papers in the written exam consisting of **400 Marks** together.

Paper 1: General Studies – 75 questions, 150 marks, 1 hr

Paper 2: Main Subject – 125 questions, 250 marks, 2 hr

Main Subject:- The paper of main subject will include questions on the following topics:-

Chemical constituents of foods: Desirable and Potentially undesirable food constituents and their importance. Water, carbohydrates, lipids, proteins, vitamins. **Minerals:** Classes, nomenclature, structure and their chemistry. **Enzymes:-** Nomenclature, Classification and specificity of enzymes, enzyme Kinetics, enzymes and their role in modification of foods. Single cell protein (SCP). **Metabolic Pathways:** Carbohydrates, proteins and fats, catabolism and anabolism, Digestion and absorption, Assimilation and Transport of nutrients in human beings.

General characteristics of Microorganism: Classification, morphology, physiology, growth, nutrition and reproduction; Pure culture techniques and maintenance of cultures, control of microorganism. Sources of contamination. Microbiological standards of foods. Food poisoning and food borne infections, Food toxins, food plant sanitation, inspection and control, personnel hygiene, beneficial microorganisms and their utilization in food fermentation. Balance diet, Recommended Dietary Allowances (RDA), Dietary utilization and disturbances, Functions and energy values of foods.

Basal energy metabolism: BV, NPU, BMR, PER calculations, Protein quality as reference protein. Dietary allowances and standards for different age groups, Techniques for assessment of human nutritional status, Causes and preventions of malnutrition. Biochemical, clinical manifestation & preventive measures due to vitamins deficiency.Diseases caused due to food adulteration. Basic knowledge of major Indian crops, their total production, losses in storage, storage of perishable and non-perishable foods.

Storage requirements: Storage environment and its interaction with stored product; temperature and moisture migration. Storage practices (including fumigation and aeration of stored product).

Storage structures for Perishable and non-perishables: Bulk storage structures (bins and silos) Modified and Controlled atmosphere storage systems. Technology of fruits and vegetable products: Juices, pulp, Puree, Paste, Ketchup, Sauce, soup, concentrates and powders, Squashes and cordials.

Beverage: Still and carbonated, James, Jellies and Marmalades. Preserves, candies and crystallized fruits. Processing of oilseeds Pretreatments of oilseeds, oil milling, solvent extraction, impurities present in oils and fats. Vegetable oil refining, hydrogenation, enter esterification, processing of de-oiled cake into protein products, textured protein. Peanut butter, Margarine and Spread. Different quality parameters: Peroxide value, Saponification value, Iodine value, acid value, RM value,

Polanski value, Adulteration and its detection in oils and fats. Rancidity, auto oxidation and anti-oxidants.

Fluid Milk: Physico-chemical properties, Production and collection, cooling and transportation of milk. Clarification and filtration of milk, pasteurized and homogenized milk.: Whole, Standardized, Toned, Double toned, skim and special milks, Test for milk quality and detection of dairy adulterant. Milk products: cream, butter, Butter oil/Ghee, Cheeses, Curd and Yoghurt, Sweet meat, Ice cream. Evaporated and Condensed milk, milk powders. Indian Dairy Products, Manufacture of casein, and Lactose. Causes and prevention of defects in dairy products. Scientific slaughtering, Tendering and curing of meat, Beef Mutton, Pork Sausages and other meat products. Fish and poultry processing. Physical, Chemical Nutritional and Functional characteristics of Egg. Processing of Egg and egg products.

Principle underlying spoilage and preservation of foods: Low and high temperature, drying and dehydration, chemical, salt and sugar, Radiation, HHP, hurdle technology, Parboiling and Milling of paddy, Quality characteristics, Curing and aging of rice, Processed rice products. Wheat milling into flour and semolina, Flour grades and their suitability for baking purposes, Flour quality, Macaroni products, Baked products: Bread, Biscuits and cakes, Breakfast cereals. Dry and Wet milling of corn, Starches and its conversion products, Malting of barely, beer, wine, cider, vinegar, Milling of legume-pulses. Spices: Composition, Structure and characteristics. Preservation and processing of spices, Processing of Tea and coffee, cocoa processing, chocolate and confectionary products. Concept of food packaging, polymeric, glass, metal packaging materials, Aseptic Packaging. Newer trends, Package printing, Packaging Laws and Regulations, Evaluation of food packaging materials and package performance.

Quality Control/Quality Assurance, Legislation for food safety: National and International criteria, sampling, records, risk analysis and management. Microbial contamination, Nutritional imbalance. Pesticide residues, permitted food additives. Relevant Foods laws: PFA, FPO, SWMA, MPO, AgMark, and BIS Standards. Food Safety and Standard Act (FSSA). Testing food for its safety. The HACCP system and food Safety management systems used in Controlling microbiological hazards. Food standards and Specifications, NAB Land ISO certification requirements.

Andhra Pradesh: Food Inspectors in AP Health Laboratories and Food (Health) Administration Sub-Services

Exam pattern

PART-A: Written Exam (Objective Type Questions) 300 marks

Paper 1: General Studies 150 Marks - 150 Questions - 150 Minutes

Paper 2: Subject:- (Common) 150 Marks - 150 Questions - 150 Minutes

PART-B: Oral Test (Interview) 30 Marks

1. Introduction to Nutrition, Health and Public Health. Nutrients – Proteins, carbohydrates, fat, vitamins and minerals – functions, requirements, food sources, and deficiency. Assessment of nutritional status – biochemical, anthropometry, clinical and diet surveys.

2. Food processing, types of processing methods.

3. Food Microbiology, Food spoilage-types, role of microorganisms, factors influencing spoilage, prevention of food spoilage. General methods of food preservation and food processing. Preservation of different types of foods (milk, milk products, meat and meat products). Food born hazards of microbial origin, types, bacterial infections and intoxications. Food Hazards of natural origin – see food toxins, biogenic amines, alkaloids, phenolic compounds, protease inhibiters, phytates.

4. Product development– criteria for selection of raw materials, sensory evaluationobjective evaluation, standardization, labeling.

5. Food Laws and Regulations– Essential commodities Act, Standards of Weights and Measures Act, AGMARK, Bureau of Indian Standards, Export and Quality Control, Prevention of Food Adulteration Act - Food additives and contaminants, food colours flavouring agents and related substances, sweeteners, preservatives, antioxidants, emulsifying and stabilizing agents, antimicrobial substances, -Indirect additives, residues, contaminants and adulterants, pesticide residues, contaminants from packaging material, Metallic contaminants, adulterants Irradiated Food, Genetically Modified Food.

8. Surveys – types. Sampling procedures for conducting surveys and for quality control.

9. Occupational health- health of workers in industries safety measures, occupational diseases.

10. Hygiene and sanitation in food sector– pest control measures, Garbage and Sewage disposal, Water – Sources, purification, Hazards Analysis & Critical Control Point (HACCP), Good Manufacturing Practices (GMP)

11. International Organizations – FAO (Food & Agriculture Organization), WHO (World Health Organization), Codex Alimentaruis, ISO, WTO. National Organizations – ICMR, ICAR, Council for social welfare, Ministry of Health & Family Welfare – delivery Health Services in India. Programmes to eradicate malnutrition and improve the health status of people in India.

TAMILADU FOOD SAFETY OFFICER EXAM SYLLABUS PATTERN

	Marks
Paper-I: General Studies and General Abilities	150
Paper-II: Concerned Subject (Degree Level) Common for all	150
Total	**300**

TNPSC Food Safety Officer Exam Syllabus 2021 Paper I General Studies

Current Affairs

- General Science
- Environmental science
- Economy
- Geography
- Indian Constitution
- Culture, Heritage, Arts and Literature Tamilnadu
- History of Modern India

General Abilities

- Logical Reasoning, Analytical Ability and Data Interpretation
- General english English

TNPSC Food Safety Officer Exam 2021 Paper-II: Concerned Subject

Food Chemistry

Food Microbiology, Hygiene & Sanitation

Food Processing technology

Food Laws and Organizations

Public & Occupational Health and Nutrition

1 Fundamentals of Chemistry

1. Which of the following statements is NOT CORRECT?
   a. Atomic radius of the elements increases as one moves down the first group of the periodic table
   b. Atomic radius of the elements decreases as one moves across from left to right in the 2nd period of the periodic table
   c. Amongst isoelectronic species, smaller the positive charge on the cation, smaller is the ionic radius
   d. Amongst isoelectronic species, greater the negative charge on the anion, larger is the ionic radius

2. Mg^{2+} is isoelectronic with
   a. Ca^{2+} b. Na^{+}
   c. Zn^{2+} d Cu^{2+}

3. n-allene (C_3H_4), the type(s) of hybridisation of the carbon atoms is (are)
   a. *sp* and sp^3 b. *sp* and sp^2
   c. Only sp^2 d. sp^2 and sp^3

4. The hybridization of the central carbon in $CH_3Ca \equiv N$ and the bond angle CCN are
   a. sp^2, 180° b. *sp*, 180°
   c. sp^2, 120° d. sp^3, 109°

5. Which of the following compounds has the MOST deshielded protons?
   a. CH_3Cl b. CH_3I
   c. CH_3Br d. CH_4

6. Which of the following may be separated by ordinary physical methods?
   a. a pair of identical molecules b. a pair of enantiomers
   c. a pair of diastereomers d. a pair of identical atoms

7. Which compound has the highest melting point?

a. decane
b. 2,2,3,3-tetramethylbutane
c. 2,2,3-trimethylpentane
d. 4-methylnonane

8. Which of the following occurs during the initiation stage of a radical mechanism?

a. Nonradicals are formed from radicals.
b. Radicals are formed from other radicals.
c. Radicals are formed from nonradicals.
d. Nonradicals are formed from other nonradicals.

9. A gaseous mixture consists of N_2 and O_2 in a ratio of 1 : 4 by weight. The ratio of number of molecules would be

a. 1 : 7
b. 1 : 8
c. 7 : 8
d. 7 : 32

10. Which of the following statements regarding cathode rays is NOT CORRECT?

a. Charge/mass ratio of these rays is smaller than the positive rays
b. It has negative charge
c. Rays produce mechanical effect
d. Charge/mass ratio is always same irrespective of the gas taken in the discharge tube

11. Out of the following elements, which is smallest in size?

a. C
b. N
c. O
d. S

12. At constant pressure and mass of a gas, if volume V becomes four times, the pressure p will become

a. p/4
b. p/2
c. 2p
d. 4p

13. If metals react with dilute HCl, hydrogen gas is liberated. Which of the following metals is exception to this rule?

a. Cu
b. Fe
c. Mg
d. Zn

14. Which of the following statements about *sp* hybridized carbon is NOT correct?

a. It is divalent.
b. It forms bonds that are linear.
c. It has two p orbitals.
d. It always forms triple bonds to carbon.

15. Atomic number of N is 7. What will be the atomic number of IV member of nitrogen family?

a. 14
b. 22
c. 35
d. 51

16. Which if the following elements is most metallic?

a. As
b. Bi
c. P
d. Sb

17. Which of the following has lowest dipole moment?
a. AsH_3 b. NH_3 c. PH_3 d. SbH_3

18. Which of the following is the hybridization of P in PCl_5?
a. sp^3 b. sp^3d^2 c. sp^3d d. sp^2

19. Which of the following oxides is the most acidic?
a. N_2O_5 b. P_2O_5 c. Sb_2O_5 d. As_2O_5

20. Which of the following oxides is the most basic?
a. N_2O b. P_2O_5 c. As_2O d. Bi_2O_3

21. Which of the following molecules have bond order 3?
a. H_2 b. N_2 c. O_2 d. CO_2

22. Which of the following scientific laws explains the presence of three unpaired electrons in nitrogen atom?
a. Hund's rule b. Pauli's exclusion law
c. Heinsenberg's uncertainty principle d. None of the above

23. Chemically inert nature of nitrogen is due to
a. low density b. absence of bond polarity
c. presence of triple bond d. All of the above

24. Shape of ammonia molecule is
a. tetrahedral b. pyramidal
c. planar triangle d. octahedral

25. The basicity of ortho-phosphoric acid is
a. 1 b. 2 c. 3 d. 4

26. Electron affinity of sulphur is
a. More than O and Se b. Less than both O and Se
c. Equal to O and Se d. Less than O but more than Se

27. What is the type of hybridisation in water molecule?
a. sp b. sp^2 c. sp^3 d. sp^3d

28. H_2S reacts with O_2 to form
a. $H_2O + S$ b. $H_2O + SO_2$
c. $H_2O_2 + SO_2$ d. $H_2SO_4 + H_2SO_3$

29. Which of the following halogens are present in solid state?
a. Br_2 b. Cl_2 c. F_2 d. I_2

30. Which of the following is NOT a halogen?
a. Br_2 b. O_2 c. Cl_2 d. F_2

31. Nuclear fusion produces
    a. Argon b. Deuterium
    c. Helium d. Krypton

32. The d-block elements in periodic table are called
    a. Halogens b. Inert elements
    c. Transition elements d. Radioactive elements

33. Which of the following is a transition element?
    a. Cl b. Na
    c. K d. Pt

34. Transition metals are mostly
    a. Diamagnetic b. Paramagnetic
    c. Nonmagnetic d. Super magnetic

35. Which of the following elements belong to actinoid series?
    a. Sodium b. Helium
    c. Thorium d. Uranium

36. Ligands are
    a. neutral molecules only b. negative ions only
    c. positive ions only d. either negative or positive or neutral

37. Oxidation state of oxygen in $O_2[PtF_6]$ is
    a. −1/2 b. 0
    c. +1/2 d. +1

38. Optical isomers have
    a. same physical properties
    b. same molecular formula
    c. difference in action towards plane polarized light
    d. All of the above

39. What is the IUPAC name of $CH_3CH(Cl)CH(Br)CH_3$?
    a. 2-Chloro-3-bromobutane b. 3-Bromo-3-chlorobutane
    c. 2-Bromo-3-chlorobutane d. 2-Bromo-2-chlorobutane

40. Which of the following is secondary allylic halide?
    a. 3-Bromo-2-methylbut-1-ene b. 2-Bromo-2-methylbut-1-ene
    c. 4-Bromo-2-methylbut-1-ene d. 4-Bromo-3-methylbut-1-ene

41. Toluene and Cl_2 will react in presence of $FeCl_3$ produce
    a. m-chlorotoluene b. Benzoyl chloride
    c. Benzyl chloride d. o-and-p-chlorotoluene

42. Ethyl bromide can be obtained by reaction of
a. Ethyl alcohol and hydrogen bromide
b. Ethyl alcohol and bromine
c. Ethylene and hydrogen bromide
d. All of the above

43. Sandmeyer's reaction involves
a. potassium salt
b. common salt
c. diazonium salt
d. None of the above

44. In Sandmeyer's reaction, N_2 of diazonium salt is replaced by
a. Oxygen
b. Halides
c. $-CH_3$
d. All of the above

45. Which of the following statements is/are CORRECT?
a. Halogenation of alkanes is an oxidative process
b. Darzen process is a method for preparing alkyl halide
c. Fluorobenzene cannot be prepared by direct halogenation of benzene
d. All of the above

46. Which of the following is NOT present in Grignard reagent?
a. Methyl group
b. Halogen
c. Carboxylic group
d. Magnesium

47. Which of the following compounds will be formed after reaction between methyl chloride and silver acetate?
a. Methyl acetate
b. Acetyl chloride
c. Acetic acid
d. None of the above

48. A mixture of equal parts of (+) and (–) enantiomers is called
a. homogenous mixture
b. optical mixture
c. racemic mixture
d. alkyl mixture

49. SN^1 reactions occur through the intermediate formation of
a. carbocations
b. free radicals
c. carboanions
d. All of the above

50. In nucleophilic aliphatic substitution reaction, the nucleophiles are
a. acids
b. bases
c. salts
d. All of the above

51. Racemic mixture is formed by mixing two
a. chiral compounds
b. aromatic compounds
c. enantiomers with chiral compounds
d. All of the above

52. *d* and *l* enantiomers can be separated from a racemic mixture by
a. hydrogenation
b. centrifugation
c. inversion
d. resolution

53. How many possible number of optical isomers can be formed from a compound with 2 asymmetric carbon atoms?
a. 2
b. 4
c. 8
d. 16

54. Which of the following has the weakest carbon halogen bond?
a. Bromobenzene
b. Benzyl chloride
c. Benzyl bromide
d. Vinyl bromide

55. Which of the following statements is/are correct?
a. SN^2 reactions involves two steps
b. Reaction of NaOH with dinitrofluorobenenzene is a nucleophilic aromatic substitution reaction
c. Rotation of plane polarized light is measured by refractometer
d. All of the above

56. Reaction between chlorobenzene and solid NaOH gives
a. Benzene
b. Benzoic acid
c. Phenol
d. Benzene chloride

57. Which of the following is produced by Fitting reaction?
a. Diphenyl
b. Tolunene
c. Acetic acid
d. Benzene

58. Chlorination of chlorobenzene in presence of Fe gives
a. o-Dichlorobenzene
b. m-Dichlorobenzene
c. p-Dichlorobenzene
d. o- and p-Dichlorobenzene

59. Phosgene is
a. Carbonyl chloride
b. Carbon tetrachloride
c. Ammonium chloride
d. None of the above

60. Which of the following causes depletion of ozone layer?
a. Freon
b. Oxygen
c. Neon
d. All of the above

61. Which of the following is used in fire extinguishers?
a. Methane
b. $CHCl_3$
c. Carbon tetrachloride
d. All of the above

62. Which of the following is used as anaesthetic?
a. CH_4
b. CCl_4
c. $CHCl_3$
d. All of the above

63. Which of the following is phenol?

a. CH_3OH
b. C_2H_5OH
c. C_6H_5OH
d. All of the above

64. Which of the following is functional isomer of alcohol?

a. Aldehyde
b. Ether
c. Ketone
d. Ester

65. Which of the following is a dihydric alcohol?

a. allyl alcohol
b. glycerine
c. glycerol
d. propylene glycol

66. Which of the following is seen in alcohol?

a. chair isomerism
b. position isomerism
c. functional isomerism
d. All of the above

67. An alcohol with two "–OH" groups are called

a. diols
b. sorbitol
c. aldehyde
d. None of the above

68. Which of the following compounds is obtained by hydrolysis of fats and oils?

a. Ethanol
b. Phenol
c. Glycerol
d. Methanol

69. Ethanol is obtained by the reduction of

a. acetaldehyde
b. acetic acid
c. ethylene
d. All of the above

70. Which of the following organic compounds is soluble in water?

a. $CHCl_3$
b. C_2H_5OH
c. C_6H_6
d. All of the above

71. With the increase in molecular mass of alcohol, its solubility

a. increases
b. decreases
c. remains same
d. depends on the final product formed

72. An aqueous solution of ethyl alcohol is

a. acidic
b. basic
c. neutral
d. amphoteric

73. Alcohols are miscible in water because of following

a. acidic nature of alcohol
b. basic nature of alcohol
c. presence of methyl group
d. hydrogen bonding

74. Esters are formed after reaction between acid and

a. alcohol
b. aldehyde
c. amine
d. water

75. In esterification reaction, concentrated H_2SO_4 acts as
a. dehydrating agent b. catalyst
c. Both a and b d. oxidizing agent

76. The product formed when primary alcohol undergoes catalytic dehydrogenation is
a. aldehyde b. ketone
c. alkene d. acid

77. Acidic nature of ethyl alcohol is seen when it reacts with
a. Acetic acid b. Water
c. Ester d. Alcohol

78. Which of the following explains the formation of 2-butene as on dehydration of 2-butanol?
a. Wurtz reaction b. Markownifkoff's rule
c. Peroxide effect d. Saytzeff rule

79. Lucas reagent is a mixture of
a. concentrated H_2SO_4 and anhydrous $ZnCl_2$
b. concentrated HCl and anhydrous $ZnCl_2$
c. concentrated HNO_3 and anhydrous $ZnCl_2$
d. concentrated HCl and anhydrous NaCl

80. Which of the following statements is/are CORRECT?
a. Ethanol can undergo dehydration reaction
b. Alkenes are formed from alcohols by intramolecular dehydration
c. 2-propanol is oxidized to form ethyl methyl ketone
d. All of the above

81. Rectified spirit can be dried with
a. Concentrated H_2SO_4 b. CaO
c. Anhydrous $CaCl_2$ d. All of the above

82. Phenols are hydroxyl compounds of
a. Methane b. Ethane
c. Benzene d. Propene

83. Which of the following statements regarding phenol is/are CORRECT?
a. It is a base stronger than NH_3 b. It is a base weaker than NH_3
c. It is an acid stronger than carboxylic d. It is an acid weaker than carboxylic

84. Acid nature of phenol is due to
a. Phenolic group b. Benzene ring
c. Resonance stabilization of phenoxide ion d. None of the above

85. Commercial production of phenols involves

a. Ethylene chloride
b. $CHCl_3$
c. $C_6H_5SO_3Na$
d. All of the above

86. The Fridel-Craft reaction of benzene is used to prepare

a. Phenol
b. Acetylene
c. Cumene
d. Vinegar

87. The paracetamol is prepared from

a. diethyl amine
b. ethyl alcohol
c. phenol
d. choloroform

88. According to Lewis concept of acid and base, ethers are

a. acid
b. base
c. neutral
d. amphoteric

89. C_2H_5OH and CH_3OCH_3 are

a. position isomers
b. optical isomers
c. functional isomers
d. None of the above

90. Which of the following products is formed when methyl iodide is heated with sodium methoxide?

a. diethyl ether
b. methyl alcohol
c. dimethyl ether
d. methyl ethyl ether

91. Which of the following methods is used for the preparation of ethers?

a. Wurtz synthesis
b. Hofmann's synthesis
c. Kolbe's synthesis
d. Williamson's reaction

92. Which of the following statements regarding ethers is/are CORRECT?

a. Ethers react with active metals
b. Ethers behave as oxidizing or reducing agents
c. Ethers do not react with strong base
d. All of the above

93. Which of the following statements is/are CORRECT?

a. A ketone groups is present in between carbon atoms
b. Formaldehyde does not have alpha hydrogen atom
c. Aldehydes and ketones are functional isomers
d. All of the above

94. $(CH_3)_2C{=}O$ is called

a. acetone
b. acrolein
c. dimethyl ketone
d. propanone

95. Reaction between methyl magnesium chloride and acetonitrile forms

a. acetone
b. ethanol
c. acetylene
d. methanol

96. Oxidation of which of the following compounds will form ketone?

a. 1° alcohol
b. 2° alcohol
c. 3° alcohol
d. methyl alcohol

97. Which of the following reagents reacts with both acetone and acetaldehyde?

a. Grignard reagent
b. Schiff's reagent
c. Fehling's solution
d. Tollen's reagent

98. Cannizzaro reaction involves

a. Oxidation
b. Reduction
c. Both oxidation and reduction
d. None of the above

99. In aldol condensation reaction, the intermediate ion formed is

a. carbonium ion
b. enolate ion
c. cation
d. All of the above

100. The reaction between $Ba(OH)_2$ and acetone to give diacetone alcohols is called

a. Cannizzaro's reaction
b. Clemmensen's reaction
c. Hoffmann's reaction
d. Aldol condensation

101. What is the molecular formula of urotropine?

a. $C_6H_{12}N_4$
b. $C_6H_{12}Cl_4$
c. $C_6H_{12}Cl_2I_2$
d. $C_6H_{12}Cl_3I$

102. Propanal and propanone are

a. Optical isomers
b. Enantiomets
c. Functional isomers
d. None of the above

103. Acetaldehyde reacts with hydroxyl amine to give

a. alkane
b. aldoxime
c. alcohol
d. ether

104. What is the hydrolysis product of alkyl cyanides?

a. Primary amines
b. Carboxylic acids
c. Aldehydes
d. Acid amides

105. Which of the following chemicals can be used to distinguish formic acid and acetic acid?

a. Fehling's reagent
b. Ammonium bicarbonate
c. Ammonical $AgNO_3$
d. Cuprous sulphate

106. Trifluoroperoxyacetic acid and .... is used to prepare nitroalkane.

a. Oxime
b. Amine
c. Aldehyde
d. Halide

107. Which of the following is 2° amine?

a. Aniline
b. Dimethyl amine
c. Isobutyl amine
d. Sec-butyl amine

108. Which of the following compounds will be formed when methyl cyanide is reduced with sodium and alcohol?

a. Methyl amine
b. Ethyl amine
c. Methyl amino acid
d. Ethyl amino acid

109. Chloroform is used to test the presence of

a. 1° amine
b. 2° amine
c. 3° amine
d. All of the above

110. Crowding effect of alkyl group reduces basic character of

a. 1° amine
b. 2° amine
c. 3° amine
d. All of the above

111. What is the colour of nitroso compound?

a. Blue
b. Yellow
c. Red
d. Violet

112. Which of the following compounds will be obtained after reduction of acetoxime followed by acetylation?

a. Ethyl amine
b. Isopropyl amine
c. Diacetyl isopropyl amine
d. Methyl amine

113. Which of the following is used as catalysts in Gattermann reaction?

a. Ni
b. $AlCl_3$
c. Hg
d. Na

114. Which of the following is natural occurring polymer?

a. PVC
b. Polyethylene
c. Starch
d. Amino acid

115. Which of the following polymer is obtained by the condensation of hexamethylene diamine and adipic acid?

a. Dacron
b. Nylon 66
c. Rayon
d. Polystyrene

116. Which of the following is used for making magnetic recording tape?

a. Nylon 6
b. Terylene
c. Polystyrene
d. All of the above

117. What is the meaning of trans-esterification?
a. preparation of ester from ester
b. preparation of ester from acid and alcohol
c. preparation of ester from trans fat
d. preparation of ester from aldehydes

118. Which of the following statement is correct?
a. Nylon is polystyrene
b. Nylon is polycarbide
c. Nylon is polyamide
d. Nylon is polyethylene

119. Which of the following polymers is used to make non-stick cookware?
a. PVC
b. Polystyrene
c. Polyethylene
d. Poly tetrafluoro ethylene (PTFE)

120. Terywool clothes are made up of
a. Cotton + wool
b. Rayon + wool
c. PVC + wool
d. Dacron + wool

121. What is the unit of heat?
a. °calorie
b. °Joule
c. degree
d. calorie

122. Which of the following statements regarding thermodynamics is/are CORRECT?
a. It deals with inter-conversion of different forms of energy
b. Conversion of all forms of energy into heat energy
c. Conversion of heat into work
d. All of the above

123. Which of the following statements regarding irreversible process is/are CORRECT?
a. It is spontaneous process
b. it is ideal process
c. It is theoretical process
d. All of the above

124. Which of the following is an intensive property?
a. enthalpy
b. mass
c. temperature
d. All of the above

125. After adiabatic expansion of gas, it gets cooled due to
a. decrease in temperature
b. energy spent in doing work
c. decrease in velocity
d. loss in kinetic energy

126. Under which of the following conditions work is a state function?
a. Adiabatic process
b. Isothermal process
c. Constant pressure
d. All of the above

127. Which of the following equation explains isothermal expansion of an ideal gas?
a. $\Delta P = 0$
b. $\Delta V = 0$
c. $\Delta U = 0$
d. $\Delta W = 0$

128. In a process where there is no transfer of heat is called ....

a. adiabatic
b. isothermal
c. isotropic
d. None of the above

129. Which of the following statements regarding an isothermal reversible expansion of an ideal gas?

a. Enthalpy decreases
b. Enthalpy increases
c. Enthalpy remains same
d. Enthalpy term is not at all related to isothermal reversible expansion

130. Which of the following statements is/are correct?

a. Maximum work is obtained when gas expands in vacuum
b. In isobaric process pressure of a system remains same
c. The temperature of the system decreases in an adiabatic compression
d. All of the above

131. The work done during expansion in vacuum is zero because there is

a. $P = 0$
b. $\Delta V = 0$
c. $\Delta U = 0$
d. $\Delta T = 0$

132. Which of the following statements is/are correct for 1st law of thermodynamics?

a. $\Delta U = q + w$
b. conservation of momentum
c. conservation of light
d. All of the above

133. The energy stored in a substance is called its

a. heat energy
b. kinetic energy
c. potential energy
d. internal energy

134. Which of the following statements is/are correct for an isothermal reversible cyclic process

a. the total change in internal energy is always positive
b. the total change in internal energy is always negative
c. the total change in internal energy is always zero
d. any of the above depending on the process

135. Which of the following energy is NOT part of internal energy?

a. Translational energy
b. Vibrational energy
c. Intramolecular energy
d. None of the above

136. Enthalpy of an element at its natural state and at 298 K is

a. positive
b. negative
c. zero
d. any of the above depending on the element

137. Thermochemistry is the study of relationship between heat energy and ....

a. chemical energy
b. kinetic energy
c. potential energy
d. activation energy

138. What will be ΔH in case of thermal decomposition of energy?
a. negative
b. positive
c. zero
d. depends on the substance which gets decomposed

139. Which of the following name is not associated with thermodynamics?
a. Kelvin
b. Ohm
c. Claussius
d. Kirchoff

140. What will be ΔH for combustion of a substance?
a. negative
b. positive
c. zero
d. depending on the substance which undergoes combustion

141. Heat of transition is the heat evolved or absorbed when a substance is converted from
a. solid to liquid
b. solid to vapour
c. liquid to vapour
d. one allotropic form to another allotropic form

142. The molar heat capacities of gases at constant pressure and at constant volume are
a. different and unrelated to each other
b. different and related to each other
c. same
d. same or different depending on the gases

143. Which of the following statements is/are correct?
a. Heat of reaction depends on temperature
b. Kirchoff's equation deals with effect of temperature on heats of reaction.
c. Vibrational energy is not possessed by monoatomic molecule
d. All of the above

144. According to Hess's Law
a. H = U + PV
b. Heat can neither be created nor be destroyed, but can only be converted from one form to another
c. The enthalpy change of a given chemical reaction is the same even that occurs in one or several steps
d. Energy can be absorbed or released in a reaction but the total energy of the reacting system and its surrounding remains constant

145. Which of the following law states that the enthalpy change is constant irrespective of steps involved?
a. Hook's law
b. Avogadro's law
c. Hess's law
d. Kirchoff's law

146. Which of the following parameters effect disorder of any substance?
a. mass
b. molecular structure
c. temperature and pressure
d. All of the above

147. At –273 °C the entropy of a perfectly crystalline substance is
a. negative
b. positive
c. zero
d. dependent on the substance

148. The concept of entropy is introduced in which of the following law of thermodynamics?
a. 0th law
b. 1st law
c. 2nd law
d. 3rd law

149. Which of the following statements is/are correct?
a. For a chemical reaction to occur, "G should be zero
b. Entropy is the measure of order in a system
c. The total energy of an isolated system is constant
d. All of the above

150. A reaction will complete if
a. ΔS is positive
b. ΔS is negative
c. ΔS is zero
d. A reaction does not depend on temperature

151. Hess's law is an application of
a. 0th law of thermodynamics
b. 1st law of thermodynamics
c. 2nd law of thermodynamics
d. 3rd law of thermodynamics

152. Oxidation number of S in $S_2O_2^{-2}$ is
a. – 2
b. + 2
c. + 6
d. – 6

153. Which of the following elements have highest electrical conductivity?
a. Gold
b. Iron
c. Copper
d. Silver

154. Pure water has zero conductivity because it is
a. neutral
b. almost non-ionized
c. liquid
d. colourless

155. Which of the following reactions takes place at cathode?
a. hydrolysis
b. neutralization
c. oxidation
d. reduction

156. Which of the following reasons explains the flow of electricity through an electrolyte?
a. movement of atoms
b. movement of solvent
c. movement of ions
d. movement of protons

157. During electroplating, the material to be electroplated should be made as

a. cathode
b. electrolyte
c. anode
d. solvent

158. The dimensions of cell constant are

a. cm
b. $Å^{-1}$
c. m
d. km

159. Electrolytic conduction is due to migration of

a. protons
b. ions
c. electrons
d. atoms

160. Which of the following explains the decrease in conductance of a concentrated solution due to increase in frictional resistance?

a. Kisenhuger effect
b. Arrhenius effect
c. Electrophoretic effect
d. None of the above

161. The Kohlrausch's law is connected with

a. migration of electrons from radioactive metal
b. formation of higher molecules during polymerization
c. conductance of ions at infinite dilution
d. decrease in entropy during freezing

162. Specific conductance of a solution is

a. the conductance of one cm of a solution
b. the conductance of one cm square of a solution
c. the conductance of one cm cube of a solution
d. the resistance of one cm of a solution

163. One Faraday is equal to

a. 9.65×10^2 coulombs
b. 9.65×10^4 coulombs
c. 9.65×10^6 coulombs
d. 9.65×10^8 coulombs

164. One mole of electrons is same as

a. Coulomb
b. Faraday
c. Ampere
d. Celsius

165. Which of the following will decompose if an electric current is passed through them?

a. Water
b. Starch
c. Ethyl alcohol
d. Silver nitrate

166. The theory of electrolytic dissociation was given by

a. Faraday
b. Dalton
c. Ostwald
d. Arrhenius

167. A cell in which electric current is produced by an oxidation-reduction reaction is called a/an ....

a. reversible cell
b. voltaic cell
c. adiabatic cell
d. standard cell

168. A voltaic cell stops working after some time, because the electrode potential of both the electrodes

a. increases
b. decrease
c. becomes equal
d. voltaic cell never stops working

169. If a salt bridge is removed between the two half cells, the voltage

a. does not change
b. increase rapidly
c. increase gradually
d. drops to zero

170. Daniel cell is

a. reversible voltaic cell
b. isothermic voltaic cell
c. irreversible voltaic cell
d. isobaric voltaic cell

171. Which of the following statements regarding salt bridge is/are correct?

a. It connects two half cells
b. It maintains the electrical neutrality of the two half cells
c. When salt bridge is removed between two half cells, the voltage drops to zero
d. All of the above

172. Which of the following terms is the tendency of a metal to lose electrons and pass into solution as cations?

a. solvent pressure
b. solute pressure
c. solution pressure
d. atmospheric pressure

173. The oxidation potential of an electrode is their tendency to

a. loose electrons
b. get oxidized
c. both a and b
d. get vaporized

174. According to Nernst theory, potential develop at an electrode is due to

a. only electronation
b. only de-electronation
c. both electronation and de-electronation
d. None of the above

175. Which of the following parameters affects emf of the cell?

a. Material of electrode
b. Temperature
c. Concentration of ions in solution
d. All of the above

176. Which of the following parameters affects the activation energy of any chemical reaction?

a. nature of reacting species
b. temperature
c. collision frequency
d. All of the above

177. Catalyst in a reaction helps in decreasing

a. heat of reaction b. activation energy

c. entropy d. All of the above

178. Which of the following is an example of a biological catalyst?

a. Starch b. Proline

c. Omega 3 fatty acid d. Peroxidase

179. Number of moles of a substance present in one liter volume is known as

a. molar concentration b. activity

c. active mass d. molality

180. The number of molecule or atoms whose concentration changes during a chemical change is its

a. order of reaction b. change in reaction

c. molecularity d. None of the above

181. Order of reaction can be

a. fractional b. zero

c. Both a and b d. negative

182. The minimum energy required for molecules to enter into chemical reaction is called

a. kinetic energy b. potential energy

c. sound energy d. activation energy

183. If in a reaction half-life period is directly proportional to the initial concentration of the reaction, the order of reaction is

a. 0 b. 1

c. 2 d. 3

184. The influence of temperature on reaction rate is predicted by

a. Kirchoff's equation b. Heiss equation

c. Arrhenius equation d. Hoffmann's equation

185. The order of reaction can be deduced from

a. Chemical equation b. Experiment

c. Thermodynamic equation d. It can never be deduced

186. Which of the following is the cause of chemical reaction?

a. effective evaporation b. effective diffusion

c. effective ionization d. effective collision

187. Which of the following statement best describe a collision frequency?
a. the number of collision per second per unit volume of the reaction mixture
b. the number of collision per minute per unit volume of the reaction mixture
c. the number of collision per hour per unit volume of the reaction mixture
d. the number of molecules formed per unit volume of the reaction mixture

188. Brass consists of
a. Mercury
b. Copper
c. Bismuth
d. All of the above

189. Bronze is made up of
a. Cu, Al, Ni
b. Cu, Al, Na
c. Cu, Zn, Sn
d. Cu, Al, Fe

190. Which of the following is used in dry cell?
a. Fe
b. Zn
c. Cu
d. All of the above

191. For sulphite ore which of the following method is used
a. Dry process
b. Froth floatation process
c. Sulphite process
d. None of the above

192. During metallurgy of iron, the material obtained from the bottom of blast furnance is
a. slag
b. cast iron
c. pig iron
d. steel

193. Which of the following statements regarding calcination process is correct?
a. It is heating of ore in blast furnace
b. It is heating of ore in open air
c. It is heating of ore in absence of air
d. It is heating of ore in presence of calcium

194. Which of the following is chemical formula of Bauxite?
a. Al_2O_3
b. $Al_2O_3.H_2O$
c. $Al_2O_3.2H_2O$
d. $Al_2O_3.3H_2O$

195. Which of the following alloy is used for making permanent magnet?
a. Alnico
b. Stainless steel
c. Bronze
d. Magnalium

196. The white pigment used under the name of pearl white is
a. BiO_2
b. BiOCl
c. $BiCl_2$
d. All of the above

197. Which of the following acid is present in lemon?
    a. Lactic acid
    b. Acetic acid
    c. Citric acid
    d. All of the above
198. What is the IUPAC name for valeric acid?
    a. Pentanoic acid
    b. Butyric acid
    c. Propionic acid
    d. Methanoic acid
199. Which of the following reactions will be given by only 1° amines?
    a. Acetylation
    b. Alkylation
    c. Reaction with HNO_2
    d. carbyl amine test
200. How many coordinate bonds are present in quaternary ammonium salt?
    a. 1
    b. 2
    c. 3
    d. 4

2 Fundamentals of Food Science and Nutrition

1. Simplest form of carbohydrate is

   a. Carbon b. Starch

   c. Monosaccharides d. Cane sugar

2. In disaccharides two monosaccharides are joined together by

   a. Glucosidic bond b. Glyscosidic bond

   c. Disulphide bond d. Hydrogen bond

3. In a sucrose molecule

   a. Two glucose molecules are present

   b. Two fructose molecules are present

   c. One glucose and two fructose molecules are present

   d. None of the above

4. Strecker degradation can be seen during

   a. Protein biosynthesis b. Maillard reaction

   c. Nucleotide metabolism d. None of the above

5. Sucrose molecule is a disaccharide in which two monosaccharide are joined together by

   a. α-1,4 glycosidic bond b. β-1,4 glycosidic bond

   c. α-1,2 glycosidic bond d. β-1,2 glycosidic bond

6. Which of the following statement is/are NOT CORRECT?

   a. Sucrose does not undergo Mutarotation

   b. Sucrose is reducing sugar

   c. Sucrose does not react with phenylhydrazine to form osazone

   d. All of the above.

7. Change in the optical activity of the racemic mixture is called

a. Reversion
b. Mutarotation
c. Inversion
d. Isomerization

8. What is phytin?

a. Phosphorus associated with mannitol
b. Phosphoric acid of sorbitol
c. Calcium salt of phytic acid
d. A polymer of phytic acid

9. Which vitamin is the example of sugar acids?

a. Vitamin A
b. Vitamin C
c. Vitamin D
d. Vitamin E

10. Sugar capable of reducing ———— are called reducing agents

a. Cu^{2+}
b. Ag^{+}
c. Ferricyanide
d. All of the above

11. In which of the following lipo-proteins, the major portion is cholesterol?

a. VLDL
b. LDL
c. HDL
d. All of the above

12. Honey contains which of the following sugar

a. Levulose
b. Fructose
c. Both a and b
d. None of the above

13. Which of the following is liquefying enzyme?

a. α- amylase
b. β- amylase
c. both a and b
d. none

14. Lactose is

a. Monosaccharide
b. Disaccharide
c. Oligosaccharide
d. Polysaccharide

15. Which of the following is/ are storage polysaccharide?

a. Dextran
b. Fructan
c. Starch
d. All of the above

16. Which of the following is/ are the structural polysaccharide?

a. Chitin
b. Cellulose
c. Lignin
d. All of the above

17. Number of carbon atom in stearic acid is

a. 12
b. 16
c. 18
d. 20

18. Which of the following is polyunsaturated fatty acid?
a. Stearic acid
b. Linolenic acid
c. Lauric acid
d. Oleic acid

19. The parent compound of the phosphoglycerides is
a. Phosphatidic acid
b. Phosphoric acid
c. Glycerol
d. Glyceric acid

20. Kind of lipid that is most abundant in the cell membrane is
a. Cholestrol
b. Glycolipid
c. Phospholipids
d. Waxes

21. α linolenic acid [ALA] is
a. ω – 2 fatty acid
b. ω – 3 fatty acid
c. ω – 4 fatty acid
d. ω – 6 fatty acid

22. EPA is
a. Eicosapentaenoic acid
b. Eicosapentanoic acid
c. Ethylpentaenoic acid
d. Ethylpentanoic acid

23. EPA is
a. ω – 2 fatty acid
b. ω – 3 fatty acid
c. ω – 4 fatty acid
d. ω – 6 fatty acid

24. DHA is
a. ω – 2 fatty acid
b. ω – 3 fatty acid
c. ω – 4 fatty acid
d. ω – 6 fatty acid

25. DHA is
a. Docosahexaenoic acid
b. Docosahexanoic acid
c. Docosaheptaenoic acid
d. Docosaheptanoic acid

26. Arachidonic acid contains ——— carbon atom
a. 16
b. 18
c. 20
d. 22

27. Which of the following essential fatty acid can be synthesized in body?
a. Linoleic acid
b. Linolenic acid
c. Arachidonic acid
d. None of the above

28. Essential fatty acid serve as precursors of
a. Vitamin C
b. Prostaglandin
c. Niacin
d. Retinol

29. Triglycerides, which are liquid at room temperature are often referred as

a. Fat | b. Oil
c. Steroids | d. Waxes

30. Castor seed is rich in

a. Ricinoleic acid | b. Oleic acid
c. Linolenic acid | d. Linoleic acid

31. The parent compound in phophoglycerides is

a. Phosphoric acid | b. Phosphoric ester of glycerol
c. Phosphoric ester of Fatty acid | d. Glycerol

32. The nitrogen containing compound in cephalin is

a. Guanine | b. Ethanolamine
c. Choline | d. Ammonium acetate

33. Ovomucoid is the protein found in

a. Fruits | b. Vegetables
c. Milk | d. Egg

34. The nitrogen containing compound in lecithin is

a. Guanine | b. Ethanolamine
c. Choline | d. Ammonium acetate

35. Iodine value measures

a. Degree of unsaturation | b. Degree of saturation
c. Amount of carbon present | d. Number of Iodine present

36. Which of the following gives the value of free fatty acids present in fat?

a. Iodine value | b. Acid value
c. Saponification value | d. Peroxide value

37. Which of the following is said to be hemaglutination inhibitor?

a. Lysozyme | b. Ovomucin
c. Avidin | d. Conalbumin

38. Peroxide value is the measure of

a. Degree of unsaturation | b. Degree of saturation
c. Amount of carbon present | d. Degree of oxidation

39. The average molecular weight of fatty acid is determined by

a. Iodine value | b. Acid value
c. Saponification value | d. Peroxide value

40. Hydrolytic rancidity of fat requires
   a. Oxygen b. Moisture
   c. High temperature d. Both b and c

41. For hydrogenation of oils, the catalyst required is
   a. Iron b. Aluminium
   c. Nickel d. Magnesium

42. Gelatin is
   a. Product obtained from agar – agar
   b. Partially degraded protein
   c. Important constituent of jelly responsible for its characteristic gel structure
   d. None of the above

43. Most abundant mineral present in the egg shell is
   a. Iron b. Magnesium
   c. Zinc d. Calcium

44. The protein portion of the myoglobin is called
   a. Heme b. Globin
   c. Flavone d. Myoglobin does not contain any protein

45. How many myoglobin molecules are linked together in a hemoglobin molecule?
   a. Two b. Three
   c. Four d. Five

46. Colorant used in butter is
   a. Annato b. Erythrosine
   c. Congo red d. None of the above

47. Primary structure of proteins is/are
   a. Open chain b. Cyclic
   c. Branched chain d. All of the above

48. Which of the following proteins has /have cyclic primary structure?
   a. Tyrosidin b. Ubiquitin
   c. Keratin d. All of the above

49. The basic compound involved in Maillard reaction is
   a. Fat and sugar b. Sugar and vitamins
   c. Sugar and amino acid d. Fat and amino acid

50. The SI unit to express the energy value of food is
   a. Kilo calorie b. Calorie
   c. Kilo joule d. Joule

51. Which of the following amino acids is sulphur containing amino acids?
a. Methionine
b. Alanine
c. Proline
d. Lysine

52. Measurement of energy value of food is called
a. Calorimetry
b. Joulimetry
c. Energymetry
d. None of the above

53. Calorimetric value of protein is
a. 4 kcal/g
b. 4.7 kcal/g
c. 5.7 kcal/ g
d. 6.2 kcal/g

54. Upon consumption of one gram of protein we get
a. 4 kcal
b. 4.7 kcal
c. 5.7 kcal
d. 6.2 kcal

55. Milk contains which of the flowing sugar
a. Sucrose
b. Starch
c. Cellulose
d. Lactose

56. Lactose increases the retention of
a. Calcium
b. Phosphorus
c. Iron
d. Iodine

57. When fats are not oxidized completely, ———— accumulates in blood
a. Glycerol
b. Fatty acids
c. Ketone bodies
d. Acetyl CoA

58. Which of the following protein is of high biological value
a. Soybean protein
b. Meat protein
c. Protein from legumes
d. Protein from cereals

59. Milk is deficient in
a. Methionine
b. Phenylanaline
c. Valine
d. Leucine

60. Which of the following dietary components helps in the growth of intestinal micro flora?
a. Dietary fiber
b. Cellulose
c. Hemicellulose
d. All of the above

61. Which vitamin is known to have anti-sterility factor in rats
a. Vitamin A
b. Vitamin D
c. Vitamin E
d. Vitamin K

62. Which of the following explains the protein quality is
a. Protein Efficiency Ratio
b. Net protein retention
c. PDCAAS
d. All of the above

63. Gain in weight per gram of protein eaten
a. Protein Efficiency Ratio
b. Net protein retention
c. PDCAAS
d. Digestibility

64. Thiamine is destroyed by
a. Sulphur dioxide
b. Acetic acid
c. Sorbic acid
d. Ethylene

65. Cereals are deficient in
a. Methionine
b. Phenylanaline
c. Valine
d. Lysine

66. Machine polished rice is responsible for
a. Xerophthalmia
b. Beri – beri
c. Rickets
d. Scurvy

67. Vitamin A activity is expressed in terms of
a. International Unit
b. SI unit
c. Retinol activity
d. Both a and c

68. Vitamin D helps in absorption of
a. Calcium
b. Phosphorus
c. Both a and b
d. None

69. Vitamin E favours the absorption of
a. Calcium
b. Phosphorus
c. Both a and b
d. Iron

70. Which of the following Vitamin is water soluble?
a. Vitamin A
b. Vitamin C
c. Vitamin D
d. Vitamin E

71. Vitamin responsible for blood clotting is
a. Vitamin B
b. Vitamin K
c. Vitamin C
d. Vitamin A

72. Among the fat soluble vitamins, which vitamin is most potent toxic vitamin
a. Vitamin A
b. Vitamin D
c. Vitamin E
d. Vitamin K

73. Which of the following is sensitive to light?

a. Vitamin A
b. Vitamin E
c. Vitamin C
d. All of the above

74. Which of the following is the anti-pernicious anemia factor?

a. Retinol
b. Riboflavin
c. Folic acid
d. Cobalamine

75. Irradiation of fungi produces which vitamin

a. Vitamin D_1
b. Vitamin D_2
c. Vitamin D_3
d. None of the above

76. Acid – alkali reaction of the blood is controlled by

a. Phosphorus
b. Iodine
c. Potassium
d. Sodium

77. Which of the following interferes with the effective absorption of phosphorus in human being

a. Calcium
b. Phytates
c. Both a and b
d. Iron

78. Which of the following mineral is important in maintaining electrical potential in nerves and membranes

a. Calcium
b. Magnesium
c. Selenium
d. Iron

79. Magnesium is required for the normal metabolism of

a. Vitamin D
b. Iron and Copper
c. Vitamin A and C
d. Amino acids and fatty acids

80. Copper aids in the utilization of ——— and hemoglobin synthesis

a. Iron
b. Magnesium
c. Phosphorus
d. Molybdenum

81. Chromium is required for

a. Protein metabolism
b. Glucose metabolism
c. Fatty acid metabolism
d. All of the above

82. Molybdenum is involved in

a. Protein metabolism
b. Glucose metabolism
c. Fatty acid metabolism
d. All of the above

83. PDCAAS stands for
a. Protein Deficiency Control by Amino Acid Supplementation
b. Protein Digestibility Corrected Amino Acid Score
c. Protein Deficiency and Chemical Analysis by Assay System
d. Protein Digestibility and Chemical Amino Acid Solution

84. Which vitamin is known as "sunshine vitamin"
a. Vitamin A b. Vitamin C
c. Vitamin D d. Vitamin E

85. Which of the following combination would you advise the people to consume in order to have balanced amount of all essential amino acids
a. Bread + Butter b. Bread + Dal
c. Rice + Sambar d. Rice + Bread

86. Vitamin D_3 is also known as
a. Retinol b. Tochopherol
c. Cholecalciferol d. Ergocalciferol

87. Vitamin D_2 is also known as
a. Retinol b. Tochopherol
c. Cholecalciferol d. Ergocalciferol

88. RDA stands for
a. Regional Dietary Advisor b. Recommended Dietary Allowances
c. Regional Drug Administrator d. Recent Dietary Advancement

89. Chromanol ring is basic ring structure of
a. Vitamin A b. Vitamin C
c. Vitamin D d. Vitamin E

90. Vitamin D deficiency in adults lead to
a. Rickets b. Beri-beri
c. Goitre d. Cretinism

91. Single cell protein is undesirable due to
a. High content of oleic acid b. High Content of uric acid
c. High content of citric acid d. High content of antinutritinal factor

92. BMI stands for
a. Basal Metabolic Index b. Body Mass Index
c. Body Metabolism Information d. Biotin Metabolic Index

93. Which of the following is the constituent of rhodopsin?
a. Vitamin A
b. Calcium
c. Vitamin D
d. Iron

94. Which of the following is essential fatty acid?
a. EPA
b. DHA
c. ALA
d. All of the above

95. BMI is equal to
a. Weight / (height in meter)^2
b. Weight / (height in inch)^2
c. Weight × height in inch
d. Weight × height in meter

96. Ragi is very good source of
a. Calcium
b. Vitamin C
c. Essential Fatty acids
d. Zinc

97. Which of the following nutrients is major source of energy in our diet?
a. Water
b. Carbohydrate
c. Fat
d. Protein

98. Body cannot synthesize
a. Palmitic acid
b. Linoleic acid
c. Lauric acid
d. Stearic acid

99. The Egg white is rich in
a. Carbohydrates
b. Minerals
c. Proteins
d. Fat

100. Which vitamin is the example of sugar acids?
a. Vitamin A
b. Vitamin C
c. Vitamin D
d. Vitamin E

101. Polishing of rice removes
a. Vitamin K
b. Vitamin B_1
c. Vitamin C
d. Vitamin A

102. High temperature processing causes destruction of which of the following vitamins?
a. Vitamin A
b. Vitamin B
c. Vitamin C
d. Vitamin D

103. Karl Fischer Titration method is based on the fundamental reaction involving
a. Reduction of iodine by SO_2 in the presence of the water
b. Oxidation of iodine by SO_2 in the presence of the water
c. Reduction of iodine by CO_2 in the presence of the water
d. Oxidation of iodine by CO_2 in the presence of the water

104. Amount of fatty acids which is insoluble in water is called
a. Acetyl value
b. Hehner value
c. Koettstorfer Number
d. Kirschner value

105. ——— measures the potential amount of soluble silver salts in the *Reichert Meissl* distillate
a. Acetyl value
b. Hehner value
c. Koettstorfer Number
d. Kirschner value

106. Koettstorfer number is also called as
a. Iodine value
b. Saponification value
c. Hehner value
d. Kirschner value

107. Nelson – Somogyi's method is for the estimation of
a. Sugar
b. Aflatoxin
c. Vitamin C
d. Tryptophan

108. Lea method is for the determination of
a. Calcium content of milk
b. Peroxide value of fat
c. Sugar content in honey
d. Total soluble ash in ragi

109. Peroxide value is the measure of
a. Protein quality
b. Fat quality
c. Sugar quality
d. Vitamin content of food

110. Peroxide value is the measure for
a. Degree of unsaturation
b. Type of fatty acid present
c. Amount of cholesterol present
d. Rancidity

111. Reacting compounds in the measuring anisidine value of fat are
a. Anisidine, acetic acid, aldehydic compounds
b. Anisidine, benzoic acid, peroxide
c. Anisidine, gallic acid, nitrile compounds
d. Anisidine, fatty acid, amides

112. Barfoed's test is for
a. Detecting the presence of triglycerides in the sample
b. Detecting the presence of monosaccharides in the sample
c. Detecting the presence of dipeptide in the sample
d. Detecting the presence of Vitamin K in the sample

113. Which of the following test would you prefer to distinguish between pentose and hexose?
a. Bial's test
b. Molish test
c. Barfoed's test
d. We cant distinguish between the two

114. Benedict's test is to identify
a. carbohydrate in a given sample
b. reducing sugar in a sample
c. hexoses in a sample
d. ketoses in a sample

115. Selivanoff's test is for detection of
a. Pentoses
b. Ketoses
c. Aldoses
d. Hexoses

116. Molisch's test is done to identify the presence of
a. Calcium
b. Carbohydrates
c. Copper
d. Cadmium

117. Biurett test is for the qualitative analysis of
a. Reducing sugar
b. Proteins
c. Saturated fatty acids
d. Vitamin K

118. Ninhydrin test gives blue colour with
a. Proline
b. Methionine
c. Ribose
d. Stearic acid

119. Ninhydrin gives yellow colour with
a. Leucine
b. Valine
c. Tryptophan
d. Hydroxy proline

120. Fiske and Rao method is used for the estimation of
a. Phosphorus
b. Pentathonic acid
c. Pectin
d. Phytates

121. Folin – Lowry method is for the estimation of
a. Sugar
b. Protein
c. Vitamin K
d. Copper

122. Wongs method is used for the estimation of
a. Reducing sugar
b. Iron
c. Biotin
d. Aflatoxin

123. Soxhlet method is used for the estimation of
a. Crude fat
b. Crude protein
c. Crude fiber
d. None of the above

124. Soxhlet method is based on the principle of
a. Chemical analysis
b. Solvent extraction
c. Colorimetry
d. Chromatography

125. Kjeldahl method is for the estimation of

a. Crude fiber
b. Crude fat
c. Crude protein
d. None of the above

126. What is/are the basic step/s in the Kjeldahl's method?

a. Digestion
b. Distillation
c. Titration
d. All of the above

127. Paper chromatography is based on

a. Ion – exchange chromatography
b. Size- exclusion chromatography
c. Partition chromatography
d. Adsorption chromatography

128. In ion – exchange chromatography, the cation exchanger contains

a. Negative charge
b. Positive charge
c. No charge
d. Both positive and negative charge

129. PAGE is

a. Partition, adsorption and gel electrophoresis
b. Polyacrylamide gel elecrophoresis
c. Principle adsorbent for gel electrophoresis
d. None of the above

130. Ergotism is due to

a. Polypeptides
b. Alkaloids
c. Phenolic compounds
d. None of the above

131. Which crop is responsible for ergotism?

a. Rice
b. Wheat
c. Barley
d. Rye

132. Cardiac beri – beri is the symptom of which of the following mycotoxin infection?

a. Citreoviridin
b. Psoralens
c. Fumagillin
d. Viridicatin

133. Turkey X disease is due to

a. Aflatoxin
b. Islanditoxin
c. Citrinin
d. Moniliformin

134. Which of the following fungi is/are responsible for the production of Aflatoxin?

a. *Aspergillus flavus*
b. *A. paraciticus*
c. *A. normius*
d. All of the above

135. Kojic acid is
   a. An acid produced during carbohydrate metabolism
   b. A mycotoxin
   c. An acidulant used in food processing
   d. None of the above

136. Slaframine is found in ———— infected by *Rhizoctonia leguminicola*
   a. red pepper b. red clover
   c. red meat d. red wine

137. Roquefortine is found in
   a. Cheese b. Meat
   c. Egg d. Fruits

138. Double vision may be evident due to
   a. Aflatoxin b. Botlulism
   c. Ochratoxin d. Raffinose

139. Argemone oil is used to adulterate
   a. Mustard oil b. Milk
   c. Tea d. All of the above

140. In Keshar adulterant used is
   a. Starch powder b. Safflower petals
   c. Argemone seeds d. All of the above

141. Ghee is adulterated with
   a. Vanaspati b. Starch
   c. Stones d. Khesari dal

142. Black pepper is sometimes adulterated by
   a. Fibres of cotton b. Stones
   c. Water d. Papaya seeds

143. Adulteration of Vanaspati in ghee can be identified by
   a. Halman's test b. Baudoduim test
   c. Holde's test d. Carl's test

144. Adulteration of edible oil by mineral oil can be identified by
   a. Halman's test b. Baudoduim test
   c. Holde's test d. Carl's test

145. Chicory is used to adulterate
   a. Tea b. Coffee
   c. Saffron d. Milk

146. Which of the following hazards can be detected by metal detector?
a. Physical
b. Chemical
c. Microbiological
d. All of the above

147. Rancidity is observed in
a. Fat
b. Protein
c. Starch
d. All of the above

148. Alzheimer's disease can be seen due to deficiency of
a. Selenium
b. Sodium
c. Silicon
d. Sulphur

149. Minamata disease is due to consumption of fishes contaminated with
a. Silicon
b. Mercury
c. Potassium
d. Calcium

150. Ropiness in bread is caused by
a. *Bacillus lichenformis*
b. *Serratia marcescens*
c. *Geotrichum auranticum*
d. None of the above

151. Which of the following yeasts is / are responsible for the spoilage of honey?
a. *Zygosaccharomyces richteri*
b. *Saccharomyces cerevisae*
c. *Padeococcus cerevisae*
d. All of the above

152. Downy mildew is due to
a. *Diplodia*
b. *Fusarium*
c. *Cladosporium*
d. *Phytophthora*

153. In jam and jellies, which of the following is most likely to be responsible for the spoilage?
a. Bacteria only
b. Molds only
c. Yeast and molds
d. Yeasts, molds and bacteria

154. Anthracnose in fruits and vegetables is caused due to
a. *Colletotrichum linemuthianum*
b. *Aspergillus niger*
c. *Triochothesmium roseum*
d. *Botrytis cinerea*

155. Putrefaction of meat is caused by
a. *Alkaligens*
b. *Clostridium*
c. *Geotrichum*
d. *Thamnidium*

156. *Coxiella burnetti* is responsible for
a. Tuberculosis
b. Q fever
c. Cerebral malaria
d. It is not pathogenic

157. Rind rot is being observed in
   a. Raw milk b. Cheese
   c. Evaporated milk d. Butter

158. Maltiness in milk is due to
   a. *Streptococcus lactis* b. *Alkaligens viscolactis*
   c. *Clostridium botulinum* d. All of the above

159. Blue milk is caused by
   a. *Pseudomonas syncyanea* b. *Streptococcus lactis*
   c. *Pseudomonas synxantha* d. *Pseudomonas putrefaciens*

160. Flat sour spoilage of canned food is caused due to
   a. *Pseudomonas* b. *Bacillus*
   c. *Clostridium* d. *Serratia*

161. TA spoilage of canned food is called so because it is being caused by ———and ——— bacteria
   a. Thermophilic, aerobic b. Thermophilic, anaerobic
   c. Thermoduric, aerobic d. Thermoduric, anaerobic

162. *Clostridium botulinum* is
   a. Mesophilic non spore forming b. Thermophilic non spore forming
   c. Mesophilic spore forming d. Thermophilic spore forming

163. Microorganism involved in spoilage of canned fruits
   a. *Clostridium botulinum* b. *Bassochlamys fulva*
   c. *Pseudomonas putrefaciens* d. *Bacillus stearothermophilus*

164. Appearance of objectionable flavours from less oxidation than is to produce rancidity
   a. Putrefaction b. Reversion
   c. Oxidative rancidity d. Autolysis

165. Anaerobic degradation of the protein with the production indole, skatole etc.
   a. Putrefaction b. Reversion
   c. Oxidative rancidity d. Autolysis

166. Which of the following microorganisms is/are involved in spoilage of prepared mustard?
   a. *Bacillus* b. Salmonella
   c. *Aspergillus* d. All of the above

167. TA spoilage in case of spices is caused by
   a. *Saccharomyces cerevisae* b. *Saccharomyces citri*
   c. *Saccharomyces heterogenicus* d. *Clostridium thermosaccharolyticum*

168. Which of the following pesticides are not allowed in India?
a. Aluminium phosphide
b. Ethylene dibromide
c. Methyl bromide
d. All of the above

169. The proportion of absorbed nitrogen retained in the body after digestion of protein is ——————— of protein
a. Protein efficiency ratio
b. PDCAAS
c. Biological value
d. Digestibility

170. Thiamine is destroyed by
a. Sulphur dioxide
b. Acetic acid
c. Sorbic acid
d. Ethylene

171. Net Protein Utilization is
a. Biological value × digestibility
b. Biological value / Digestibility
c. Digestibility / Biological value
d. Biological value – Digestibility

172. Vitamin A as such naturally occurs in
a. Animals only
b. Plant only
c. Both animals and plants
d. Neither animals nor plants

173. Dry and scaly skin disease in children is caused by the deficiency of
a. Vitamin D
b. Essential fatty acids
c. Essential amino acids
d. Magnesium

174. Vitamin E prevent carotene and vitamin from ——————— destruction
a. Thermal
b. Reductive
c. Oxidative
d. Microbiological

175. Glycemic index is related to
a. High protein food
b. High fat food
c. High carbohydrate food
d. High vitamin food

176. Which of the following statements is the most appropriate?
a. Glycemic index of complex carbohydrate is high
b. Glycemic index of complex carbohydrate is low
c. Glycemic index of complex protein is high
d. Glycemic index of complex protein is low

177. Which of the following carbohydrates has least impact on blood sugar level?
a. Sucrose
b. Maltose
c. Glucose
d. Fructose

178. The term "roughage" is used for which of the following food components?
a. Saturated fats
b. Essential amino acids
c. Minerals
d. Dietary fibers

179. Putrefaction is observed in
a. Fat
b. Protein
c. Starch
d. All of the above

180. Which of the following statements is/are correct?
a. Soluble fibers reduce LDL cholesterol
b. Insoluble fibers reduce LDL cholesterol
c. Soluble fibers reduce HDL cholesterol
d. All of the above

181. Which of the following statements is/are correct?
a. Soluble fibers add bulk to stool
b. Insoluble fibers add bulk to stool
c. Insoluble fibers regulate blood sugar
d. All of the above

182. Trans fats are
a. Type of saturated fatty acids
b. Isomers of unsaturated fatty acids
c. Type of bad cholesterol
d. Oxidized fat

183. Which of the following amino-acids is NOT an essential amino acids?
a. Methionine
b. Lysine
c. Leucine
d. Proline

184. Limiting amino-acid in rice is
a. Methionine
b. Lysine
c. Leucine
d. Proline

185. Biological value of egg white is around
a. 1
b. 10
c. 100
d. 1000

186. Pellagra disease is due to deficiency of which of the following nutrients in food?
a. Essential fatty acids
b. Essential amino acids
c. Niacin
d. Mercury

187. Megaloblastic anemia is due to deficiency of which of the following nutrients in food?
a. Vitamin K
b. Vitamin A
c. Vitamin C
d. Vitamin B_{12}

188. Heterocyclic Amines (HCAs) are formed when
   a. Creatine-rich foods are roasted in high temperature
   b. Sugar reacts with amino acids under high temperature
   c. Sugar is heated under moist condition for longer time
   d. Fat reacts with amino acids under low pH

189. Gelatinization is observed in
   a. Fat
   b. Protein
   c. Starch
   d. All of the above

190. Adulterants in food can be identified by which of the following methods?
   a. Visual tests
   b. Physical tests
   c. Chemical tests
   d. All of the above

191. Honey is generally adulterated with
   a. Mustard oil
   b. Vanaspati
   c. Sugar solution
   d. All of the above

192. Fruits are good source of
   a. Proteins
   b. Fats
   c. Vitamins
   d. All of the above

193. Vitamin D_2 is also known as
   a. Retinol
   b. Tochopherol
   c. Cholecalciferol
   d. Ergocalciferol

194. RDA stands for
   a. Regional Dietary Advisor
   b. Recommended Dietary Allowances
   c. Regional Drug Administrator
   d. Recent Dietary Advancement

195. Green Tea is good source of
   a. Protein
   b. Antioxidants
   c. Fats
   d. All of the above

196. NIN stands for
   a. National Institute of Nutrition
   b. National In-charge for Nutrition
   c. National Industrial Network
   d. None of the above

197. NIN is situated at
   a. New Delhi
   b. Nagpur
   c. Chennai
   d. Hyderabad

198. Glycogen is polymer of

a. Maltose
b. Glucose
c. Amino acids
d. Glycerine

199. ICMR stands for

a. Indian Council for Medical Research
b. Indian Chambers for Marine Research
c. Indian Centre for Meteorological Research
d. Incoming Call and Message Recovery

200. Which of the following is essential fatty acid?

a. EPA
b. DHA
c. ALA
d. All of the above

3 Fundamentals of Food Processing and Technology

1. Which chemical preservative is added to tomato sauce to extend the shelf life
   a. Sodium benzoate
   b. Calcium propionate
   c. Tocopherol
   d. All of the above

2. Nisin is a
   a. narrow spectrum antibiotic
   b. broad spectrum antibiotic
   c. stabilizer
   d. nutrient supplement

3. Sorbic acid is mostly used as preservatives in which of the following food products?
   a. Meat
   b. Milk
   c. Baked products
   d. All of the above

4. Which of the following preservatives has found to be much effective to prevent ropiness of bread?
   a. Sugar
   b. Sulphite
   c. Propionic acid
   d. Acetic acid

5. Which component of cinnamon has antimicrobial effect?
   a. Eugenol aldehyde
   b. Eugenol
   c. Cinnamic acid
   d. Thymol

6. Which of the following is/are the class I preservative?
   a. Sugar
   b. Sorbic acid
   c. Calcium propionates
   d. All of the above

7. Which acid is found in carbonated non-alcoholic beverages?
   a. Propionic acid
   b. Acetic acid
   c. Citric acid
   d. Phosphoric acid

8. What is the proposed mode of action of citric acid?
   a. Dehydration
   b. Osmosis
   c. Chelation
   d. None of the above

9. Mustard shows antimicrobial effect because it contains
   a. Allyl sulphide
   b. Allyl isosulphide
   c. Allyl isothiocyanate
   d. Allyl thiocyanate

10. Hydrogen peroxide is used as the preservative ion for which of the following food commodity?
   a. Meat
   b. Bread
   c. Confectionary
   d. Milk

11. In Asceptic packaging, the most preservative used to sterilize the packaging material is
   a. Phosphoric acid
   b. Sulphuric acid
   c. Hydrogen peroxide
   d. All of the above

12. Which of the following compounds acts as both synergists and antioxidants?
   a. Ascorbic acid
   b. Citric acid
   c. Phosphoric acid
   d. Tartaric acid

13. Dimethyl dicarbonate has got application in preservation of
   a. Bread
   b. Jellies
   c. Oils
   d. Wine

14. Sucrose esters are
   a. emulsifiers
   b. antimicrobial agents
   c. Both a and b
   d. None of the above

15. Which component of garlic have antimicrobial effect?
   a. Allicin
   b. Allyl isothicyanate
   c. Methyl sulphide
   d. All of the above

16. Cyclamate is
   a. a leavening agent
   b. an antimicrobial agent
   c. a non-nutritive sweetener
   d. a shortening

17. Anticaking agents are
   a. Those used to destroy the cake while disposing the spoiled cakes
   b. Those used to maintain the free flowing nature of granular or powdered products
   c. Those used to kill microorganisms growing in cakes
   d. Those used to maintain the shape of cakes and pastries

18. Calcium stearate is used as an
   a. anticaking agent
   b. antifungal agent
   c. antifoaming agent
   d. antibacterial agent

19. Which of the following is used as the clarifying agent?
a. Gelatin
b. Bentonite
c. Diatomacious earth
d. All of the above

20. Monosodium glutamate is used as
a. artificial sweetener
b. anticaking agent
c. flavour enhancer
d. cleaning agent

21. Which of the following preservatives is NOT recommended in food application?
a. Formaldehyde
b. Sorbic acid
c. Benzoic acid
d. None of the above

22. Lecithin is used as
a. stabilizer
b. emulsifier
c. leavening agent
d. None of the above

23. Carboxymethyl cellulose is used as
a. stabilizer
b. colouring agent
c. detergent
d. emulsifier

24. Which of the following colorant is NOT recommended for food applications?
a. Malachite green
b. Carotenoids
c. Coal tar
d. None of the above

25. Baking powder is used in baking as
a. antimicrobial agent
b. anticaking agent
c. leavening agent
d. None of the above

26. Vinegar is used as the preservatives in
a. confectionary
b. ketchup
c. jelly
d. oils

27. Which of the following acts as chelating agent?
a. Sulphur dioxide
b. Chromium oxide
c. Sorbic acid
d. Citric acid

28. Process responsible for the preservative nature of sugar is
a. osmosis
b. reverse osmosis
c. chelation
d. toxicity

29. Nitrate and Nitrite is helpful in meat processing as it
a. increases tenderness
b. increases Juiciness
c. improves colour
d. prevents from microbial deterioration

30. Which of the following acts as dough softener?
a. Benzene hexachloride
b. Sodium metabisulphide
c. Calcium oxalate
d. All of the above

31. Bacterial cells shows maximum resistance against the heat during
a. Logarithmic phase
b. Lag phase
c. Late lag phase
d. Decline phase

32. Canning is also sometime called as
a. Appertization
b. Pasteurization
c. Sterilization
d. Cold sterilization

33. The time of heating at a temperature to cause 90% reduction in count of viable spores is called
a. D value
b. F value
c. Z value
d. Lethal rate

34. The degree in Fahrenheit required to reduce the thermal death time ten fold is
a. D value
b. F value
c. Z value
d. Lethal rate

35. Time in minute required to destroy the organism in a specified medium at 250°F is
a. D value
b. F value
c. Z value
d. Lethal rate

36. The lethal rate is reciprocal of
a. Z value
b. Thermal death time
c. F value
d. None of the above

37. Both extra cellular and intracellular crystallization takes place in
a. Slow freezing only
b. Fast freezing only
c. Both in fast as well as slow freezing
d. Neither slow nor fast freezing

38. Blast freezing is preferred to slow freezing because
a. Large ice crystals are formed in food
b. Very small crystals are formed
c. Food freezes gradually in a blast of cold air
d. Food can be stored indefinitely in the refrigerator

39. What is the strength of the brine solution for the canning of vegetables?
a. 2%
b. 8%
c. 15%
d. 67%

40. In slow freezing
a. Crystal size is big
b. Crystal size is small
c. Both extra cellular and intracellular crystallization takes place
d. Quality of product is better than fast freezing

41. Which of the following is being used in immersion freezing?

a. Glycol b. Dry ice

c. Ammonia d. All of the above

42. In canned fruit, major function of syrup is

a. Conduction of heat b. Provide taste

c. Preserve fruit d. Kill microorganisms

43. In CA storage, the ethylene scrubber uses which of the following oxidizing compound?

a. Nitric acid b. Potassium permangante

c. Hydrogen peroxide d. All of the above

44. Death of bacteria follows

a. Zero order reaction b. First order reaction

c. Second order reaction d. It does not follow any pattern

45. Corn gluten is rich in the corn protein known as

a. Zein b. Glutenin

c. Glutelin d. Prolamin

46. For manufacturing of biscuits, wheat variety used is

a. Soft wheat b. Hard wheat

c. Durum wheat d. None of these

47. Which protein fraction constitutes gluten

a. Prolamin and Proteose b. Gliadin and Zein

c. Gliadin and Glutenin d. Prolamin and Gliadin

48. Which of the following function sugar performs in biscuits

a. Imparts tenderness

b. Provides food for yeast during fermentation

c. Helps in formation of gluten

d. Both a and b

49. Water used in biscuits

a. Helps in formation of gluten

b. Helps in maintenance of particular temperature during mixing

c. Facilitates activities of enzymes and yeast in dough

d. All of the above.

50. Flour and eggs used as baking ingredients acts as

a. Tenderizers b. Toughners

c. Structure builders d. Both b and c

51. Which of the following processes is responsible for the staling of bread?

a. Gelatinization
b. Retrogradation
c. Hydrolysis of starch
d. All of the above

52. Food products under batter systems include

a. Cookies
b. Cakes
c. Biscuits
d. All of the above

53. Pasta products are prepared from

a. Hard wheat
b. Soft wheat
c. Durum wheat
d. Buckwheat flour

54. Straight flour is

a. Finest stream of flour produced during milling
b. Most coarse stream of the flour produced during milling
c. Flour containing all the different types of stream produced during milling
d. None of the above

55. Quick bread is

a. A cereal product made from rye flour and mimic wheat flour bread
b. A bread which is prepared very quickly- ready to eat bread
c. A bread leavened with air, steam, and/ or CO_2 from baking soda or baking powder
d. A bread which is easily digested

56. Patent flour is

a. Finest stream of flour produced during milling
b. Flour making method which has been patented
c. Flour of mixed cereals
d. None of the above

57. The cell structure appearing when a baked product is sliced is called

a. Crust
b. Crumb
c. Crush
d. Cracks

58. An extruded product with no expansion in volume is called

a. Collet
b. Dellet
c. Pellet
d. Sellet

59. Milk powder provides ———— to the bread

a. Nutritive value
b. Crust colour
c. White colour to crumb
d. Milk is not added in bread

60. Shortenings,

a. Impart colour to bread
b. Provide soft texture to bread
c. Aerate dough
d. Increases the strength of bread

61. Water inside coconut is
    a. Rain water that might have leached in to its center
    b. Endosperm
    c. Juice of the mesoderm
    d. Molten seed

62. As per FSSAI, what should be the minimum TSS of a tomato sauce?
    a. 20% b. 25%
    c. 10% d. 5%

63. For many fruits the tartness and flavour are determined by
    a. Sugar to acid ratio b. Acid to salt ratio
    c. Sugar to salt ratio d. Sugar to pectin ratio

64. Which of the following fruit is having the highest amount of fat?
    a. Peach b. Avocado
    c. Coconut d. Banana

65. As per FSSAI, what should be the minimum acidity of tomato ketchup?
    a. 0.5% b. 1.0%
    c. 1.5% d. 2.0%

66. As per FSSAI, what should be the minimum TSS of fruit squash
    a. 12% b. 25%
    c. 30% d. 40%

67. The sparkling, clear sweetened fruit juice is
    a. RTS b. Squash
    c. Puree d. Cordial

68. Climacteric fruits
    a. Show sudden increase in the respiration
    b. Change colour with change in colour
    c. Shows increase in total solid content
    d. Are those which grow at different climate

69. Sourkraut is the
    a. Fermented product b. Dairy product
    c. Fruit juice d. Meat product

70. Wax coating of fruits is done to reduce
    a. Total soluble solids b. Rate of transpiration
    c. Surface gloss d. All of the above

71. Ethylene increases the rate of .... of fruits
a. transpiration
b. respiration
c. reproduction
d. excretion

72. Sliced potatoes are kept in saline water to prevent
a. Respiration
b. Microbial deterioration
c. Enzymic browning
d. None of the above

73. Pineapple is a good source of
a. Amylase
b. Bromelin
c. Palmolive
d. None of the above

74. Pineapple is a good source of
a. Invertase enzyme
b. Proteolytic enzyme
c. Saccharifying enzyme
d. Lypolytic enzyme

75. Papain is obtained from
a. Papaya
b. Pineapple
c. Pomegranate
d. Pear

76. Which of the following chemicals is used for the inhibition of the sprouting of onion?
a. Maleic hydrazide
b. Maleic acetate
c. Maleic stearate
d. All of the above

77. Primary aim of blanching of fruit is
a. To destroy surface microorganisms
b. To increase softness of the fruits
c. To destroy the enzyme
d. To increase the palatability of the fruit

78. Renin causes
a. Separation of oil and water phase
b. Coagulation of casein
c. Solublization of lactose
d. Dispersion of milk fat

79. Which of the following pigments is present in a mature tomato?
a. Chlorophyll
b. Lycopene
c. Bixin
d. Anthocyanin

80. Which of the following is the phase transformation method?
a. Vacreation
b. Working
c. Churning
d. Homogenization

81. In cola soft drinks the common colorant is
a. coal tar
b. tannins
c. caramel
d. charcoal

82. Butter flavour is due to

a. Ammonia
b. Diacetyl
c. Ethylene
d. Vanillin

83. Carbon dioxide in carbonated beverages acts as

a. Preservative
b. Sparkling agent
c. Enhancement of flavour
d. All of the above

84. After harvesting fruits should be dipped in cold water immediately to remove

a. Soils from the surface
b. Remove microorganism from the surface
c. Field heat
d. All of the above

85. What acts as the preservatives in mango pickle?

a. Salt
b. Mango
c. Oil
d. Sodium benzoate

86. Which of the following statement is/are correct?

a. Jam is made from fruit pulp
b. Jelly is made from fruit juice
c. Jam have better spreadability than jelly
d. All of the above

87. Which of the following type of pectin can be used for making gel by cross linking with divalent ions?

a. High methoxy
b. Low methoxy
c. Both a and b
d. Neither can form cross linking with divalent ions

88. Which of the following is/are the reasons for the syneresis in jellies?

a. Excess of acid
b. Low pectin content
c. Low sugar
d. All of the above

89. Which of the following is/are class I preservative?

a. Sodium benzoate
b. Calcium propionate
c. Sugar
d. All of the above

90. Yellow orange colour in saffron is due to

a. Xanthophyll
b. Chlorophyll
c. Crocetin
d. None of the above

91. Chill injury is most common in
a. Banana
b. Apple
c. Mango
d. Grape

92. Strength of brine is being measured by
a. Salometer
b. Salinometer
c. Baume's hydrometer
d. All of the above

93. Which of the following storage designs makes piles of vegetables and cover it with straws?
a. Barns
b. Clamps
c. Pits
d. Cellars

94. A confectionary having air and water as main ingredient
a. Eclairs
b. Batasa
c. Marsh mallow
d. All of the above

95. Fat bloom is
a. Increase in the fat level in chocolate leading to the formation of soft texture
b. Coating the sugar candy with cocoa butter
c. Defect found in chocolate
d. None of the above

96. Fat bloom can be reduced by the use of
a. Sorbitan oxalate
b. Sorbitan acetate
c. Sorbitan ester
d. Sorbitan amide

97. Which of the following is/are common gelling agents used in confectionary industries?
a. Carrageenan
b. Alginate
c. Gelatin
d. All of the above

98. Feather is
a. A coating on the sugar crystal
b. Doctor used in confectionary
c. Stage in boiling sugar syrup
d. None of the above

99. Casein present in milk is found in the form of
a. Magnesium caseinate-phosphate complex
b. Calcium caseinate-phosphate complex
c. Potassium caseinate-phosphate complex
d. None of the above

100. Clot-on-boiling is the test carried out to
a. Determine both heat-stability and pH of the milk
b. Determine the heat-stability of the milk
c. Determine the extent of bacterial contamination and growth in milk
d. Detect adulteration in milk

101. Blue cheese is also called as
a. Roquefort cheese
b. Cottage cheese
c. Camembert cheese
d. Soft cheese

102. Lactometer can be used to
a. Find adulteration of milk by water
b. Find the specific gravity of milk
c. Both a and b
d. Neither a nor b

103. As per FSSAI, minimum SNF content of buffalo milk is
a. 5%
b. 7%
c. 9%
d. 13%

104. As per the FSSAI, minimum amount of fat in toned milk should be
a. 3%
b. 4%
c. 5%
d. 6%

105. The product remaining after the removal of most of the casein and fat from milk in the process of cheese making
a. Whey butter
b. Whey cheese
c. Whey
d. Condensed whey

106. Milk fat is
a. Oil-in-water type emulsion
b. Water-in-oil type emulsion
c. Colloidal state
d. None of the above

107. Which of the following test is used to detect sesame oil in milk
a. Halphen test
b. Baudouin test
c. Kreis test
d. Polenske value

108. The coagulation of milk proteins by heat consists of
a. Denaturation
b. Agglutination
c. Denaturation and agglutination
d. None of the above

109. Phosphatase test is not applicable for
a. Pasteurized milk
b. Sterilized milk
c. Both a and b
d. None of the above

110. Which of the following is a lactic acid-alcohol fermented milk, originated in Russia
a. Kumiss
b. Kefir
c. Yoghurt
d. Bulgarian Buttermilk

111. While manufacturing the toned milk,
a. Both the fat and solid-not-fat are reduced
b. Fat content is reduced and solid-not-fat is increased
c. Fat content is increased and solid-not-fat is reduced
d. None of the above

112. Churning is a process of phase reversal in which
   a. Water-in-oil type emulsion is changed to oil-in-water type emulsion
   b. Oil-in-water type emulsion is changed to water-in-oil type emulsion
   c. Oil-in-water type emulsion is changed to colloidal suspension
   d. None of the above

113. Sugar as constituent of ice-cream has following limitation
   a. High calorific value
   b. Lowers whipping ability
   c. Excess body and melting resistance
   d. None of the above

114. The only carbohydrate present in the milk is
   a. Maltose
   b. Sucrose
   c. Glucose
   d. None of the above

115. Cheese is classified on the basis of
   a. The fat content
   b. The moisture content
   c. Both a and b
   d. The protein content

116. The father of White Revolution is
   a. Dr. M. Kurien
   b. Dr. V. Kurien
   c. Dr. S. Kurien
   d. Dr. A. Kurien

117. As per the FSSAI, minimum fat % in double toned milk is
   a. 0.5
   b. 1.5
   c. 2.5
   d. 3.5

118. Marinades are prepared from
   a. Egg
   b. Meat
   c. Fish
   d. Cereals

119. Nitrate and nitrite are helpful in meat processing as it
   a. Increases tenderness
   b. Increases Juiciness
   c. Improves colour
   d. Prevent from microbial deterioration

120. Nitrate and Nitrite along with Sodium Chloride is called as
   a. Curing agent
   b. Emulsifier
   c. Anticaking agent
   d. Fumigating agent

121. Veal meat is obtained from
   a. Sheep
   b. Buffalo
   c. Goat
   d. Calf

122. Condition of toughening of the muscle of the meat after slaughtering of animals is called
   a. Rigor toughening
   b. Rigor mortis
   a. Rigor hardening
   b. Rigor tightening

123. The chief muscle pigment is
a. Myoglobin
b. Myoerythrim
c. Myocyanin
d. Myocholine

124. Smoking in used for the preservation of
a. Cereals
b. Meat
c. Egg
d. Fruits

125. Deposition of fat within the lean muscle is called
a. Curing
b. Marbling
c. Homogenization
d. None of the above

126. Tenderization of meat leads to the
a. Softening of muscles
b. Retaining the colour of meat
c. Prevention of microbial deterioration
d. All of the above

127. Pork is never aged because
a. It is not consumed largely
b. Ageing of pork is not liked by consumers
c. It has high fat content
d. None of the above

128. The tenderness of meat is determined by
a. The amount and distribution of connective tissues
b. The size of both muscle fibers and bundles of fibers
c. Moisture content of muscle
d. Both a and b

129. Meat is tenderized by
a. Using proteolytic enzymes
b. Using low levels of salts
c. Changing the pH of meat
d. All of the above

130. The proteolytic enzymes used in tenderization of meat are
a. Papain
b. Bromelin
c. Ficin
d. All of the above

131. A component of the egg which is responsible for holding the yolk in the centre of egg is
a. Air cell
b. Chalazae
c. Shell
d. Vitelline membrane

132. Which of the following statement is correct?
a. As the egg become older, white of the egg becomes thinner and yolk membrane becomes weaker
b. As the egg become older, white of the egg becomes thicker and yolk membrane becomes weaker
c. As the egg become older, white of the egg becomes thinner and yolk membrane becomes stronger
d. As the egg become older, white of the egg becomes thicker and yolk membrane becomes stronger

133. The thin surface layer of proteinaceous material acts as protective layer in egg is

a. cuticle
b. chalazae
c. vitelline membrane
d. shell membranes

134. Enzymatic meat tenderization methods are

a. Injection of an enzyme into the animal before slaughter
b. Introducing enzyme through fork holes into meat after cooking
c. Dipping the meat pieces in enzyme solution
d. Freeze drying the meat and rehydrating it with the water containing enzyme after cooking

135. Saffron is obtained from

a. Seed
b. Root
c. Fruit
d. Flower

136. Clove is

a. Root
b. Bark
c. Bud
d. Fruit

137. Extraction of aromatic compound into fat is called

a. expression
b. super critical extraction
c. enfluerage
d. Soxhlet extraction

138. Limonene is present in

a. orange
b. mandarin
c. lime
d. lemon

139. Linalool is present in

a. clove
b. coriander
c. cardamom
d. cinnamon

140. Which of the following is used as sparkling agent in carbonated beverages?

a. Sodium benzoate
b. Sparkling colorant
c. Sugar
d. Carbon dioxide

141. Edible portion of apple is

a. epicarp
b. mesocarp
c. thalamus
d. leaf

142. Which of the following is observed exclusively in meat?

a. Rigor mortis
b. Fat bloom
c. Enzymatic browning
d. All of the above

143. Which of the following is least nutritive?

a. Mango
b. Asparagus
c. Cucumber
d. Papaya

144. If potato is stored at more than 10°C
   a. There is increase in starch content
   b. There is increase in glucose content
   c. There in increase in both glucose and starch
   d. No change in either glucose or starch

145. Which of the following preservatives should not be used for the mango pulp which is to be canned?
   a. KMS   b. Vinegar
   c. Citric acid   d. Benzoic acid

146. Which of the following compounds is said to be "the doctor" in confectionary?
   a. Invertase   b. Mono Sodium Glutamate
   c. Sorbitol   d. Aspartame

147. In high fructose corn syrup preparation the enzyme used for the conversion of glucose to fructose is
   a. Epimerase   b. Isomerase
   c. Invertase   d. Amylase

148. Liquorice as a confectionary contains
   a. Wheat flour   b. Gelatin
   c. Caramel   d. All of the above

149. Quality of sugar is determined by the process specified by
   a. ICMUSA   b. IUCMSA
   c. ICUMSA   d. ISUCMA

150. Which of the following makes excellent whipping agent?
   a. Carbohydrate   b. Protein
   c. Inorganic acid   d. Fat

151. Unplanned crystallization of sugar in a confection is called
   a. Winnowing   b. Panning
   c. Engrossing   d. Fudging

152. Silver coating in confectionary is also called as
   a. Panning   b. Gilding
   c. Polishing   d. None of the above

153. Which of the following statements describes the characteristics of a good jelly?
   a. Should be cut easily
   b. Retain shape of edge and show clear cut surface
   c. Tender enough to quiver
   d. All of the above

154. Syneresis is a defect seen in

a. Egg
b. Jelly
c. Chocolate
d. None of the above

155. In fruit candy, the mode of preservation is

a. osmosis
b. decrease in temperature
c. addition of Class II preservatives
d. decrease in pH

156. Which of the following statements is/are correct?

a. Optical isomers have different organoleptic properties
b. Threshold quantity of two optical isomers are same under constant condition
c. Dill caraway have (–)ve carvone
d. All of the above

157. Spear mint and dill caraway have

a. Flavouring compounds which are optical isomers of each other
b. Carvone as the flavouring compound
c. Different threshold quantity
d. All of the above

158. Sausage is

a. an emulsion
b. a solution
c. a precipitate
d. None of the above

159. Poor quality egg floats in the water due to

a. Microbial spoilage
b. Increase in air cell
c. Decrease in air cell
d. Air cell has no relation to quality of egg

160. The major duty of two muscle proteins filaments actin and myosin is

a. to provide colour to muscle
b. to facilitate muscle contraction
c. to bind the endomysium to the sarcolemma
d. None of the above

161. When two isoprenes are joined it is called

a. monoterpene
b. diterpene
c. triterpene
d. None of the above

162. Sharp smell of onion is due to

a. Ammonia
b. Sulphur
c. Chlorine
d. Combined effect of above

163. Lard is obtained from

a. Coconut
b. Pigs
c. Soybean
d. Beef

164. White deposition on the surface of the chocolate is due to faulty

a. Winterization
b. Plasticization
c. Tempering
d. None of the above

165. Which type of fat would you prefer for the chocolate manufacture?

a. Fat with high linolenic content
b. Fat with short plastic range
c. Fat with α crystal form
d. All of the above

166. The surface active agents used in water in oil emulsion have

a. Higher HLB value
b. Lower HLB value
c. Higher peroxide value
d. Low peroxide value

167. What is HLB value?

a. Hydrogen linolenic bond
b. High lipophilic bond
c. Hydrophilic lipophilic balance
d. None of the above

168. Fat bloom is the defect found in

a. Margarine
b. Chocolate
c. Ghee
d. Yoghurt

169. Decrease in smoke point is the indication of

a. high shelf life of oil
b. low quality of oil
c. high quality of oil
d. It has no relation with the quality of oil

170. During the extraction of oil from oil seeds the process of removal of mucilaginous material is termed as

a. Tempering
b. Winterizing
c. Bleaching
d. Degumming

171. Storage of food under reduced pressure is called

a. Aseptic packaging
b. Hyperbaric storage
c. Hypobaric storage
d. Gas packaging

172. Lacquering of cans helps in

a. Preventing cans from discolouration
b. Providing cheaper way of colouring the can
c. Providing mechanical strength
d. Preventing can from shock during transportation

173. Lamination is

a. The method of wrapping the food article with certain packaging material and storing them at ambient temperature

b. Combination of two or more materials into a single homogenous packaging web by means of adhesive, solvent or heat

c. A type of packaging where the material used for packaging is made from substance obtained from middle lamella of cell wall

d. Coating of zinc on the surface of iron to prevent it from rusting

174. Shrink wrapping is

a. Dehydrating the food material to reduce the volume so that it can be adjusted in a given volume of packaging material

b. Method of packaging the material to give skin tight wrap

c. Type of packaging material used for packing marine foods

d. None of the above

175. Retort pouches are

a. Equipment used for the sterilization of pouches

b. Pouch shaped retort used for the sterilization of packaging material

c. Type of colour used for printing the LDPE used to pack low acid food

d. Heat sterilizable flexible packs

176. What is WVTR?

a. Water to vapour transient rate b. Water to vapour transfer rate

c. Water vapour transfer rate d. Water to vapour total ratio

177. What is OTR?

a. Odour transfer rate b. Oxygen transfer rate

c. Oxygen testing result d. Odour testing result

178. WVTR is expressed as

a. $g/cm^2/24$ hr b. g/cm^2

c. g/m^2 d. $g/m^2/24$ hr

179. Aluminium foil acts

a. as good barrier for vapour b. as good barrier for oxygen

c. as good barrier for light d. all of the above

180. Which of the following packaging material has perfect barrier properties

a. Paper and board b. Metal

c. Glass d. Plastics

181. A secondary package is that
   a. Directly holds the product for sale
   b. Contains the primary package
   c. Whose prime purpose is to protect the product during distribution
   d. None of the above

182. Modified atmospheric packaging (MAP) involves
   a. Monitoring & adjustment of the gases
   b. Introduction of a gas mixture other than air into a package
   c. Introduction of a gas mixture same as the air into a package
   d. Both a and b

183. What is the first thing the consumer notices about a package?
   a. What is this and what is it going to do for me
   b. Date of manufacture and expiry
   c. Both a and b
   d. Which packaging material is used in package

184. EVOH stands for
   a. Ethylated Vinyl Alcohol
   b. Ethylene Vinyl Alcohol
   c. Ethyl Vinyl Alcohol
   d. Ethylidene Vinyl Alcohol

185. The actual material used to make a tin can is
   a. High-carbon steel
   b. Low-carbon steel
   c. Bronze and Copper
   d. None of the above

186. BOPP stands for
   a. Biaxially Oriented Polypropylene
   b. Biodegradable Oxidized Polypropylene
   c. Biodegradable & Oriented Polypropylene
   d. None of the above

187. Sulfide process of pulping is a
   a. Mechanical method
   b. Chemical method
   c. Semi chemical method
   d. None of the above

188. Casein is present in milk in
   a. Dispersed form
   b. Colloidal form
   c. Emulsion form
   d. All of the above

189. Site of rennin action is
   a. κ casein
   b. γ casein
   c. α lactalbumin
   d. β lactglobulin

190. Which of the tests comes under the 'platform tests' of milk?
a. Appearance
b. Lactometer reading
c. Acidity
d. All of the above

191. In butter making, the term 'working' means
a. Kneading of butter
b. Pasteurization of cream
c. Salting of butter
d. Addition of colour

192. Which of the following is the phase transformation method?
a. Vacreation
b. Working
c. Churning
d. Homogenization

193. Clove contains
a. Carveol
b. Indole
c. Clovonol
d. Eugenol

194. Equipment should be cleaned
a. as soon as you finish using it
b. before you go home
c. according to fix schedule
d. as soon as you arrive

195. The most hygienic way of drying hands is by using
a. a warm air drier
b. a hand towel
c. the dish cloth
d. the lab coat

196. Instructions for operating a machine
a. Should be distributed as handouts
b. Displayed on a plaque near the machine
c. Pasted on the machine
d. Explained verbally when the machine is purchased

197. Which of the following factors affect/s the ease of cleaning of a machine?
a. Material used for the machine fabrication
b. Machine design
c. Ease of dismantling
d. All of the above

198. Ideal flooring of a processing area is
a. carpet
b. wooden
c. ceramic tiles
d. without any plastering

199. Hot water should be used for cleaning equipment because
a. it increase chemical activity of the detergent
b. it melts fats
c. it has sanitizing affect
d. All of the above

200. Wound like cuts, burns, etc. should be covered with

a. waterproof dressing | b. antiseptic ointment
c. cotton and bandage | d. anything available

201. According to GMP, food handlers should keep their fingernails

a. short | b. manicured
c. unvarnished | d. All of the above

202. Which of the following spices is known as the KING of spices?

a. Aniseed | b. Chili
c. Pepper | d. Ginger

203. Which of the following is sulphur containing spice?

a. Dill | b. Asafoetida
c. Clove | d. Pepper

204. Principle component of pepper is

a. d-pinene | b. limonene
c. euginol | d. anethole

205. The deep red, pungent powder prepared from the ground, derived pods of sweet pepper is

a. pepper unit | b. paprika
c. pepprinol | d. None of the above

206. Chief carotenoid present in chili is

a. xanthophyll | b. capsanthin
c. lycopene | d. All of the above

207. Pungency factor present in chili is

a. capsorubin | b. capsanthin
c. capsine | d. capsaicin

208. Compounding step is involved in the processing of

a. asafoetida | b. dill
c. caraway | d. All of the above

209. Curcumin is the pigment found in

a. turmeric | b. ginger
c. saffron | d. clove

210. Curing step is involved in the processing of

a. vanilla | b. green cardamom
c. saffron | d. All of the above

211. Withering step is seen during the processing of
a. coffee
b. tea
c. clove
d. cocoa

212. Rolling is done in the processing of
a. coffee
b. cocoa
c. tea
d. cashew

213. Objective of withering process is
a. crush leaf
b. condition leaf
c. dry leaf
d. All of the above

214. Caffeine is a/an
a. carbohydrate
b. alkaloid
c. amino acid
d. steroid

215. The enzyme playing central role in black tea processing is
a. protease
b. polyphenol oxidase
c. papain
d. phosphatidase

216. Green tea is
a. double distilled tea
b. unfermented tea
c. chlorophyll rich tea
d. fresh leaf to tea plant

217. Which of the following is/are the tea pigments?
a. Theaflavin
b. Thearubigin
c. Both a and b
d. Neither a nor b

218. Decaffeination of tea can be done by which of the following methods?
a. Use of adsorbents
b. Use of cyclodextrin
c. Biotechnology
d. All of the above

219. Wet processing of coffee beans yields which kind of coffee?
a. Parchment coffee
b. Cherry coffee
c. Kerala coffee
d. Ivory coffee

220. Aim ~~of~~ polishing of coffee beans is
a. cosmetic
b. to increase shelf life
c. decaffeination
d. All of the above

221. Roasting of coffee beans leads to
a. Moisture reduction
b. Flavour generation
c. Both a and b
d. Either a or b

222. Chicory is obtained from
a. Leaf
b. Stem
c. Flower
d. Root

223. Astringency of coffee is attributed to the presence of
a. chicory
b. caffeine
c. chlorogenic acid
d. insulin

224. Bitterness of coffee is attributed to
a. caffeine
b. chlorogenic acid
c. insulin
d. None of the above

225. Espresso coffee is
a. African traditional drink
b. Indian traditional drink
c. Italian traditional drink
d. Sri Lankan traditional drink

226. Which of the following steps are NOT included in cocoa processing?
a. Fermentation
b. Drying
c. Roasting
d. None of the above

227. Cocoa fermentation is dominated by
a. Bacteria
b. Yeast
c. Fungi
d. All of the above

228. Alkalization is a method generally done during the process of
a. cocoa
b. coffee
c. tea
d. cashew nut

229. Cocoa contain which of the following alkaloids?
a. Theanine
b. Theobromine
c. Thearubigin
d. Theaflavin

230. Winnowing step is seen during processing of
a. Tea
b. Cocoa
c. Tomato
d. Milk

231. Heating of cream at low pressure is called
a. Pasteurization
b. Sterilization
c. Vacreation
d. Thermo-sterilization

232. In a spray dryer, rotating discs make use of ———— energy for atomization
a. Gravitational
b. Centrifugal
c. Potential
d. Heat

233. _______ is the basis for checking pasteurization efficiency of milk
a. Peroxidase and catalase test
b. Phosphatase test
c. Amylase test
d. None of the above

234. Eyes are the characteristic feature of
a. Icecream
b. Khoa
c. Swiss cheese
d. Cottage cheese

235. Butter flavour is due to
a. Ammonia
b. Diacetyl
c. Ethylene
d. Vanillin

236. Chief source of rennin is
a. Microorganisms
b. Papaya seed
c. Stomach of calf
d. Reacting urea with sulphuric acid

237. The father of White Revolution is
a. Dr. M. Kurien
b. Dr. V. Kurien
c. Dr. S. Kurien
d. Dr. A. Kurien

238. Marinades are prepared from
a. Egg
b. Meat
c. Fish
d. Cereals

239. Churning process is used during
a. Butter making
b. Chocolate making
c. Marinade making
d. None of the above

240. A component of the egg which is responsible for holding the yolk in the centre of egg is
a. Air cell
b. Chalazae
c. Shell
d. Vitelline membrane

241. Poor quality egg floats in the water due to
a. Microbial spoilage
b. Increase in air cell
c. Decrease in air cell
d. Air cell has no relation to quality of egg

242. In controlled atmospheric storage
a. CO_2 is used
b. N_2 is used
c. O_2 is used
d. All of the above

243. Which of the following gas is gaseous hormone?
a. Carbon dioxide
b. Ethane
c. Ethylene
d. Methane

244. Which of the following statements is/are correct?
a. Retrogradation is seen in starch
b. Rancidity is seen in fat
c. Putrefaction is seen in protein
d. All of the above

245. Which of the following condition is for pasteurization of milk?
a. 50 °C for 1 hr
b. 65 °C for 45 min
c. 72 °C for 15 sec
d. 85 °C for 2 sec

246. Which of the following statements is/are CORRECT?
a. Ham is from pork thighs
b. While conventional Bacon is from pork bellies
c. Sausage is a minced meat product
d. All of the above

247. Maize is milled to obtain
a. starch
b. germ oil
c. liquid starch
d. All of the above

248. Which of the following process is seen in sorghum processing?
a. Winnowing
b. Pearling
c. Curling
d. All of the above

249. Which of the following process is seen in barley processing?
a. Pearling
b. Blocking
c. Milling
d. All of the above

250. Blocking processing during barely processing is
a. rounding of grains
b. shelling of grains
c. milling of grains
d. weighing of grains

251. Oolong variety is found in
a. Tea
b. Coffee
c. Cocoa
d. Barley

252. 'Cupping' is process of
a. using cup for grading of apple
b. closing carbonated beverage bottle with cap
c. testing of coffee for quality and taste
d. None of the above

253. Pyrolysis process is seen during processing of
a. Tea
b. Coffee
c. Chocolate
d. All of the above

254. Which of the following is called 'queen of spice'?
a. Pepper
b. Turmeric
c. Chilli
d. Cardamom

255. Curcumin is obtained from
a. Pepper
b. Turmeric
c. Chilli
d. Cardamom

256. In modified atmosphere packaging
a. Amount of oxygen is increased inside pack
b. Amount of oxygen is decreased inside pack
c. Amount of oxygen is kept at atmospheric level inside pack
d. Any of the above depending on the fruit to be packed

257. Lyophilization is
a. Pasteurization
b. Radiation
c. Homogenization
d. Freeze drying

258. PVA stands for
a. Polyvinyl Alcohol
b. Post Vacreation Activity
c. Potassium Valeric Acid
d. None of the above

259. Fillers in paper (packaging material) improve
a. Opacity
b. Brightness
c. Gloss
d. All of the above

260. Enamels in cans are
a. their material of construction
b. their secondary packaging
c. their colour
d. their protective coating

261. R-enamels are used for packing ______________ foods
a. strongly coloured acidic food
b. strongly acidic colourless food
c. high sulphur containing colourless food
d. high protein colourless food

262. E-enamels are used for packing ______________ foods
a. strongly coloured acidic food
b. strongly acidic coloured food
c. high sulphur containing colourless food
d. high protein colourless food

263. Which of the following is the major chemical process used for pulping of wood during paper manufacturing?
a. Birch's process
b. Kraft's process
c. Paine's process
d. Parker's process

264. Controlled atmosphere packaging (CAP) involves
a. Monitoring and adjustment of the gases
b. Introduction of a gas mixture other than air into a package
c. Introduction of a gas mixture same as the air into a package
d. Both a and b

265. Which of the following is not a packaging material used in food industry?
a. RR
b. EVOH
c. PP
d. None of the above

266. Which of the following statements regarding non-climacteric fruits is/are CORRECT?
a. they ripen on the tree
b. they are not capable of continuing their ripening process once removed from the plant.
c. they do not respond to ethylene treatment for ripening
d. All of the above

267. Which of the following changes are seen in in cell wall during ripening of fruits?
a. Loss of arabinan
b. Loss of galactan
c. Solubilization of pectin
d. All of the above.

268. Which of the following parameters generally describes quality specifications of fruit juice?
a. Fermentable sugar, acidity
b. Composition, color, texture, flavor
c. Acidity, sugar content, flavor
d. Texture, acidity, consistency

269. Which of the following statements regarding pre-cooling is/are CORRECT?
a. High humidity is maintained during room cooling is to avoid desiccation and weight loss during cooling
b. Cooling time in forced air cooling is more than the room cooling
c. In hydro-cooling products are by spraying or flooding the commodity with hot water
d. All of the above

270. Which of the following statements regarding fumigation is/are CORRECT?
a. Methyl bromide is used for fresh produce
b. Phosphine is used for dry produce
c. Thiabendazole and dichloran are effective against fungi
d. All of the above

271. Which of the following sequence of unit operations shows correct steps of pulse dry milling?
a. Cleaning → Conditioning → Dehusking & splitting → Pretreatment with oil → Polishing
b. Cleaning → Dehusking & splitting → Conditioning → Pretreatment with oil → Polishing
c. Cleaning → Pretreatment with oil à Conditioning → Dehusking & splitting → Polishing
d. Cleaning → Conditioning → Pretreatment with oil → Dehusking & splitting → Polishing

272. Conditioning process during pulse processing there is
a. alternate wetting and drying of pulses
b. treating with sunflower oil
c. rubbing pulses between two rubber rollers
d. None of the above

273. Fundamental objective of polishing step in pulse milling process is to
a. Increase the vitamin content of pulse
b. Decrease the anti-nutritional factors in pulses
c. Increase the consumer acceptability of pulses
d. All of the above

274. Which of the following is a naturally occurring gaseous plant growth hormone?
a. Ethylene
b. Methane
c. Nitrogen
d. Carbon dioxide

275. Which of the following chemicals is/are the index of spoilage of fish?
a. Diacetyl
b. TMA
c. Carbon Monoxide
d. All of the above

276. Drip loss is seen in fishes and other seafood products when
a. water-holding capacity falls below the water content of the muscle
b. when fish is stored in dried area, there is water loss from the surface
c. when fish stored in water filled container, excess water is lost
d. All of the above

277. Electrical stimulation is the post slaughter application of an electrical current to the animal carcass to
a. Increase the rate of bleeding
b. accelerate postmortem glycolysis
c. kill the microbes
d. All of the above

278. Which of the following statements regarding meat processing is/are CORRECT?
a. The muscle undergo rigor mortis when supplies of ATP are depleted
b. Electrical stimulation decreases tenderness, color, and palatability of meat
c. Pale, Soft, and Exudative (PSE) condition is most often observed in canned fish
d. The Dark Firm and Dry (DFD) phenomenon is typically characterized by pasteurized egg

279. Which of the following statements is/are CORRECT?
a. Drip loss is one of the most important problems in frozen meat
b. The loss of fluid reduces the eating quality, binding ability, and the weight of the meat
c. Freezing initiates several physical and physico chemical changes in meat that lead to the deterioration in quality
d. All of the above

280. The lactoperoxidase system which have antimicrobial effect in milk consists of
a. Lactoperxidase .
b. Thiocyanate
c. Hydrogen peroxide
d. All of the above

281. Common characteristics of a Lactic Acid Bacteria is/are?
a. Gram positive
b. Fermentative aerobes
c. Spore forming
d. All of the above

282. Which of the following is the most important for cheese making?
a. Rennin
b. Hydrogen peroxide
c. Sodium nitrite
d. All of the above

283. Which of the following shows correct sequence of cheese making?

a. Curdling of milk → draining of whey → salting → cooking → pressing → ripening

b. Curdling of milk → draining of whey → salting → pressing → cooking → ripening

c. Curdling of milk → cooking à draining of whey → salting → pressing → ripening

d. Curdling of milk → draining of whey → salting → pressing → ripening → cooking

284. Hops are added during the manufacture of

a. cheese b. beer

c. kefir d. chocolate

284. Which of the following statements is/are CORRECT?

a. Sourdough bakery products have an extended shelf life

b. *Saccharomyces cerevisiae* is commonly known as baker's yeast

c. Vinegar contains a minimum of 4% w/v acetic acid

d. All of the above

285. Which of the following statements with respect to Modified Atmospheric Packaging (MAP) is/are CORRECT?

a. The MAP of respiring food products is different from those MAP of non-respiring foods products

b. In MAP, the gas composition within the package is not monitored or adjusted

c. The MAP of fresh fruits and vegetables is a preservation system that is non-sterile by design.

d. All of the above

286. Which of the following statement is CORRECT for controlled atmospheric packaging and modified atmospheric packaging?

a. In both CAP and MAP gas composition is controlled

b. Neither in CAP nor in MAP gas composition is controlled

c. In CAP gas composition is controlled but not in MAP

d. In MAP gas composition is controlled but not in CAP

287. The main purpose of ______________ is to inactivate the naturally occurring enzymes present in vegetable.

a. Curing b. Blanching

c. Winnowing d. Smoking

288. ______________ is classified as enzymatic and non enzymatic

a. Brownian movement b. Blanching

c. Browning reaction d. Bloom

289. ______________ is the condition where the surface of food yield a skin practically impervious to moisture during drying process.

a. Case hardening b. Blooming

c. Maillard reaction d. Caramelization

290. ________________ is the process of moistening dry material.

a. Osmosis
b. Dehydration
c. Rehydration
d. None of the above

291. Which of the following statements related to caking is/are correct?

a. It is desirable for tablet formation
b. It is undesirable when a dry free-flowing material is required
c. Calcium triphosphate is used as anti-caking agent
d. All of the above

292. Which of the following is an/are example of an emulsion?

a. Cream
b. Mayonnaise
c. Butter
d. All of the above

293. Which of the following is/are used for coating of food?

a. Resins
b. Wax
c. Shellac
d. All of the above

294. ________________ technology is the coating of food ingredient particles with more stable medium so as to ensure controlled release of the ingredients?

a. Enrobing
b. Encapsulation
c. Hurdle
d. None of the above

295. "Halal" method is a type of

a. Baking
b. Brewing
c. Slaughtering
d. None of the above

296. ________________ is a type of pasteurizing apparatus used particularly in the butter industry?

a. Churner
b. Homogenizer
c. Vacreator
d. None of the above

297. Which of the following is an example of dry heat cooking?

a. Stewing
b. Baking
c. Frying
d. Poaching

298. ________________ is the process where frozen foods are brought to ambient temperature.

a. Crystallization
b. Homogenization
c. Thawing
d. Nucleation

299. Which of the following is NOT associated with meat processing?

a. Curing
b. Winnowing
c. Sausage
d. Smoking

300. Which of the following is NOT associated with chocolate manufacturing?

a. Refining
b. Conching
c. Blanching
d. Moulding

4 Advances in Food Science and Technology

1. Which of the following microbes is used in the developing insect resistance crop?
   a. *Bacillus cereus*
   b. *Bacillus thuringiensis*
   c. *Bacillus okhensis*
   d. All of the above
2. Genetic engineering can help in
   a. slow down the natural senescence processes
   b. prevention from insect attack
   c. increasing shelf life of fruits and vegetables
   d. All of the above
3. Which of the following statements related to genetically modified foods?
   a. GM foods are not permitted in India
   b. Only GM corns are allowed in India
   c. Only GM wheat are allowed in India
   d. Only GM potato are allowed in India
4. Which of the following techniques is NOT a membrane processing technology?
   a. Reverse osmosis
   b. Ultra filtration
   c. Micro filtration
   d. Super critical extraction
5. Which of the following membrane processing technology is NOT based on the principle of sieving?
   a. Reverse osmosis
   b. Ultra filtration
   c. Micro filtration
   d. All of the above
6. Which of the following wavelength range is detrimental on microbes and thus helpful in preserving foods?
   a. 50 to 100 nm
   b. 100 to 150 nm
   c. 170 to 800 nm
   d. 900 to 1250 nm

7. High intensity light kills microbes by
   a. denaturation of proteins
   b. inactivation of functional enzymes
   c. disruption of the functional components of nucleoproteins
   d. All of the above

8. Which of the following non-conventional preservation techniques is based on cavitation and de-cavitation?
   a. Irradiation
   b. Reverse osmosis
   c. Ultrasound
   d. All of the above

9. Which of the following frequency ranges can be used in preservation of food?
   a. < 10 Hz
   b. 10 Hz to 200 Hz
   c. 5 kHz to 10 kHz
   d. > 20 kHz

10. Ultra-sonication can be used for
    a. accelerated freezing
    b. accelerated oxidation and ageing
    c. crystallization of fats
    d. All of the above

11. Which of the following process involves semi permeable membrane?
    a. Reverse osmosis
    b. Ultra filtration
    c. Micro filtration
    d. All of the above

12. Which of the following factors affect the microwave heating?
    a. Frequency
    b. Moisture content of food
    c. Dielectric constant of food
    d. All of the above

13. Science of chemical reactions performed under an acoustic field is called ....
    a. Sonography
    b. Sonochemistry
    c. Aerodynamics
    d. Stoichiometry

14. Which kind of sound wave is called shear wave?
    a. Magnetic wave
    b. Longitudinal wave
    c. Transverse wave
    d. None of the above

15. Which of the following statements is CORRECT?
    a. Longitudinal waves can move through solid, liquid and gas
    b. Transverse waves can move through solid, liquid and gas
    c. Transverse waves cannot move through solid
    d. Longitudinal waves cannot move through solid

16. Which of the following waves are widely used in ultrasonic applications?
    a. Longitudinal
    b. Transverse
    c. Both a and b
    d. None of the above

17. In the liquid media, the best-known effect of ultrasound is ________
a. caramelization b. putrefaction
c. gelatinization d. cavitation

18. Application of ultrasound in food industry can be in
a. homogenization b. emulsification
c. protein denaturation d. All of the above

19. Ohmic heating is also known as
a. Pascal heating b. Nicholas heating
c. Joule heating d. Pasteur heating

20. Effectiveness of Ohmic heating depends on ________ of food
a. electrical conductivity b. solid content
c. specific heat d. All of the above

21. Which of the following statements is/are CORRECT?
a. moisture mobility increase electrical conductivity
b. salt increase electrical conductivity
c. fat decrease electrical conductivity
d. All of the above

22. Which of the following statement is CORRECT with respect to Ohmic heating?
a. In a mixture of solid and liquid, component with lower heat capacity will tend to heat faster
b. DC current is used in Ohmic heating
c. Higher viscosity fluids heat slower than lower viscosity fluids
d. All of the above

23. Ohmic heating has found its application in
a. sensor to detect starch gelatinization b. dehydration of vegetables
c. extraction of components from food d. All of the above

24. Optimal wavelength of light wave for maximum germicidal effect is
a. 1200 Å b. 2600 Å
c. 3150 Å d. 4800 Å

25. Which of the following is food preservation technique?
a. Irradiation b. Hurdle technology
c. Fermentation d. All of the above

26. Which of the following electromagnetic wave spectrum have shown germicidal effect during food processing?
a. Violet b. Red
c. Ultraviolet colour d. Green

27. Proposed mode of action of UV rays on microbes leading to their germicidal effect is/are
    a. formation of lethal organic peroxide b. disruption of DNA of microbes
    c. disruption of cell wall of bacteria d. All of the above

28. Which of the following radioactive element is used in irradiation of food?
    a. ^{60}Co b. ^{137}Cs c. Both a and b d. None of the above

29. Which of the following is/are unit of irradiation dose?
    a. Gray b. Rad c. Curie d. All of the above

30. At what dose of irradiation, we can achieve disinfestation in fruits and vegetable?
    a. Upto 3 kGy b. Upto 30 kGy c. Upto 300 kGy d. Upto 3000 kGy

31. Sprouting of potato can be prevented at what dose of irradiation?
    a. 0.05 – 0.15 kGy b. 0.5 – 1.5 kGy c. 5.0 – 15 kGy d. 50 – 150 kGy

32. Which of the following doses of irradiation can be used for pasteurization of food?
    a. 1.0 – 2.0 Gy b. 10 – 20 Gy c. 1.0 – 2.0 kGy d. 10 – 20 kGy

33. Which of the following doses of irradiation is generally used for sterilization of food?
    a. 1.0 – 2.0 kGy b. 3.0 – 20 kGy c. 30 – 80 kGy d. >100 kGy

34. Pasteurization by irradiation is also called as
    a. Radio pasteurization b. Sonic pasteurization
    c. Radurization d. Radappertization

35. Sterilization by irradiation is also called as
    a. Radio pasteurization b. Sonic pasteurization
    c. Radurization d. Radappertization

36. Cobalt 60 is source of which kind of radiation which is used for preservation of food?
    a. alpha b. beta c. gamma d. X ray

37. Mode of action of irradiation on microbe can be explained by
    a. effect on nucleic acid of microbes b. alteration of membrane lipids
    c. change in activity of membrane enzymes d. All of the above

38. The factors that affect the susceptibility of microorganisms to irradiation is/are
    a. dose level b. temperature
    c. type of organism d. All of the above

39. Softening of fruits and vegetables at higher dose of irradiation is due to
    a. breaking of higher polysaccharides b. formation of soft tissues due to genetic mutation
    c. formation and accumulation of soft lipids d. All of the above

40. Which of the following changes can be seen due to irradiation of food?
    a. Hydrolization of sugar b. Autoxidation of fat
    c. Degradation of vitamin C d. All of the above

41. High intensity pulsed electric field cause the lysis of microbial cell due to
   a. reverse osmosis b. surface desiccation
   c. pore formation in cell membrane d. All of the above
42. Which of the following is the non-thermal method of food preservation?
   a. Microwave processing b. Retorting
   c. Pulsed electric field processing d. High pressure processing
43. Which of the following methods is called cold sterilization?
   a. Reverse osmosis b. Irradiation
   c. High pressure processing d. All of the above
44. Microbes which can survive high pressure applied for prolonged time is called
   a. barophiles b. baroduric
   c. barophobic d. barolovers
45. Barophiles are organisms that
   a. can grow at higher pressure b. are killed at higher pressure
   c. hates higher pressure d. None of the above
46. High pressure processing inactivates microbes as it affects microbes in following way
   a. affecting the cell membrane
   b. inactivation of membrane bound enzyme
   c. decrease in pH due to the enhancement of the ionic dissociation
   d. All of the above
47. Which of the following statements is NOT correct regarding high pressure processing?
   a. It is a non-thermal process
   b. It adversely decrease the nutritional value of food
   c. It causes denaturation of protein
   d. All of the above
48. Hurdle technology is a food preservation technique using
   a. magnetic fields b. electric fields
   c. high pressure d. different preservation techniques together
49. Principally, hurdle technology disrupts which of the following phenomena in microbes
   a. Homeostasis b. Respiration
   c. Photosynthesis d. Osmosis
50. In osmotic dehydration process, water is removed from tissues by immersing them in ________ solution.
   a. hypertonic b. hypotonic
   c. dilute d. All of the above

51. Which of the following statements related to osmotic dehydration is correct?
    a. It is used for partial removal of moisture before any other processing
    b. Osmotic dehydration before frying helps in getting a final product with less fat
    c. Osmotic dehydration as pre-freezing treatment helps in decreasing the enzymatic browning of product
    d. All of the above

52. Which of the following methods is/are a thermal process for removal of water from food?
    a. Osmotic dehydration
    b. Osmotic membrane distillation
    c. Direct osmosis
    d. All of the above

53. Osmotic membrane distillation process requires
    a. high pressure
    b. ambient temperature
    c. hydrophilic membrane
    d. All of the above

54. Osmotic membrane distillation process is also known as
    a. osmotic evaporation
    b. membrane evaporation
    c. isothermal membrane distillation
    d. All of the above

55. Better inactivation of microbes has been observed at radio frequencies near
    a. 2.5 kHz
    b. 5.0 kHz
    c. 10 kHz
    d. 20 kHz

56. Which of the following statement regarding irradiated packed foods is/are CORRECT?
    a. In India irradiation of any kind of food products is prohibited
    b. Label of an irradiated packed food should clearly mention that the product is irradiated
    c. Irradiation can only kill microbes but cannot inhibit sprouting in potato
    d. All of the above

57. Which of the following statements regarding non-traditional preservatives is/are CORRECT?
    a. Phytoallexins are effective against bacteria only
    b. Chitins have both bactericidal and fungicidal effect
    c. Lactoperoxidase enzyme shows best antimicrobial effect at neutral pH
    c. All of the above

58. The concept of triple point is used in which of the following processing method?
    a. Microwave heating
    b. Dehydrofreezing
    c. Freeze drying
    d. Osmotic drying

59. Freeze drying process involves the phenomena of
    a. Diffusion
    b. Browning reaction
    c. Blooming
    d. Sublimation

60. A freeze dried product is superior to a tray dried product because it has
    a. superior nutritional value
    b. superior flavour retention
    c. superior texture
    d. All of the above

61. Supercritical fluid extraction method uses ________ as solvent

a. methanol | b. hexane
c. liquid carbon dioxide | d. All of the above

62. If we say nanotechnology, it uses particles in the size range of

a. 10^{-3} m | b. 10^{-6} m
c. 10^{-9} m | d. 10^{-12} m

63. Nanotechnology in food technology has promising potential in

a. improving barrier properties of packaging material
b. enhancing the nutritional delivery
c. decreasing the time of emulsification
d. All of the above

64. Which of the following is/are source of alpha linolenic acid:

a. Flax seeds | b. Walnut
c. Soyabean | d. All of the above

65. A dietary supplement is a product that contains nutrients derived from food products that are concentrated in liquid or capsule form:

a. True | b. False

66. The word "nutraceutical" was coined by:

a. Dr. Aldrin W. Norwen | b. Dr. Stephen L. Defelice
c. Dr. Stanley S. Wood | d. None of the above

67. Which of the following is source of lutein?

a. Carrot | b. Beet root | c. Spinach | d. Red wine

(Lutein is one of the naturally occurring carotenoids)

68. Prebiotics are

a. Phytochemicals | b. Nutrients
c. Dietary supplements | d. None of the above

69. Vitamin E is fat soluble vitamin

a. True | b. False

(Vitamin E is important for human vision and also has antioxidant properties)

70. Food should be fortified with which of the following vitamins to avoid the case of no blood clotting

a. A | b. E | c. D | d. K

71. Below given Vitamin helps to produce essential proteins:

a. B_1 | b. B_2 | c. B_6 | d. B_{12}

72. Which mineral helps in haemoglobin production?

a. Cobalt | b. Copper | c. Iodine | d. Chromium

73. Benefit(s) of phytochemicals is/are

a. Substrate for biochemical reactions | b. Cofactors of enzymatic reactions
c. Scavengers of reactive or toxic chemicals | d. All of the above

74. Which of the following statements is/are correct?
   a. Coffee is packed in metal container
   b. Coffee is packed in glass container
   c. Potato chips are packed in metalized laminates
   d. All of the above

75. Disadvantage(s) of nutraceuticals is/are
   a. Not subjected to same testing and regulations as pharmaceuticals
   b. Bioavailability of nutrients is less
   c. No regulatory definition
   d. All of the above

76. Organic food certification is certification process for
   a. producing organic foods
   b. marketing organic foods
   c. Both a and b
   d. None

77. Which of the following is/are considered as nutraceutical?
   a. Lycopene
   b. Flavonoid
   c. Allium compounds
   d. All of the above

78. Which of the following statements regarding "dietary supplement" is/are correct?
   a. is intended for ingestion in pill, capsule, tablet, or liquid form.
   b. is not represented for use as a conventional food or as the sole item of a meal or diet.
   c. includes products such as an approved new drug or certified antibiotic
   d. All of the above

79. Chemical substances present in food which might have important function in human body are
   a. Plantochemicals
   b. Phytoceuticals
   c. Phytochemicals
   d. Phytotoxicants

80. Which of the following is/are phytoestrogens?
   a. β-carotene
   b. Zeaxanthin
   c. Isoflavones
   d. All of the above

81. Genetic engineering can be used to make
   a. disease resistant variety of plant
   b. enhanced flavour in food
   c. new colour development in food
   d. All of the above

82. Which of the following methods of extraction uses liquified carbon dioxide as solvent?
   a. Super critical fluid extraction
   b. Hyper critical fluid extraction
   c. Carbon dioxide fluid extraction
   d. None of the above

83. Hurdle technology is used in
   a. Oil extraction process
   b. Ketchup preservation.
   c. Wheat milling
   d. All of the above

84. There are some concerns about Genetically modified (GM) foods. Which of the following reasons is/are cited by experts for not allowing GM foods to be used commonly?
   a. It is very expensive
   b. It decreases the nutritional value of food
   c. It may form some proteins which can cause allergy
   d. All of the above

85. Which of the following statements regarding organic foods is/are correct?
   a. These are grown without synthetic pesticides
   b. They are safer than those grown using synthetic fertilizers
   c. Taste of food is not drastically different from those grown using synthetic fertilizers
   d. All of the above

86. Which of the following statements is perfect definition for "100% organic" as per USDA?
   a. No synthetic ingredients are allowed by law.
   b. At least 95% of ingredients are organically produced.
   c. At least 70% of ingredients are organic; the other 30% are from a list approved by the USDA.
   d. None of the above

87. Which of the following statements is perfect definition for "organic food" as per USDA?
   a. No synthetic ingredients are allowed by law.
   b. At least 95% of ingredients are organically produced.
   c. At least 70% of ingredients are organic; the other 30% are from a list approved by the USDA.
   d. None of the above

88. Which of the following labelled foods need not to have USDA Organic seal?
   a. 100% organic food b. Organic food
   c. Made with organic ingredients d. All of the above

89. Issues expected from Genetically Modified foods is/are
   a. toxicity b. allergenicity
   c. Both a and b d. None of the above

90. Which of the following statements is/are CORRECT?
   a. In India GM crops are regulated under the Environment Protection Act
   b. In India GM crops are regulated under the Ministry of Agriculture
   c. In India all kinds of GM crops permitted for consumption
   d. All of the above

91. Which of the following is/are issues related to GM foods?
   a. Potential human health impacts, including allergens, transfer of antibiotic resistance markers, unknown effects
   b. Increasing dependence on industrialized nations by developing countries
   c. Tampering with nature by mixing genes among species
   d. All of the above

92. Which of the following is/are the scope for application of nano-technology?
    a. Nano-modification of seed and fertilizers b. Food fortification
    c. Smart food packaging d. All of the above
93. In hurdle technology, which of the following is/are the hurdles?
    a. High temperature as physical hurdle b. Lactic acid as chemical hurdle
    c. Protective culture as biological hurdle d. All of the above
94. The biologically active compounds present in plant (other than nutrients) which have potential to reduce diseases in human beings are called ______
    a. DHA b. Phytochemicals
    c. Naturochemicals d. None of the above
95. Which of the following present in oats acts phytochemicals and reduces LDL in blood?
    a. Starch b. Beta glucan
    c. Phytosterone d. All of the above
96. Food or food product that provides health and medical benefits, including the prevention and treatment of disease is called ______
    a. Aromatic food b. Unsatuarted food
    c. Nutraceuticals d. Phytochemcials
97. Which of the following statements is CORRECT?
    a. Dietary supplement is a product taken by mouth that contains a "dietary ingredient" intended to supplement the diet
    b. Dietary supplement is a product taken during fasting
    c. Dietary supplement is a product taken by mouth that contains a "nutraceuticals and phytochemicals only" intended to supplement the diet
    d. None of the above
98. The term 'pascalization' is another word for
    a. Hurdle technology b. Irradiation
    c. High pressure processing d. Supercritical processing
99. Which of the following is/are used in supercritical fluid extraction method?
    a. Hexane b. CO_2
    c. Ethanol d. All of the above
100. Stage-Gate process is widely used in
    a. Cleaning in place of food machinery b. New product development cycle
    c. Rework utilization d. Effluent treatment plant

5 Fundamentals of Food Safety

1. As per GMP guidelines the refrigerated food should be stored below
   a. 5°C or below b. 0°C or below
   c. 4°C or below d. 8°C or below
2. As per GHP water used in food processing units should meet the
   a. Non portability test b. Drinkability test
   c. Cleaning test d. Portability test
3. HACCP has shifted emphasis from end product inspection & testing to
   a. Preventive control of hazards at all stages of food production
   b. Predictive control of hazards at all stages of food production
   c. Managing control of hazards at all stages of food production
   d. Corrective control of hazards at all stages of food production
4. HACCP has defined CCP as
   a. Critical Care Points b. Critical Control Process.
   c. Critical Control Points d. Coded Control Points
5. What is the objective of ISO 22000?
   a. To establish a food safety management system
   b. Certification for production plant
   c. Minimize resource d. None of the above
6. Which is National accreditation body for India with respect to ISO/IEC 17021:2006 and also member of IAF.
   a. Quality Council of India b. BIS
   c. FSSAI d. FDA
7. Following are three main Hazards defined in HACCP
   a. Chemical/Biological and Physical Hazards b. Organic/Biological and Physical Hazards
   c. Non living/Living and Physical Hazards d. Chemical/Biological and Viral Hazards

8. How many principals are in HACCP?
   a. 6 b. 7 c. 5 d. 4
9. Which method is used in HACCP to identify the CCPs?
   a. Checklist b. 5 Why analysis
   c. Elimination techniques d. Decision tree method
10. ISO 9001 is which kind of management system
    a. Quality management b. Food safety
    c. Environment d. Food security
11. FAO, WHO & CODEX have membership of how many countries?
    a. 165 b. 200 c. 240 d. 100
12. Ergot disease is caused by which mycotoxin?
    a. Aflatoxin b. Ergotin c. botulin d. pathogens
13. Food hazard is?
    a. a biological, chemical, or physical agent with the potential to cause an adverse health effect
    b. a chemical agent with the potential to cause an adverse health effect
    c. a physical agent with the potential to cause an adverse health effect
    d. a biological agent with the potential to cause an adverse health effect
14. Which of this is biological hazard?
    a. Metal pieces b. Bacteria
    c. Stone d. Agricultural waste
15. Which of this is chemical hazard?
    a. Virus b. Fungi
    c. Stones d. Aflatoxin
16. Which of this is physical hazard?
    a. Pesticides b. Bacteria
    c. Wood d. Aflatoxin
17. Which code/system to be followed in LAB area?
    a. GMP b. GLP
    c. GCP d. GAP
18. Which of these is food safety tool?
    a. tree diagram b. HACCP
    c. control chart d. pareto analysis
19. Which of these is not TQM tool?
    a. affinity diagram b. tree diagram
    c. interrelationship diagram d. 5s system

20. Which of these is secondary level of processing?
    a. sorting
    b. crushing
    c. grading
    d. canning
21. Microbial contamination can cause which disease?
    a. cancer
    b. meningitis
    c. food poisoning
    d. constipation
22. Which bacteria cause botulism?
    a. *S. typhi*
    b. *S. aureus*
    c. *E. coli*
    d. *Clostridium*
23. Which of these is emerging food contaminant?
    a. Benzene
    b. Aldehyde
    c. Ketones
    d. Esters
24. What are agrochemicals?
    a. Chemical used in animal husbandry
    b. Chemical used for packaging
    c. Chemicals used in agricultural practices and animal husbandry with the intent to increase crops and reduce costs
    d. None of the above
25. According to GMP food handlers should keep their fingernails
    a. short
    b. manicured
    c. unvarnished
    d. All of the above
26. Chemical additive which when added to food retards or prevents oxidative deterioration of food is?
    a. Antioxidant
    b. Emulsifier
    c. Stabilizer
    d. Colourant
27. AGMARK logo with blend B is for?
    a. Admixture of any Refined edible oil with Rice bran oil
    b. Blend of only Refined edible oil
    c. Blend of only Rice bran oil
    d. None of the above
28. GHP has how many principal
    a. 6
    b. 3
    c. 7
    d. 8
29. GHP full form is
    a. Good health practice
    b. Good hygiene practice
    c. Good healthcare practice
    d. Good human resource practice

30. Environmental hygiene means
    a. sources of contamination from the production place
    b. sources of contamination from the nearby place
    c. sources of contamination from the environment
    d. sources of contamination from the warehouse

31. GRAS means?
    a. Good product
    b. Genetically modified
    c. Generally recognized as safe
    d. All of the above

32. Which was the widely used food preservative in 1920?
    a. Benzol
    b. Boric Acid
    c. Sugar
    d. Acetaldehyde

33. The food additive cyclamate was banned in 1969 in which country?
    a. Mexico
    b. Russia
    c. USA
    d. All of the above

34. Ingredient listing in food must be as follow?
    a. In descending order of weight.
    b. Increasing order of weight
    c. Declaration as portion size
    d. All of the above

35. Cross contamination in food can be avoided by
    a. Pest control
    b. GMP
    c. Design layout
    d. None of the above

36. Which of these is true?
    a. Structure & design layout important for production plant
    b. Quality products mandatory to produce
    c. Quality control for product to be done
    d. All of the above

37. ISO 9001 is for
    a. Environment safety standard
    b. Occupational health & safety
    c. Quality management system
    d. Co-operate service

38. Claims that say food can cure diseases are prohibited?
    a. May be allowed
    b. False
    c. True
    d. None of the above

39. ISO 22000 is for
    a. QMS
    b. HACCP
    c. FSMS
    d. 5 Why system

40. ISO 14001
    a. QMS
    b. HACCP
    c. EMS
    d. FSMS

41. The GHP for food processing comes under which schedule of FSSAI
a. Schedule 3
b. Schedule 5
c. Schedule 6
d. Schedule 4

42. Which of these is 2nd principle of HACCP?
a. Identify CCP
b. Set critical limit
c. Layout design
d. Identify hazard

43. ISO 22000 comprise of?
a. HACCP
b. PRP
c. FSM
d. All of the above

44. Which of these is true?
a. Ventilation systems should be designed and constructed so that air does not flow from contaminated areas to clean areas
b. Ventilation systems is constructed that air to flow from negative pressure to positive pressure area
c. Ventilation systems designed and constructed so that air flow from contaminated areas to clean areas
d. Ventilation systems designed and constructed that air flow to be continuous.

45. What are PRP?
a. HACCP Analysis
b. Pre-Innovative approach
c. Prerequisite Programme
d. Quality control

46. "Use by date" is used for products?
a. Shelf life less than 7 days
b. Shelf life of 24 hrs
c. Shelf life less than 1 month
d. Shelf life less than 6 month

47. Which of these is CCP?
a. Sieving of RM
b. Magnet screening machine
c. Nut & bolt of machine
d. All of the above

48. Which of these is safety procedure before entry in production area?
a. Sanitization of hand
b. Hair tied neatly with hair net
c. Proper glove & apron wear
d. All of the above

49. Quality check of RM, sample done by?
a. Random sampling
b. Cross checking
c. Parameter analysis
d. Control check

50. AGMARK logo with blend A is for?
a. Admixture of any two refined edible oil except Rice bran oil
b. Blend of only Refined edible oil
c. Blend of only Rice bran oil
d. None of the above

51. Which disinfectant commonly used in food handling as sanitization of hands
a. Denatured alcohol
b. Isopropyl alcohol
c. Benzoic phenol
d. formaldehyde

52. In year 1986 the important Act has been enacted called as ——
a. Export act
b. Essential commodities act
c. Consumer Protection act
d. None of the above

53. GMP full form is
a. Good method practice
b. Good Manufacturing practice
c. Good manual practice
d. Good marketing practice

54. Pasteurizing of milk means?
a. Rapid heating at high temperature
b. Rapid heating at high temperature & cooling at very low temperature
c. Rapid coolingat low temperature
d. None of the above

55. Which of these gas is used as preservation technique in potato chip packaging?
a. Helium gas
b. Oxygen gas
c. Nitrogen gas
d. All of the above

56. Raw milk storage done at temperature?
a. 4 °C
b. 10 °C
c. 20 °C
d. 35 °C

57. Process Validation means?
a. Quality Test analysis
b. Documentation of process
c. Evaluation of data that a process is capable of consistently delivering quality products
d. All of the above

58. Finished product to be kept in?
a. conditions that will protect food against physical, chemical, and microbial contamination
b. conditions that will protect food against physical contamination
c. conditions that will protect food against chemical contamination
d. conditions that will protect food against microbial contamination

59. Cleaning of food equipment to be done with?
a. Benzyl products
b. Cold water
c. Toxic product
d. Hot water jet

60. Raw material used in agro production to be checked for?
a. Fat content
b. Aflatoxin
c. Protein content
d. Fibre content

61. HACCP defined as codex
    a. identifies and evaluates the hazards
    b. identifies and controls hazards
    c. identifies, evaluates, and controls hazards
    d. identifies and controls hazards after verification

62. Risk assessment, risk management, risk communication are part of———?
    a. Hazard analysis
    b. Risk analysis
    c. Preventive action
    d. Control of non-conformance

63. The efficacy of HACCP system rely on
    a. Management
    b. Employee
    c. Lead auditor
    d. Management & employee

64. Risk assessment comprise of?
    a. Hazard identification
    b. Hazard characterization
    c. Risk characterization
    d. All of the above

65. Which of these is true?
    a. Critical control point need to be monitored
    b. Critical limit is set for CCP to keep in check
    c. Corrective action to be taken at time of any non-conformance
    d. All of the above

66. Records help maintain?
    a. Deviation in the process
    b. Nutritional information
    c. Control chart
    d. CCP critical limit list

67. Which of these is a Prerequisite programme?
    a. Validation
    b. GMP & GHP
    c. Codex
    d. FSSAI

68. In food factory the ISO 22000 is for?
    a. Increasing profits
    b. Managing food safety
    c. Employee welfare
    d. None of the above

69. ISO stands for?
    a. International standard of organization
    b. Indian stand of organization
    c. International organization for standard
    d. Indian organization of standard

70. BIS stands for?
    a. Bureau of Indian standards
    b. British international standards
    c. Bureau of standards association
    d. British association standards

71. The National Codex Contact Point (NCCP) for India is at ______
   a. Ministry of health and family welfare
   b. Ministry of commerce
   c. FDA
   d. Food safety and standard's authority of India, Delhi.

72. HACCP means
   a. Hazard advancement control critical point
   b. Hazard analytical critical control parameter
   c. Hazard analysis critical control point
   d. Hazard advancement control critical parameter

73. Recall procedure applied for?
   a. Product manufacturing
   b. Raw material intake
   c. Finished product with safety issues
   d. Quality check

74. Safety protective gear to wear during entry into manufacturing is part of?
   a. CCP
   b. GAP
   c. GMP
   d. FIFO

75. Vehicle inspection during transportation is to?
   a. Reduce hazard risk
   b. Avoid contamination
   c. Safety of product
   d. All of the above

76. In codex how many General subject committees are there?
   a. 10
   b. 5
   c. 6
   d. 20

77. Validation of a process to be done after interval of?
   a. 2 months
   b. 3 months
   c. 6 months
   d. 9 months

78. In Codex Horizontal committees are also called?
   a. Vertical committees
   b. Quality Check
   c. FSM
   d. General subject committees

79. A person by whom the business is carried on or owned and is responsible for ensuring the compliance is?
   a. FSM
   b. FBO
   c. PRP
   d. All of the above

80. Traceability of goods done with help of?
   a. Numbering the products
   b. Batch code
   c. Barcode system & Batch code records
   d. Document record

81. Corrective action is?
   a. Monitoring indicates a deviation from a critical limit
   b. Monitoring indicates a deviation in process of RM
   c. Monitoring indicates a shift in production quality
   d. Monitoring indicates a defect in production

82. Preventive action is?
   a. Monitoring indicates a deviation from a critical limit
   b. Monitoring indicates a deviation in process of RM
   c. Monitoring indicates a shift in production quality
   d. Determination of causes of potential non-conformities

83. CAPA applied in?
   a. GHP
   b. ISO 9001
   c. GMP
   d. None of the above

84. ISO is mostly?
   a. Process specific certification
   b. Product specific
   c. Both (*a*) and (*b*)
   d. None of the above

85. ISO 9001 has how many clauses?
   a. 5
   b. 6
   c. 9
   d. 8

86. Quality manual is reviewed periodically by?
   a. Administration
   b. Employee & staff
   c. Top management
   d. None of the above

87. Which of these is a safety gear?
   a. Gloves
   b. Apron
   c. Safety shoes
   d. All of the above

88. Which of these is corrective action for food recall for unsafe food products?
   a. Destroying of products
   b. Replacing of product
   c. Altering of products
   d. All of the above

89. Which of these is a class 1 recall?
   a. Hazard that cause serious health consequences or death effect
   b. Food will not or is not likely to cause adverse health consequences
   c. Probability of adverse health consequences from eating the food
   d. All of the above

90. BIS is mostly for?
   a. Product specific standard
   b. Process specific
   c. Both (*a*) and (*b*)
   d. None of the above

91. Safety precaution & environment safety guideline is given under?
a. ISO 9001
b. ISO 14001
c. ISO 18000
d. ISO 23000

92. Protocol for recall is given in?
a. ISO 22000
b. ISO 9001
c. ISO 18000
d. ISO 14001

93. Non conformance of product analyzed by?
a. Control chart
b. Pareto analysis
c. Affinity diagram
d. All of the above

94. CCP helps to control?
a. Hazard risk
b. Quality checklist
c. New product development
d. Quality Assurance

95. Standards laid for product is given by?
a. BIS
b. ISO
c. ISI
d. WHO

96. Process flow to be maintained constant we should follow?
a. Random sampling
b. Verification
c. Standard operating procedure
d. Inspection of finished product

97. FIFO is?
a. First in final release
b. First leave first out
c. All of the above
d. First in first out

98. As per NLEA food are exempted from Nutritional Labelling for?
a. Food served for immediate consumption
b. Shops
c. Retail Market
d. Consumers

99. Audit to be carried
a. To help improvement of quality
b. To maintain records
c. To remove faults
d. None of the above

100. Quality is defined by Juran as?
a. Safe for consumer use and hazard free
b. Fitness for intended use
c. Quality product
d. Product free from any disease causing agents

101. Double vision, muscle paralysis and breathing problems are symptoms of :

a. *E. coli* b. *C. botulism*

c. *Staphylococcus aureus* d. *Salmonella*

102. Which of the following is at lowest risk of foodborne illness?

a. Adolescents b. Alcoholics

c. Elderly people d. Pregnant women

103. Spreading bacteria to clean food from contaminated work surfaces, hands, utensils, or food is called:

a. Botulism b. Cross-contamination

c. Hygiene d. Food-borne illness

104. Perishable foods can be left out at room temperature for :

a. There is no safe time for foods to be left out

b. More than four hours

c. Not more than two hours

d. As long as you want as long as they are covered

105. The "temperature danger zone" is:

a. 40 degrees-140 degrees F. b. 65 degrees-140 degrees F

c. 0 degrees-100 Degrees F. d. 180 degrees-350 degrees F.

106. Growth of bacteria can be prevented by:

a. Thawing food in the microwave

b. Putting perishable foods in the refrigerator

c. Keeping cooked food out for less than 2 hours

d. All of the above

107. The Third Party audit is

a. Customer audit b. Internal Audit

c. Audit by an external/certification body d. None of the above

108. Which of the following is NOT an example of Verification?

a. Routine hygiene monitoring

b. Trials to standardize the amount of sodium benzoate in the ketchup

c. Analysis of customer complaints

d. CCP compliance checks

109. Which of the following is NOT identified as an allergen by European Union (EU)?

a. Mustard Oil b. Gluten containing cereals

c. SO_2 more than 10 ppm d. Peanuts

110. How many principles are identified by Codex Alimentarius Commission (CAC)

a. 12 b. 5

c. 7 d. 8

111. Food Safety Management System consists of

a. Pre-requisite program b. HACCP Principles

c. System Elements d. All of above

112. Which of the following is a source and NOT description of hazard

a. *Bacillus spp.* b. Water

c. Glass particle d. Lead

113 FSSC 22000 consists of

a. ISO 22000 b. ISO 22002-1

c. FSSC Part I d. All of the above

114. Which of the following metal is recommended for food industry?

a. Mild Steel b. Galvanized Iron

c. Stainless Steel d. Aluminium

115. The definition of the hazard is

a. Probability of the presence of pathogen micro-organisms in the foodstuff.

b. Agent in, or condition of, food with the potential to cause an adverse health effect

c. Contamination with broken pieces of glass

d. Inadequate freezing and heat treatment

116 An action taken to eliminate a detected non conformity is:

a. Corrective Action b. Preventive Action

c. Control Measure d. Correction

117 Product that will undergo no further processing or transformation by the organization

a. Finished Product b. Intermediate Product

c. End Product d. Raw Material

118. Requirements for bodies providing audit and certification of FSMS

a. ISO/TS 22003:2007 b. ISO 22000:2005

c. ISO 22001:2007 d. ISO 22005:2007

119. To raise a non conformity there must be:

a. A failing b. A requirement

c. Evidence d. All of the above

120. ISO 19011 is the guideline for

a. Auditing b. Writing non conformities

c. Food Safety Management System d. Customer complaint Management

121. In case of non-compliance with company's food safety policies or procedures, the managers should ideally

   a. Immediately punish the personnel responsible
   b. Analyse the cause and take corrective action
   c. Concentrate on how to recover from the harm rather than on the culprit
   d. None of the above

122. BIS standard which prescribes the requirements and the methods of sampling and test for synthetic food colour preparation and food colour mixtures.

   a. IS : 5346 : 1994
   b. IS : 5342 : 1992
   c. IS : 5346 : 1990
   d. None

123. The Operational PRP are

   a. Identified by hazard analysis
   b. Are not identified by hazard analysis but are intended to control likelihood of food safety hazard by prevention or reduction.
   c. Are identified by hazard analysis, intended to control likelihood of food safety hazard by prevention or reduction.
   d. None of the above

6 Introduction to Food Safety and Standards Act, 2006

1. Food Safety and Standards act, 2006 contains ______ number of sections
   a. 83 b. 97
   c. 101 d. 113
2. According to FSS Rules, ______ shall not be below the rank of a Sub-Divisional Officer, to be in-charge of food safety administration in such area as may be specified by regulations.
   a. Food Safety Officer b. Designated Officer
   c. Assistant Commissioner d. Commissioner
3. According to FSS Rules, ______ shall be responsible for inspection of food business, drawing samples and sending them to Food Analyst for analysis.
   a. Food Safety Officer b. Designated Officer
   c. Assistant Commissioner d. Commissioner
4. NABL stands for ______
   a. National Analytical Board for Laboratories
   b. National Accreditation Board for Testing and Certification of Laboratories
   c. National Analytical Board for Testing and Calibration of Laboratories
   d. National Accreditation Board for Testing and Calibration of Laboratories
5. According to FSSA, Food Safety audit and checking compliance with Food Safety Management systems required under this act and regulations can be done by
   a. FSSAI authority only b. Accreditation body only
   b. Certification bodies only d. Any organization recognized by food authority

6. Any sample taken by Food Safety Officer should be divided into _____ parts
   a. 2 b. 4
   c. 6 d. 8
7. According to FSS Rules, Food Analyst shall analase or cause to be analysed the samples and shall send the four copies of report as per form VII A to ________
   a. Food Safety Officer b. Designated Officer
   c. Commissioner d. FSSAI
8. According to FSS Rules, appeal against the report of Food Analyst by FBO shall lie before the ___________
   a. Food Safety Officer b. Designated Officer
   c. Commissioner d. FSSAI
9. According to FSS Rules, Food Safety Officer should retain ________ part/(s) of sample with him
   a. 0 b. 1
   c. 2 d. 3
10. According to FSS Rules, Food Safety Officer should send ________ parts of sample to Designated Officer if fourth sample analysis is requested by FBO.
    a. 0 b. 1
    c. 2 d. 3
11. Under Food Safety and Standards (Laboratory and Sample Analysis) Regulations, 2011 what is the desired quantity of sample is required to be sent to food analyst in case of 'Milk' as a food article.
    a. 700 ml b. 600 ml
    c. 500 ml d. 250 ml
12. According to FSS Regulations, _________ means an article of food for which standards have not been specified under these regulations but shall comply with other FSS regulations.
    a. Proprietary food b. Novel food
    c. Organic food d. Both a & b
13. Under Food Safety and Standards (Laboratory and Sample Analysis) Regulations, 2011 what is the desired quantity of sample is required to be sent to food analyst in case of 'Artificial Sweetener' as a food article.
    a. 200 gm b. 150 gm
    c. 1000 gm d. 100 gm
14. According to FSSA, _______ include the parent compounds or their metabolites or both in any edible portion of any animal product and include residues of associated impurities of the veterinary drugs concerned.
    a. Residues of veterinary drugs b. Insecticide residue
    c. Pesticide residues d. Toxicants

15. According to FSSA, _______ means the interactive exchange of information and opinions throughout the risk analysis process concerning risks, risk-related factors and risk perceptions, among risk assessors, risk managers, consumers, industry, the academic community and other interested parties, including the explanation of risk assessment findings and the basis of risk management decisions

a. Risk Assessment b. Risk Management
c. Risk Analysis d. Risk Communication

16. According to FSSA, _______, in relation to any article of food, means the probability of an adverse effect on the health of consumers of such food and the severity of that effect, consequential to a food hazard;

a. Risk Assessment b. Risk
c. Risk Analysis d. Risk Communication

17. If FBO goes in appeal to go against the report of Food analyst, then the test report of _______ shall be considered as final.

a. FSSAI b. Central laboratory
c. Referral laboratory d. Food Analyst

18. According to Section 50 of FSSA, the penalty for selling any food which is not in complaince with the provisions of this Act or the regulations made thereunder, or of the nature of substance or quality demanded by the purchaser shall be liable to a penalty not exceeding Rs _______

a. 2 lakh rupees b. 3 lakh rupees
c. 5 lakh rupees d. 10 lakh rupees

19. According to FSSA Section 52, Penalty for misbranded food may extend to ———

a. 2 lakh rupees b. 3 lakh rupees
c. 5 lakh rupees d. 10 lakh rupees

20. According to FSSA Section 53, Penalty for misleading advertisement may be extended to

a. 2 lakh rupees b. 3 lakh rupees
c. 5 lakh rupees d. 10 lakh rupees

21. Under Food Safety and Standards (Prohibition and Restrictions on sales) Regulations, 2011, *Carvia callosa* and Honey dew shall be sold only in sealed containers bearing _______ seal.

a. AGMARK b. BIS
c. FSSAI d. Legal Metrology

22. According to FSSA Section 55, Penalty for failure to comply with the directions of Food Safety Officer may be extended to

a. 1 lakh rupees b. 2 lakh rupees
c. 3 lakh rupees d. 5 lakh rupees

23. According to FSSA, penalty for unhygienic or unsanitary processing or manufacturing of food may extend to

a. 1 lakh rupees b. 2 lakh rupees
c. 3 lakh rupees d. 5 lakh rupees

24. According to FSSA Section 57, Penalty for possessing adulterant for a person who whether by himself or by any other person on his behalf, imports or manufactures for sale, or stores, sells or distribute any adulterant shall be liable: where such adulterant is injurious to health, to a penalty not exceeding

a. 2 lakh rupees b. 3 lakh rupees
c. 5 lakh rupees d. 10 lakh rupees

25. The Food Authority shall consist of a Chairperson and the following ____ number of members

a. 18 b. 20
c. 22 d. 25

26. Under Food Safety and Standards (Prohibition and Restrictions on sales) Regulations, 2011 ________ shall be sold only in high density polyethylene bag (HDPE) 14 mesh, density 100 kg/m^3, unlaminated package which shall bear the lable as specified in the Regulation 2.4.5 (21 & 42) of Food Safety and Standards (Packaging and Labelling) regulations, 2011.

a. Rock salt b. Iron fortified common salt
c. Double fortified salt d. Iodized Salt

27. The maximum age limit for the chairperson of Food Authority is ____ years

a. 60 b. 62
c. 63 d. 65

28. If any petty manufacturer commits an offence then as per Section 69 of the FSSA, the matter can be comounded as per the guidelines and amount shall not be more than Rs ________

a. 1 lakh b. 2 lakh
c. 3 lakh d. 5 lakh

29. FSSA has not repealed ________

a. Consumer protection act b. Prevention of Food Adulteration Act
c. The Fruit Product Order 1955 d. The meat food product order 1973

30. Under Food Safety and Standards (Packaging and Labelling) Regulations, 2011, exemption for Nutritional information is given when the surface area of the package is not more than ________ square centimeters, but this information is to be given on wholesale packages or Multipiece packages.

a. 50 b. 100
c. 30 d. 10

31. Under Section 92 of FSS Act the power of making regulations are given to ________

a. Food Authority b. Central Government

c. State Government d. Both b & c

32. ________ is appointed under section 36 of FSSA

a. Food Safety Officer b. Designated Officer

c. Commissioner d. Food Authority

33. Under Food Safety and Standards (Packaging and Labelling) Regulations, 2011, Nutrition claim" is defined as ________

a. any representation which states, suggests or implies that the relationship exisit between a food and health.

b. any representation which states, suggests or implies that a food has particular nutritional properties which are limited to the energy value but include protein, fat carbohydrates,vitamins and minerals

c. any representation which states, suggests or implies that a food has particular nutritional properties which are not limited to the energy value but include protein, fat carbohydrates,vitamins and minerals

d. None of above

34. ________ is the highest position of State Food safety and standards agency

a. Food Safety Officer b. Designated Officer

c. Food safety Commissioner d. Food Authority

35 ________ means an article of food offered or promoted for sale with false, misleading or deceptive claims either;

a. Prohibited food b. Deceptive food

c. Misbranded food d. None of these

36. The Food Authority shall establish scientific panels up to the number

a. 5 b. 17

c. 22 d. No limit

37 Which of the following has/have the power to cancel the licence?

a. Food Safety Officer b. Designated Officer

c. Food analyst d. All of these

38. According to section 42 of FSSA, ________ shall be responsible for inspection of food business, drawing samples and sending them to Food Analyst for analysis.

a. Food Safety Officer b. Designated Officer

c. Adjudicating Officer d. Both A & C

39. According to section 42 of FSSA, Designated Officer after scrutiny of the report of Food Analyst shall decide as to whether the contravention is punishable with imprisonment or

fine only and in the case of contravention punishable with imprisonment, he shall send his recommendations within ______ days to the Commissioner of Food Safety for sanctioning prosecution.

a. 7 b. 14
c. 21 d. 30

40. Guidelines relating to food recall procedures as the Food Authority may specify by regulations should be followed by ______

a. Only Manufacturer b. Only Retailer
c. Only Distributor d. Every food business operator

41. The head office of the Food Authority is located at

a. Mumbai b. Noida
c. Hyderabad d. New Delhi

42 According to FSSA, No insecticide shall be used directly on article of food except fumigants registered and approved under the act:

a. FSSA b. Insecticides Act, 1968
c. Pesticide Residue act, 1969 d. Pesticide & Fumigants act, 1969

43 Under Food Safety and Standards (Food Products Standards and Food Additives) Regulations, 2011, Infant milk should contain Vitamin B12, μg per 100 g. (not less than) ______

a. 0.6 μg b. 0.7 μg
c. 0.5 μg d. 0.4 μg

44 Under Food Safety and Standards (Food Products Standards and Food Additives) Regulations, 2011, Moisture requirement of table Butter is ______

a. Maximum 14% b. Maximum 18 %
c. Maximum 20 % d. Maximum 16 %

45 "Food Authority" means the Food Safety and Standards Authority of India established under ______ of FSSA, 2006

a. Section 30 b. Section 4
c. Section 36 d. Section 45

46 "Tribunal" means the Food Safety Appellate Tribunal established under ______ of FSSA, 2006

a. Section 43 b. Section 37
c. Section 45 d. Section 70

47 "Authorities responsible for enforcement of Act" in FSSA, 2006 are discussed under ______

a. Section 29 b. Section 30
c. Section 31 d. Section 32

48. "General principles to be followed in Administration of Act", in FSSA, 2006 are discussed under section ——

a. 17 b. 18
c. 19 d. 20

49. "Food Recall Procedure" in FSSA, 2006 are discussed under

a. Section 27 b. Section 28
c. Section 29 d. Section 30

50. "Use of food additive or processing aid", in FSSA, 2006 is covered under section ——

a. Section 19 b. Section 21
c. Section 25 d. Section 27

51. THE FIRST SCHEDULE of FSSA, 2006 has how many Zones

a. 3 b. 5
c. 2 d. 10

52 Responsibilities of Designated Officer for enforcement of FSSA, 2006 are discussed under section ——

a. 29 b. 31
c. 36 d. 39

53 "Procedure for launching prosecution" in enforcement of FSSA, 2006 is discussed under ——

a. 36 b. 42
c. 46 d. 52

54 ENFORCEMENT OF THE ACT in FSSA, 2006 are covered in ——

a. Chapter IV b. Chapter V
c. Chapter VI d. Chapter VII

55 "Central Advisory Committee" in FSSA, 2006 is discussed under section ——

a. 7 b. 9
c. 11 d. 13

56 "Duties and functions of Food Authority" in FSSA, 2006 is discussed under section ——

a. 6 b. 16
c. 4 d. 14

57 "Sampling and Analysis" in FSSA, 2006 is discussed under ——

a. Section 43 b. Section 45
c. Section 47 d. Section 49

58 Which of the following is/are source of alpha linolenic acid: ——

a. Flax seeds b. Walnut
c. Soyabean d. All of the above

59. Under Food Safety and Standards (Food Products Standards and Food Additives) Regulations, 2011, iodine value for coconut oil is in range of ——
a. 4 to 9
b. 7 to 11
c. 6:5 to 10
d. 7.5 to 10

60. Ingredient listing in food must be as follow?
a. In descending order of weight
b. Increasing order of weight
c. Declaration as portion size
d. All of the above

61. Proprietary foods are covered under ———— section of FSSA, 2006.
a. 19
b. 20
c. 21
d. 22

62. If purchaser wants to analyze the sample under FSSA, 2006, which section will be applicable?
a. Section 40
b. Section 41
c. Section 42
d. Section 43

63. Accounts and Audit of Food Authority in FSSA, 2006 is discussed in ———
a. Section 81
b. Section 82
c. Section 83
d. Section 84

64. OFFENCES AND PENALTIES in FSSA, 2006 is covered in ———
a. Chapter IX
b. Chapter X
c. Chapter XI
d. Chapter XII

65. "Punishment for false information" in FSSA, 2006 is discussed under ——
a. Section 59
b. Section 60
c. Section 61
d. Section 62

66. Under FSS Act the Punishment for subsequent offences are discussed under which section ——
a. 64
b. 66
c. 68
d. 70

67. Description about Annual Report of Food Authority in FSSA, 2006 is discussed in ——
a. Section 81
b. Section 82
c. Section 83
d. Section 84

68. "Prohibition orders" in FSSA, 2006 are covered in ———
a. Section 31
b. Section 32
c. Section 33
d. Section 34

69. "Penalty for misbranded food", is discussed in ______ of FSSA, 2006.
a. Section 50
b. Section 52
c. Section 54
b. Section 56

70 "Power of court to implead manufacturer etc.", are covered under ______ section of FSSA, 2006

a. 77 b. 78

c. 79 d. 80

71. Under Food Safety and Standards (Food Products Standards and Food Additives) Regulations, 2011, Palm oil acid value should not be more than ______

a. 5 b. 6

c. 10 d. 0.5

72. Section 101 of FSSA, 2006 deals with

a. Reward by State Government b. Recovery of Penalty

c. Repeal and Savings d. Power to remove difficulties

73. "Who will appoint the Food Analyst" as per Section 45 of FSSA2006?

a. Food Safety Officer b. Designated Officer

c. FSSAI c. Food Safety Commissioner

74. Which of the following laws/acts got repealed after commencement of FSS Act, 2006?

a. PFA, 1954 b. FPO, 1955

c. MFPO, 1973 d. All of the above

75. Which of the following is the administrative Ministry for the implementation of FSSAI

a. Ministry of Food processing, Govt. of India

b. Ministry of Parliamentary affairs, Govt. of India

c. Ministry of Health and family welfare, Govt. of India

d. Ministry of Agriculture, Govt. of India

76. Improvement notice can be issued to FBOs under which section

a. 28 b. 29

c. 30 d. 31

77. As per Section FSS Act 71, any person aggrieved by any decision or order of the Tribunal may file an appeal to the High Court within ______ days from the date of communication of the decision

a. 30 b. 45

c. 60 d. None of above

78. The Solvent Extracted Oil, De oiled Meal, and Edible Flour (Control) Order, was established in the year

a. 2006 b. 1967

c. 1966 d. 2011

79. Licensing and registration of food business" in FSSA, 2006 are covered in

a. Section 29 b. Section 31

c. Section 30 d. Section 32

80. Compounding of an offense is applicable to only following ________ under section 69.
a. Small industrialist
b. Medimum industrialist
c. Petty manufacturer who is temporary a stall holder
d. All of the above

81. Section 96 of FSSA, 2006 deals with
a. Reward by State Government
b. Recovery of Penalty
c. Repeal and Savings
d. Power to remove difficulties

82. "Adjudication" in FSSA, 2006 is described in section
a. 68
b. 70
c. 72
d. 74

83 "Overriding effect of this Act over all other food related laws" is covered under Section ________ of FSSA, 2006.
a. 87
b. 88
c. 89
d. 90

84 Under Food Safety and Standards (Food Products Standards and Food Additives) Regulations, 2011, Moisture level of ATTA should not be more than ______ percent
a. 14
b. 13
c. 12
d. 11

85. The biologically active compounds present in plant (other than nutrients) which have potential to reduce diseases in human beings are called ________
a. DHA
b. Phytochemicals
c. Naturochemicals
d. None of the above

86. Which of this is physical hazard?
a. Pesticides
b. Bacteria
c. Wood
d. Aflatoxin

87. GRAS means?
a. Good product
b. Genetically modified
c. Generally recognized as safe
d. All of the above

88. There are some concerns about genetically modified (GM) foods. Which of the following reasons is/are cited by experts for not allowing GM foods to be used commonly?
a. It is very expensive
b. It decreases the nutritional value of food
c. It may form some proteins which can cause allergy
c. All of the above

89. Organic food production certification is certification process for
    - a. Producing organic foods
    - b. Marketing organic foods
    - c. Both
    - d. None

90. Prebiotics are
    - a. Phytochemicals
    - b. Nutrients
    - d. Dietary supplements
    - d. None of the above

91. The word "nutraceutical" was coined by:
    - a. Dr. Aldrin W. Norwen
    - b. Dr. Stephen L. Defelice
    - c. Dr. Stanley S. Wood
    - d. None of the above

92. Which of the following statements related to genetically modified foods?
    - a. GM foods are not permitted in India
    - b. Only GM corns are allowed in India
    - c. Only GM wheat are allowed in India
    - d. Only GM potato are allowed in India

93. Values of sugar /Protein and Fats to be displayed as part of ——————
    - a. Control chart
    - b. Deviation in the process
    - c. Nutritional information
    - d. CCP critical limit list

94. "Use by date" is required to be given for which product as per FSS regulations?
    - a. Bread
    - b. Canned foods having shelf life 1 yr
    - c. Soft drinks with shelf life 6 months
    - d. None of above

95. A person by whom the business is carried on or owned and is responsible for ensuring the compliance is?
    - a. FSM
    - b. FBO
    - c. PRP
    - d. All of the above

96. Traceability of goods is done with help of?
    - a. Quantity of the product
    - b. Batch code
    - c. Barcode system & Batch code records
    - d. MRP of the product

97. Recall procedure is applied for?
    - a. Product manufacturing
    - b. Raw material intake
    - c. Finished product with safety issues
    - d. Quality check

98. GMP full form is
    - a. Good Method Practice
    - b. Good Manufacturing Practice
    - c. Good Manual Practice
    - d. Good Analytical Method

99. What does FSSAI stand for?
    - a. Food Security and Standards Authority of India
    - b. Food Standards and Safety Authority of India
    - c. Food Safety and Standards Authroity of India
    - d. Food Standards and Security Authority of India

100. What does FSSA stand for?
 a. Food Security and Standards Act
 b. Food Safety and Standards Act
 c. Food Standards and Security Act
 d. Food Standards and Safety Act

101. What does FLRS stand for?
 a. Food Licesning and Regulations System
 b. Food Licensing and Registration System
 c. Food Licensing and Recording System
 d. Food Licesing and Resgitration Society

102. What does FSMS stand for?
 a. Food Security Management System
 b. Food Safety and Management Scheme
 c. Food Safety Management System
 d. Food Security and Management Scheme

103. The officer appointed under Section 36 of the Act is called
 a. Food Safety Officer
 b. Designated Officer
 c. None of the above
 d. both a and b

104. The officer appointed under Section 37 of the Act is called
 a. Food Safety Officer
 b. Designated Officer
 c. None of the above
 d. both a and b

105. What does CAC in Section 11 of FSSA stand for?
 a. Codex Adminstrative Committee
 b. Codex Alimentarius Committee
 c. Central Advisory Committee
 d. Central Administrative Committee

106. The application for the grant of license to carry out food business has to be addressed to
 a. Food Safety Officer
 b. Designated Officer
 c. Food Commisioner
 d. None of the above

107. In case the application of grant of license is not rejected, in how much time shall the license be granted from the date of making the application
 a. 1 month
 b. 2 months
 c. 4 months
 d. 15 days

108 In case the application of grant of license is not rejected, but the license has not been granted within 2 months of making the application, can the FBO start operating the food business
 a. Yes
 b. No

109. _________ means any substance or material, not including apparatus or utensils, and not consumed as a food ingredient by itself, used in the processing of raw materials, foods or its ingredients to fulfil a certain technological purpose during treatment or processing and which may result in the non-intentional but unavoidable presence of residues or derivatives in the final product
 a. Food Additive
 b. Processing aid
 c. Contaminant
 d. Adulterant

110. No insecticide shall be used directly on article of food except ________ Registered and approved under the Insecticides Act, 1968

a. Fumigants b. Chloradanes

c. Bromates d. None of the above

111. Which of the following drugs as defined under Drugs and Cosmetcis Act, are included in the category of FSDU

a. Unani drugs b. Siddha drugs

d. Ayurvedic drugs d. None of the above

112. During the course of lifting samples, FSO serves the notice to the FBO in which form

a. Form B b. Form VI

c. Form V A d. None of the above

113. Which of the following is not required on the container label when the FSO sends a sample to the lab for food analysis

a. Code number of sample

b. Name of the sender with its official designation

c. Date and place of collection

d. List of all the ingredients in the sample

114. When an FSO sends a sample to the food analyst, the memorandum sent along with the sample is given in which of the following forms

a. Form B b. Form VI

d. Form V A d. None of the above

115. If the FBO does not request to send the fouth part of the sample for testing, to whom it is submitted to

a. FSO b. DO

c. FBO d. None of the above

116. If the sample container received by the Food Analyst is found to be in broken condition or unfit for analysis, within how many days should the analyst request the DO to send the second part of sample for analysis

a. 5 days b. 10 days

c. 7 days d. 15 days

117. Tea means tea other than ________ obtained by acceptable processes, exclusively from the leaves, buds and tender stems of plant of the Camellia sinesis.

a. Darjeeling tea b. Assam tea

c. Kangra tea d. None of the above

118. According to GHP for catering businesses, frozen food should be thawed at ________ Temperature

a. 10 °C b. 5 °C

c. 2 °C d. 12 °C

119. No irradiation facility shall be used for the treatment of food unless such facility has been approved and licensed under the ________Rules

a. Atomic Energy Rules
b. Radiation Energy Rules
c. Renewable Energy Rules
d. Green Energy Rules

120. The TSS of thermally processed fruit nectars should be minimum

a. 12%
b. 20%
c. 15%
d. 10%

121. The TSS of thermally processed fruit beverages/fruit Drink/Ready to Serve Fruit Beverages should be minimum

a. 12%
b. 20%
c. 15%
d. 10%

122. The TSS of thermally processed tomato puree should be minimum

a. 12%
b. 20%
c. 15%
d. 9%

123. The TSS of thermally processed tomato paste should be minimum

a. 25%
b. 20%
c. 35%
d. 30%

124. While filling fruit beverages or juices in containers, the container shall be filled upto not less than _______% of the water capacity of the container

a. 95%
b. 88%
c. 90%
d. 99%

125 While filling fruit beverages or juices in containers, the container shall be filled upto not less than 90% of the water capacity of the container, where the water capacity of the conatainer is defined as the volume of distliied water at .... °C which the sealed container is capable of holding when completely filled.

a. 25
b. 20
c. 30
d. 15

126. Which of the following is not a regulatory requirement on the food product label

a. Name of the Food
b. Lot/Batch code
c. Name of the company owner
d. Veg/Non-Veg logo

127. The nutriotinal information on the label may not be necessary for which of the following

a. Agricultural commodities
b. Table salt
c. Packaged drinking water
d. All of the above

128. On which of the products, instead of Best Before date, Use by date/recommended last consumption date/ expiry date shall be given

a. Aspartame
b. Infant Milk Substitute
c. Alcoholic beverage
d. Both a and b

129. In addition to the declarartion of net quantity, a food packed in a liquid medium shall carry a declaration of the ______ weight of the food

a. drained
b. dehydrated
c. dried
d. liquid

130. The month and year of manufacture, packing or pre-packing shall be given if the 'Best Before Date' of the products is more than ______ months

a. Two
b. Three
c. Six
d. Five

131. What is the area on which the information under FSS (Packaging and Labeling) is given, called

a. Principal Display Panel
b. Primary Display Panel
c. Primary Display of Product
d. Principal Display of Product

132. What does PDP in the labeling regulations stand for?

a. Principal Display Panel
b. Primary Display Panel
c. Primary Display of Product
d. Principal Display of Product

133. The date of manufacture is not required on the label of pre packaged foods, when the shelf-life is not not more than

a. 2 days
b. 7 days
c. 10 days
d. 5 days

134. When the net quantitiy of the the commodity contained in the package is declared, the weight of the wrappers and packaging materials is

a. included
b. excluded
c. partially included
d. none of the above

135. For which of the following, the net weight declared on the package may include the weight of immediate wrapper

a. Milk carton
b. Juice tetra pack
c. Multipiece pack of confectionery
d. Small Water Botlle

136. If a manufacturer bought cheese from Italy and converted it into cheese spread after importing into India, the country of origin will be

a. Both Italy and India
b. Italy
c. India
d. None of the above

137. Which of the following is not a regulatory requirement on the food product label

a. Instruction of use
a. List of ingredients
c. Suggested receipe
d. Nutrional information

138. Which of the following does not come under the declaration as 'Instructions for Use'
   a. Garnish with coriander
   b. Reconstitute with water
   c. Pour boiling water and cover for 3 minutes
   d. All of the above

139. Which of the following is a mandatory requirement for Infant Milk Substitute Labeling
   a. A statement "MOTHER'S MILK IS BEST FOR THE BABY"
   b. A warning that infant milk substitute is not the sole source of nourishment of an infant
   c. Quantity per scoop of the measuring scoop provided
   d. All of the above

140. Which of the following artificial table top sweeteners need the declararion "Not for Phenylketonurics"
   a. Acseulfame K　　b. Aspertame (Methyl Ester)
   c. Sucralose　　d. Neotame

141. What does INS, with respect to additives stand for in Labeling Regulations?
   a. International Numbering System　　b. Indian Numbering System
   c. International Numbers for Sweetners　　d. Inspection Numbering System

142. Which of the following is not true for best before date
   c. The food may still be perfectly safe to consume
   b. The quality of food may have diminished
   c. The food is still fully marketable
   d. The food may have become unsafe for usage

143 "Infant" means a child of not more than _________ months of age
   a. Six　　b. Eight
   c. Ten　　d. Twelve

144. A lot number can contain
   a. Numbers　　b. Alphabets
   c. Combination of numbers and alphabets　　d. All of the above

145. Contents of 'Multipiece packages' can be sold
   a. Together only　　a. Can be sold indivisually or together
   c. Individually only　　d. None of the above

146. "Non Vegetarian food" means an article of food, which contains whole or part of any animal including birds, fresh water or marine animals or eggs or products of any animal origin, but excluding __________
   a. Liver　　b. Protein extract from animal muscles
   c. Milk and milk products　　d. None of the above

147. For the purpose of labeling what is the class title for "All types of gum or preparations used in the manufacture of gum base for chewing gum"

a. Gums b. Gums and resins

c. Gum base d. Chewing gums

148. For the purpose of labeling what is the class title for "All milk and milk products derives solely from milk"

a. Milk and milk products b. Dried milk

c. Milk concentratres d. Milk solids

149. For the purpose of labeling what is the class title for "Cocoa bean, coconib, cocoamass, cocoa press cakes, cocoa powder (Fine/Dust)"

a. Cocoa prodcuts b. Cocoa solids

c. Cocoa dusts d. Cocoa by-products

150. Butter is what type of emulsion

a. Oil in water b. Water in oil

c. Oil in oil d. None of the above

151. Which of the following is not an important parameter for Oil standards

a. Unsaponifiable matter b. Acid Value

c. Total Ash d. Refractive Index

152 The quorum of the meeting of Scientific Committee or Panel shall be________ at least

a. One-fourth b. One-third

c. Two-third b. Half

153. Which of the following are required for applying for a new license

a. Form-B duly signed

b. List of food category desired to be manufactured

c. Proof of possession of premise

d. All of the above

154. In case of injury or death of consumer the maximum compensation is

a. One lakh b. Three lakhs

c. Five lakhs c. Ten lakhs

155. No court shall take cognizance of an offence under this Act after the expiry of the period of __________ Year from the date of commission of an offence : Provided that Commisioner of Food Safety may, for reasons to be recorded in writing, approve prosecution within an extended period of upto _____ years

a. Two, three b. One, three

c. Three, five d. One, five

156. The provision of Recovery of penalty through arrear of land revenue, in case it is not paid, is given under which clause

a. Clause 96 b. Clause 31

c. Clause 95 d. Clause 32

157. Under which clause is MMPO deemed to be a regulation made under FSSA

a. Clause 96 b. Clause 100

c. Clause 99 d. Clause 98

158. Every appeal arising out of a decision of the Adjudicating Officer shall be filed within a period of ______ days from the date on which the order is received by appealant. Though it can be extended by ______ more days by Appellate Tribunal

a. 30,30 b. 30,60

c. 60,30 d. 20,30

159. Which of the following FBOs does not fall under the central licensing purview

a. Dairy Unit processing 70,000 litres of liquid milk per day

b. Refinery having an installed caapacity of 5MT per day

c. A slaughter house slaughtering 20 large animals per day

d. 100% export oriented units

160. Edible Casein Products is the product obatined by separating, washing and drying the coagulum of ______ Milk

a. Skimmed b. Full cream

c. Toned d. Double toned

161. For which of the Oil the quantity of gossypol is an important parameter

a. Til Oil b. Coconut Oil

c. Cottonseed Oil d. Mustard Oil

162. The quantitiy of milk sample to be sent to the Food Analyst for analysis is

a. 200 ml b. 1000ml

c. 500ml d. 250ml

163. The preservative used in case of any samples of any milk shall be

a. Citric acid b. Formalin

c. Vitamin A d. Ascorbic acid

164. The common name of *Lathyrus sativus*, a kind of pulse which is prohibited from sale is

a. Kesari dal b. Arhar dal

c. Chana dal d. Moong dal

165. The acidity of Vinegar should be calculated in reference to which acid

a. Tartaric acid b. Acetic acid

c. Citric acid d. Ascorbic acid

166. The acidity of pickles should be calculated in reference to which acid

a. Tartaric acid
b. Acetic acid
c. Citric acid
d. Ascorbic acid

167. Which of the following is allowed in Table margerine

a. Rancidity
b. Mineral oil
c. Animal body fats
d. Skimmed milk powder

168. Maximum amount of common salt allowed in table margarine is

a. 2%
b. 2.50%
c. 3%
d. 5%

169. What is the maximum limit of Aspartame allowed in carbonated water

a. 500 ppm
b. 700 ppm
c. 300 ppm
d. 1000 ppm

170. How many parts of scheduele IV are there

a. 4
b. 2
c. 5
d. 6

171. Saint paulin is a type of

a. Fat
b. Butter
c. Oil
d. none of the above

172 ________ means the product obtained by partial removal of water from milk of cow and/ or buffalo by heat or any other process which leads to a product of the same composition and charectersitcis

a. Dehydrated milk
b. Dried milk
c. Evaporated milk
d. None of the above

173. What does a cleaning scheduele at a catering process include

a. What needs to be cleaned
b. How often it needs to be cleaned
c. How the cleaning should be done
d. All of the above

174. The chopping instruments used in slaughter houses should be cleaned with hot water at a temperature of ________ °C

a. 82
b. 90
c. 95
d. 80

175. What should be the minimum iodine content of edible common salt at manufacturing level (on dry weight basis)

a. 50 ppm
b. 30 ppm
c. 20 ppm
d. 25 ppm

176. What should be the minimum iodine content of edible common salt at distribution channel and retail level (on dry weight basis)

a. 20 ppm
b. 40 ppm
c. 15 ppm
d. 10 ppm

177. What should be the range of iron content in iron fortified salt
   a. 850-1100 ppm b. 900-1000 ppm
   c. 700-1000 ppm d. 950-1150 ppm

178. What is the common term for iron fortified iodised salt
   a. Fortified salt b. Double fortified salt
   c. Iodized fortified salt d. Twin fortified salt

179. Which of the following is not a characteristic of mineral water
   a. It is obtained directly from natural or drilled sources from underground water
   b. It is obtained from public water supply
   c. It is collected under conditions that gurantee the original micorbiological purity and chemical composition of essential components
   d. It has certain mineral salts and their relative proportions and presence of trace elements

180. _______ is natural mineral water which after possible tretament as given hereunder and after packaging has less carbon dioxide content than at the emergence and does not visibly and spontaneously give off carbon dioxide under normal conditons of temperature and pressure
   a. Decarbonated Natural Mineral Water b. Non-Carbonated Natural Mineral Water
   c. Ntaural mIneral water d. Carbonated natural mineral water

181. Which of the following can be used to act as the acid-reacting material of baking powder
   a. Trataric acid or its salts, or both b. Acid salts of phosphoric acid
   c. Acid compounds of aluminium d. All of the above

182. Which of the following terms is not allowed to be used on the label of oil
   a. Double refined b. Extra refined
   c. Micro refined d. All of the above

183. ___________ means any substance not intentionally added to food, but which gets added to articles of food in the process of their production, manufacture, processing, preparation, treatment as a result of environmental contamination
   a. Environmental contaminant b. Natural contaminant
   c. Crop contaminant d. Adulterant

184. Which of the following is not a metal contaminant
   a. Lead b. Copper
   c. Arsenic d. Carbaryl

185. Which of the following is a naturally occuring toxic substance
   a. Agaric acid b. Aflatoxin
   c. Patulin d. Ochratoxin A

186. Which of the following is not a function of referral laboratory

a. Analysis of samples sent by FSO

b. Investigation for the purpose of fixation of a standard

c. Ensuring that the laboratory follows the scientific protocols laid down for handling/ testing the articles of food

d. Development of new' food products

187. Condensed milk, sweetened milk, condensed skimmed milk sweetened, milk powder, skimmed milk powder, partly skimmed milk powder and partly skimmed sweetened condensed milk shall not be sold except under _________ mark

a. Agmark b. Indian standards institution certification

c. BIS d. HACCP

188. All the irradiated food can be sold

a. Loose b. Pre-packed only

c. Both a and b d. e-business only

189. No solvent except ________ shall be used in the extraction of cocoa butter, oils and fats and edible soya flour

a. n-hexane b. Butane

c. Ethanol d. None of the above

190 Minimum nnumber of meeting that CAC should hold in a year is

a. 5 b. 4

c. 3 d. 2

191 The notice of every CAC has to be signed by the _______and circulated to the members at least 15 days before the date of meeting

a. Chairperson b. CEO

c. DO d. FSO

192. The maximum temperature at which pasteurized milk may be stored untill it leaves the treatment establishment shall not exceed _________ °C

a. 10 b. 5

c. 4 d. 2

193. Fees for registeration with FSSAI is

a. Rs 100 b. Rs 200

c. Rs 500 d. Rs 50

194 A registeration or License granted shall be valid for maximum upto

a. 2 years b. 3 years

c. 5 years d. none of the above

195 For electric stunning minumum level of current levels for head-only stunning for cattle is

a. 2.0 amps b. 1.5 amps

c. 1.0 amps d. 3.0 amps

196. Making the animal unconcious before slaughtering is called

a. Stunning
b. Fainting
c. Resting
d. None of the above

197. Which of the following is a petty food manufacturer

a. FBO with 90 kilolitre per day production capacity
b. Street hawker
c. Person distributing prasad in a religious place
d. All of the above

198 Food Safety and Standards Act, 2006 - passed by Indian Parliament and notified on

a. 24th July, 2006
b. 24th June, 2006
c. 24th August, 2006
d. 24th November, 2006

199. Food Safety and Standards Act, 2006 - operationalised on

a. 5th August, 2007
b. 5th August, 2011
c. 5th August, 2012
d. 5th August, 2013

200. How many acts are repealed by Food Safety and Standards Act, 2006

a. 4
b. 5
c. 7
d. 8

201. Agencies involved behind "Plant Quarantine (Regulation of Import into India) Order, 2003

a. Ministry of Health & Family Welfare
b. Ministry of Food Processing Industries
c. Department of Agriculture & Cooperation
d. Directorate General of Health Services

202. Coffee is adulterated with

a. Saw dust
b. Chicory
c. Ghee
d. All of these

203. Ghee is adulterated with

a. Vanaspathi
b. Oil
c. Artificial fat
d. Rancid fat

204. The MSNF means

a. Milk Solid Natural Fat
b. Milk Solid Non Fat
c. Milk Standardized Natural Fat
d. Milk Solid Not Fat

205. Cow milk contains ______% MF and ______% MSNF

a. 5.0-6.0, 9.0
b. 3.0-4.0, 8.5
c. 3.0-3.5, 9.0
d. 4.5, 8.5

206. Which of the following has highest protein content ?

a. Oat
b. Ragi
c. Wheat
d. Bajra

207. FSSAI has launched which logo for fortified foods?
a. Circle with an F and a + sign with a ring
b. Square with an F and a + sign with a ring
c. Rectangle with an F and a + sign with a ring
d. None of the above

208. Regulator FSSAI has joined hands with which organisation to check misleading ads in the foods and beverages sector?
a. ASCI
b. ASDI
c. ASOI
d. ASBI

209 FSSAI has issued an advisory banning the use of which material for wrapping and packaging of food items?
a. Newspaper
b. Plastic
c. Polythene
d. None of the above

210. Who has been appointed as CEO of FSSAI on 22nd December 2015?
a. Prem Kumar Singh
b. Pawan Kumar Agarwal
c. Ashok Singh Malik
d. Ashish Bahugana

211. Who is responsible for implementation & Enforcement of FSSA, 2006? Or Who is the regulatory authority under the Food Act in India?
a. Food Safety and Standards Authority of India
b. State Food Authorities
c. Both a and b
d. None of the above

212. Who issues improvement notice?
a. Designated Officer
b. Food business operator
c. Food Safety Commissioner
d. Food safety officer

213. Who has the rights to suspend the license if the food business operator fails to comply with an improvement notice
a. Food Safety Commissioner
b. Designated Officer
c. FSSAI
d. Food business operator

214. Which chapter provides information on Offences and Penalties
a. Chapter XII
b. ChapterVIII
c. Chapter VII
d. Chapter IX

215. Under Food Safety and Standards (Laboratory and Sample Analysis) Regulations, 2011 what is the desired quantity of sample required to be sent to food analyst in case of 'Artificial Sweetener' as a food article.
a. 200 gm
b. 150 gm
c. 1000 gm
d. 100 gm

216. The Food Authority shall consist of a Chairperson and the following ____ number of members
a. 18 b. 20
c. 22 d. 25

217. Under Food Safety and Standards (Prohibition and Restrictions on sales) Regulations, 2011 ________ shall be sold only in high density polyethylene bag (HDPE) 14 mesh, density 100 kg/m^3, unlaminated package which shall bear the lable as specified in the Regulation 2.4.5 (21 & 42) of Food Safety and Standards (Packaging and Labelling) regulations, 2011.
a. Rock salt b. Iron fortified common salt
c. Double fortified salt d. Iodized Salt

218. The maximum age limit for the chairperson of Food Authority is _____ years
a. 60 b. 62
c. 63 d. 65

219. ________ shall be in close proximity to the name or brand name of the product
a. Veg/Non-Veg logo b. Lot/Batch code
c. Name of the company owner d. Name or brand name

220. According to FSSA Section 34 provides
a. Prohibition orders b. Notification of food poisoning
c. Emergency prohibition notices and orders d. Powers of food safety officers

221 According to FSSA Section 47 provides
a. Sampling and analysis b. Functions of food Analyst
c. Improvement notices d. None of the above

222. Recall procedure is applied for?
a. Product manufacturing b. Raw material intake
c. Finished product with safety issues d. Quality check

223. "Appeal" in FSSA, 2006 is described in section
a. 76 b. 70
c. 72 d. 74

224. Adjudication and Food safety applellate tribunal is covered in which chapter
a. Chapter XII b. Chapter X
c. Chapter VIII d. Chapter IX

225. Under Food Safety and Standards (Food Products Standards and Food Additives). What is the maximum Acid value of coconut oil
a. Not more than 6.0 b. Not more than 6.5
c. Not more than 0.50 d. None of the above

226. The word "Tilsiter" means
a. Cream cheese b. Soft unripened cheese
c. Ripened semi-hard cheese d. Ripened soft cheese

227. Evaporated Milk contains ______ % MF
a. Not less than 8.0 percent m/m
b. Not less than 26.0 percent m/m
c. Not less than 8.2 percent m/m
d. Not less than 1.0 percent m/m

228. Khoya contains ______ % of citric acid
a. Not more than 6.0
b. Not more than 2.5
c. Not more than 0.5
d. Not more than 0.1

229. What is the source of Provitamin A
a. Beta-carotene
b. Rentinyl Acetate
c. Riboflavin
d. Retinyl palmitate

230. Synthetic vinegar shall be distinctly labelled as
a. Synthetic Vinegar
b. Vinegar
c. Synthetic-prepared from Acetic acid
d. None of the above

231. The Acidity of the Synthetic vinegar shall not be less than
a. 3.50 percent m/v
b. 3.75 percent m/v
c. 5.0 percent m/v
d. 1.0 percent m/v

232 ________syrup obtained by blending syrup made from sugar, dextrose or liquide glucose
a. Sharbat
b. Synthetic syrup
c. Both a and b
d. None of the above

233. Selection committee for selection of chairperson and members of food authority is given in which section
a. Section 6
b. Section 8
c. Section 7
d. Section 10

234. Section 24 of FSSA, 2006 deals with
a. Packaging and labelling of foods
b. Duties and functions of food authority
c. Restrictions of advertisement and prohibition as to unfair trade
d. use of food additive or processing aid

235. A single license may be issued by the Designated officers for one or more articles of food and also for different establishments or premises in the same area
a. Designated Officer
b. Food business operator
c. Food Safety Commissioner
d. Food safety officer

236. Who is responsible for sanction or launch prosecution in cases of contraventions punishable with fine
a. Food business operator
b. Food Safety Commissioner
c. Designated Officer
d. Food safety officer

237 ________means food products that have been produced in accordance with specified organic production standards

a. Organic food
b. Genetically modified food
c. Novel food
d. None of the above

238. Provisions relating to import is given in _____chapter

a. Chapter VIII
b. Chapter VII
c. Chapter VI
d. Chapter V

239. Special Responsibilities of Food business operator is provided in section

a. 30
b. 25
c. 26
d. 28

240. The food temperature 'danger zone' is between what temperature range?

a. 15°C-75°C
b. 5°C-80°C
c. 5°C-60°C
d. 0°C-15°C

241. Foods not likely to support bacterial growth are:

a. Fresh meat and poultry
b. Fish and seafood
c. Dried pasta, noodles or bread
d. Milk and cream

242. According to FSSA Section 51, Penalty for Sub-standard food may be extended to

a. 2 lakh rupees
b. 3 lakh rupees
c. 5 lakh rupees
d. 10 lakh rupees

243. According to FSSA Section 54, Penalty for food containing extragenous matter may be extended to

a. 1 lakh rupees
b. 5 lakh rupees
c. 10 lakh rupees
d. 3 lakh rupees

244. Punishment for false information is covered in section

a. 60
b. 58
c. 62
d. 61

245. Punishment for carrying out a business without license is covered in section

a. 62
b. 60
c. 63
d. 65

246. Punishment for interfering with seized items is covered in section

a. 60
b. 58
c. 62
d. 61

247. Functions of food analyst is given in section

a. 40
b. 42
c. 49
d. 46

248. Clause ______enumerates the functions of the food analyst

a. 46
b. 42
c. 49
d. 40

249. Analysis is covered in chapter

a. VIII
b. VII
c. XI
d. VI

250. Clause ______ provides general provisions relating to offences

a. 49
b. 50
c. 48
d. 42

7 Introduction to Codex Alimentarius

1. The major objective of Codex Alimentarius Commission [CAC] is
   a. To protect the health of the consumers and ensure fair practices in the food trade as well as to facilitate national trade in food.
   b. To protect the health of the country and ensure fair practices in the food trade as well as to facilitate international trade in food.
   c. To protect the health of the consumers and ensure fair practices in the food trade as well as to facilitate international trade in food.
   d. To protect the wealth of the consumers and ensure fair practices in the food trade as well as to facilitate international trade in food.

2. The National Codex Contact Point (NCCP) for India is at
   a. Ministry of Health and Family welfare
   b. Ministry of Commerce
   c. FDA
   d. Food Safety and Standard's Authority of India, Delhi.

3. Codex Alimentarius Commission was created in year
   a. 1963 b. 1965
   c. 1947 d. 1990

4. Codex standards are accepted by
   a. FSSAI b. BIS
   c. FDA d. WHO

5. Codex Alimentarius Commission was created by joint efforts of
   a. WHO and FOO b. WHO and FAO
   c. WHO and FSO d. WHO and World Bank

6. Core function of NCC India is
   a. Act as a link between the international industries and India Member Body;
   b. Act as a link between the Codex Secretariat and FSSAI
   c. Act as a link between the Codex Secretariat and Consumers
   d. Act as a link between the Codex Secretariat and India Member Body

7. In india, the membership of the NCC was reconstituted in 1999 through Govt GSR _____
   a. GSR 763 b. GSR 762
   c. GSR 761 d. GSR 760

8. Codex Alimentarius is a collection of standards, ___________, guidelines and other recommendations.
   a. SOPs b. Work instructions
   c. Codes of Practice d. None of the above

9. The Codex General Principles of Food Hygiene introduces the use of___________
   a. The critical control points
   b. The Hazard Analysis and Critical Control Point (HACCP)
   c. GMP for food
   d. ISO 22000

10. There are _______of food additives and contaminants and toxins in foods that contain both general and commodity- specific provisions
    a. Specifications b. Codex special standards
    c. Codex general standards d. MRL

11. Codex methods of analysis and sampling covers contaminants and residues of pesticides and _________in foods,
    a. Heavy metals b. Veterinary drugs
    c. Allopathy drugs d. None of the above

12. Following commodity standards are not covered by codex
    a. Fish and fishery products
    b. Fresh fruits and vegetables
    c. Processed and quick-frozen fruits and vegetables
    d. Indian traditional foods

13. The procedures for preparing standards are well defined, open and ___________
    a. Transparent b. Detailed
    c. Science base d. None of the above

14. As part of development of standard, The submission of a proposal by a national government or a subsidiary committee is done by circulating ________
    a. Distribution paper b. Draft standard
    c. Discussion paper d. Edited paper

15. Codex horizontal standard does not cover following
    a. Contaminants in Foods
    b. Food Hygiene
    c. Food Labeling
    d. Fish and Fish products standards

16. The responsibility for developing standards for specific foods or classes of food lies with the_____________
    a. Commodity Committees
    b. Vertical Committee
    c. Special committee
    d. None of the above

17. The ____________ on the Application of Sanitary and Phytosanitary Measures and on Technical Barriers to Trade (SPS and TBT Agreements) both encourage the international harmonization of food standards.
    a. Zurich Round Agreement
    b. Uganda Round Agreement
    c. India Round Agreement
    d. Uruguay Round Agreement

18. Function of India Codex Contact Point is to formulate __________ position in consultation with the members of NCC in the matters of Codex;
    a. National
    b. International
    c. Expert
    d. None of the above

19. The ________ has been authorized to appoint Shadow Committees (sub-committees) on subject matters corresponding to the Codex subcommittees.
    a. FSSAI
    b. Health Ministry
    c. NCC
    d. BIS

20. NCC does not have following shadow committee.
    a. Food Additives and Contaminants
    b. Food Export and Import and Certification Systems
    c. Sugar and Honey
    d. Fish and Fishery Products

21. Good Agricultural Practice in the Use of Pesticides (GAP)includes
    a. Review of residue data from supervised trials
    b. Nationally authorized safe uses of pesticides
    c. Toxicological assessment
    d. Consideration of the various dietary residue

22. ____________ means any addition, change or deletion of text or numeric values in a Codex standard
    a. Categorization
    b. Revision
    c. Monitoring
    d. Amendment

23. The *ad hoc* Inter Governmental Task Force shall report to the
    a. Task Force
    b. FAO
    c. The Codex Alimentarius Commission and to the Executive Committee
    d. Only Executive Committee

24. The Criteria applicable to commodities are
    a. Amenability of the commodity to standardisation
    b. Consideration of the global magnitude of the problem or issue
    c. Scope of work and establishment
    d. Amenability of the subject of the proposal to standardization

25. Codex general subject committees include the committees on
    a. Food Hygiene
    b. Food Packaging
    c. Food Shelf life
    d. Food Research

26. The Committee on Methods of Analysis and Sampling will assess
    a. Elaboration of specific method
    b. Actual analytical performance of the method
    c. Request for advice
    d. Sampling for endorsement

27. When commodity committees includes provisions on microbiological methods of analysis and sampling for the purpose of verifying hygiene provisions, they should be referred to the
    a. Committee of Food Additives
    b. Committee of Food Labelling
    c. Committee of Food Pesticides
    d. Committee of Food Hygiene

28. JECFA stands for
    a. Joint FAO/WHO Expert Committee on Food Additives
    b. Joint FAO Expertise Committee on Food Additives
    c. Joint FAO/WHO Expert Committee on Food Hygiene
    d. Joint WHO Expertise Committee on Food Additives

29. Codes of Hygienic Practice applicable to specific food items or food groups shall refer to
    a. General Principles of Food Hygiene
    b. General Practices of Food Hygiene
    c. General Problems of Food Hygiene
    d. General Provision of Food Hygiene

30. There are _____ general subject committees, _____ commodity committees and _____ regional co-ordinating committees
    a. 7, 11, 5
    b. 12, 6, 8
    c. 11, 7, 6
    d. 10, 8, 5

31. Following is not a part of Codex Documentation:
    a. Codex Procedural Manual
    b. Provisional Agenda
    c. Committee Working Papers
    d. Information documents

32. How many members countries at present in the Codex Alimentarius Commission

a. 187 b. 188

c. 189 d. 190

33. Specific Sampling Plans for health-related properties are

a. applied to analytically determine compositional criteria

b. applied to heterogeneous conditions

c. applied to visual defects

d. applied to pre-packaged foods

34. After endorsing, any changes that influence performance characteristics must be reported to

a. JECFA b. FAO

c. CCMAS d. FDA

35. Meetings of Codex and Coordinating Committees shall be held a

a. Private b. Secret Rooms

c. Conference Rooms d. Public

36. In the report of meetings of Codex and Coordinating Committees

a. Decision should be clearly stated

b. All decisions on draft standards should not be accompanied

c. Action to be taken should not be included

d. Decision should be hidden

37. The Host is responsible for providing all conference services, including

a. Secretariat b. Chairperson

c. Members d. Observer

38. The secretariat of the Host should circulate the papers ______ before the opening of the session.

a. At least three months b. At least six months

c. At least twelve months d. At least two months

39. Codex Committees, when deciding to undertake work between sessions, should give the first priority to

a. Establishment of electronic working groups

b. Minimal Use of technology

c. Maximum Oral work

d. Establishing new committee members

40. _________ should notify the Chairperson of the Committee and the host country secretariat of the Committee

a. Organizer b. Producer

c. Observer d. CCMAS

41. The conclusions of an electronic working group and the list of participants shall be distributed to
    a. Codex Contact Points
    b. Host
    c. FAO
    d. HACCP

42. __________ is an inherent element of risk analysis
    a. Preservation
    b. Processing
    c. Precaution
    d. Analysis

43. The ______ given by risk managers to risk assessors should be as clear as possible
    a. Protocol
    b. Mandate
    c. Observation
    d. Report

44. Risk assessment may also take into account
    a. Quantitative Information
    b. Qualitative Information
    c. Both Quantitative And Qualitative Information
    d. None of the above

45. Risk assessments should be based on
    a. Realistic Exposure Scenario
    b. Open Scenario
    c. Production Scenario
    d. Research

46. The effect in frequency and/or concentration of a hazard in a food that must be achieved by the application of one or more control measures is known as:
    a. Hazard Identification
    b. Food safety objective
    c. Dose-Response Assessment
    d. Performance criterion

47. ________ provides an estimate as to which of the GEMS/Food Consumption Cluster Diets
    a. FAO
    b. HACCP
    c. JECFA
    d. CCCF

48. CCCF stands for
    a. Codex Committee on Cofactor in Foods
    b. Codex Council on Contaminants in Foods
    c. Codex Committee on Contamination in Foods
    d. Codex Control of Contamination in Foods

49. _____________ should provide a clear explanation and rationale for its conclusions and recommendations
    a. JECFA
    b. ADI
    c. FDA
    d. HACCP

50. The Executive Committee of the Commission does not consist of:
    a. Chairperson
    b. Regional Co-ordinators
    c. Advisors to Members
    d. Secretariat

8 Miscellaneous Laws

Consumer Protection Act 1986; The Indian Penal Code; The Criminal Procedure Code

1. The Consumer Protection Act came into force on

   a. 24th December 1986   b. 24th March 1986

   c. 15th Aug 1986   d. 26th Jan 1986

2. The following acts were implemented for consumer interest

   a. Consumer protection Act   b. FSS Act

   c. Weights & Measures act   d All of the above

3. Who is a consumer?

   a. Buys any goods for a consideration

   b. Any user of goods for a consideration

   c. Hires a service for consideration

   d. All of the above

4. Time limit for filling complaint under Consumer Act

   a. 2 Years   b. 1 Year

   c. 6 Months   d. No Limit

5. When Right to Information Act (RTI) was passed

   a. Oct 2005   b. Oct 2006

   c. Aug 2005   d. Aug 2008

6. The Definition of Public servant is given in

   a. Section 19   b. Section 21

   c. Section 23   d. Section 25

7. In market place, consumer are exploited when
   a. Shopkeeper weighs less than what they should
   b. Adulterated/ defective goods are sold
   c. Traders charges above MRP
   d. All of the above

8. How many rights of consumers are provided under Consumer Protection Act 1986?
   a. 6 b. 7
   c. 8 d. 4

9. The matters in which compensation is more than one crore are handled by
   a. District Consumer Forum b. State Consumer Forum
   c. Central Consumer Forum d. None of the above

10. The Maharashtra Consumer Protection Rules were came into force in the year
    a. Year 2000 b. Year 1999
    c. Year 1989 d. Year 1988

11. The Section in which false complaint is discharge is at
    a. Section 25 b. Section 26
    c. Section 27 d. Section 32

12. Consummation refer to movement by
    a. Government b. Society
    c. Production d. Consumers

13. World consumer day is celebrated on
    a. 15th March every year b. 26th January every year
    c. 24 December every year d. None of above

14. Under section 45 of IPC, life denotes
    a. Life of a human being b. Life of an animal
    c. Life of Human being & animal both d. Life of either human being or animal

15. How many punishments have been prescribed under India Penal Code
    a. Three b. Six
    c. Five d. Four

16. Chapter V of IPC deal with
    a. Abetment b. Attempt
    c. Elections d. Religions

17. Adulteration of food or drink intended for sale is given in Section
    a. 275 b. 274
    c. 273 d. 272

18. Hallmark is certification maintained for standardization of
    a. Milk b. Honey
    c. Package d. Gold

19. The limit for compensation for District Consumer Forum is
    a. 10 lakhs b. 15 lakhs
    c. 20 lakhs d. 25 lakh

20. Accident in doing a lawful act is contained in IPC
    a. Sec 87 b. Sec 80
    c. Sec 96 d. Sec 71

21. Food Standards for product specification is given by which Indian authority?
    a. FSSAI b. ISO
    c. FAO d. WHO

22. Provisions in Legal Metrology Act, 2009 are applicable to
    a. criminal issues in any food industry
    b. packages intended for retail sale
    c. legal action taken against the quality department of food industry
    d. All of the above

23. Export (Quality Control and Inspection) Act, 1963 comes under
    a. Department of Consumer Affairs, Govt. of India
    b. Directorate of Marketing and Inspection
    c. Export Inspection Council of India
    d. Department of Legal Metrology

24. AGMARK logo with blend B is for?
    a. Blend of only Refined edible oil
    b. Blend of only Rice bran oil
    c. Admixture of any refined edible oil with Rice bran oil
    d. None of the above

25. AGMARK was promulgated in
    a. 2004 b. 1987
    c. 1937 d. 1897

26. "AGMARK Act 1937" comes under
    a. Department of Consumer Affairs, Govt. of India
    b. Directorate of Marketing and Inspection
    c. Department of Agriculture & Cooperation
    d. Department of Legal Metrology

27. How many punishments have been prescribed under India Penal Code?

a. Three
b. Six
c. Five
d. Four

28. Causing hurt by means of poison with intent to commit an offence is given unde _________ section of IPC

a. 327
b. 328
c. 329
d. 330

29. A criminal act done by several person with common intention is given under _________ section of IPC

a. 35
b. 420
c. 34
d. 273

30. The number of members at District Consumer Forum is

a. 11
b. 7
c. 5
d. 3

31. The District Consumer Forum must have at least _________ women members

a. 1
b. 2
c. Nil
d. None of the above

32. The limit for compensation for State Consumer Redressal Forum is

a. One Crore to 2 Crore
b. 50 lakhs to 1 Core
c. 75 Lakh to 1 Crore
d. 20 lakh to 1 Core

33. Which of the following statement is false

a. The appeal against the order of District Forum can be made before State Consume Reddressal Forum.
b. The appeal against the order of State Forum can be made before Central Consume Commission.
c. The appeal against the order of State Forum can be made before High Court.
d. the appeal against the order of Centre Consumer Commission can be made before th Supreme court of India.

34. The implementation of order of Consumer Court is given in

a. Sec 24
b. Sec 25
c. Sec 26
d. Sec 27

35. Dishonesty has been defined as doing anything with intention to cause wrongful gain t one person and wrongful loss to another is given under section of IPC

a. 4
b. 23
c. 24
d. 25

36. Fraudulently has been defined as doing anything with intent to defraud given in section of IPC

a. 23
b. 25
c. 24
d. 26

37. General exceptions are mentioned in which chapter of IPC

a. III
b. IV
c. V
d. VI

38. Section 166 of IPC deals with

a. offences against public servant
b. offences against state
c. offences against private person
d. None of the above

39. Offences against state are given in which chapter of IPC

a. VI
b. III
c. IX
d. VII

40. Punishments are mentioned in which chapter of IPC

a. III
b. IV
c. V
d. VI

41. A hangman who hangs the prisoners pursuant to the order of court is exempted from criminal liability by virtue of section

a. 77 of IPC
b. 76 of IPC
c. 78 of IPC
d. 79 of IPC

42. Section 274 of IPC deals with

a. Sale of Noxious food
b. Adulteration of drug
c. Sale of Adulterated food
d. None of the above

43. Sale of Adulterated drug is given in

a. Section 274 of IPC
b. Section 275 of IPC
c. Section 276 of IPC
d. Section 272 of IPC

44. The offences relating to religion is given in

a. Chapter XV of IPC
b. Chapter XIV of IPC
c. Chapter XVI of IPC
d. Chapter XX of IPC

45. The arrest of persons is given in Chapter __________ of Cr. P.C.

a. IV
b. V
c. VI
d. III

46. Section 273 of IPC deals with

a. Sale of noxious food
b. Sale of Noxious Drink
c. Either a or b
d. None of the above

47. Essential Commodities Act came into force in

a. 1954
b. 1986
c. 1955
d. 1940

48. Which of the commodities are covered under Essential Commodities Act

a. Bakery products
b. Drugs
c. Raw jute and jute textiles
d. Both b and c

59. Traceability of goods done with help of?

a. Numbering the products
b. Batch code
c. Barcode system & Batch code records
d. Document record

50. The "*maxim ignorantia juris non excusat*" means

a. Ignorance of law is an excuse
b. Ignorance of facts is no excuse
c. Ignorance of law is no excuse
d. Ignorance of facts is an excuse

51. Why Essential commodities Act required

a. maintaining or increasing supplies
b. equitable distribution
c. Both a & b
d. None of the above

52. Who executes the Essential commodities Act

a. Food & Civil supply authorities
b. Central Committee for Food Standards
c. Department of Agriculture and Cooperation
d. All of the above

53. The Legal Metrology Act came into force in

a. 1986
b. 2009
c. 1975
d. 1940

54. Compounding of an offense is applicable to only following __________ under section 69?

a. Petty manufacture
b. Street Vendor
c. Temporary stall holder
d. All of the above

55. Section_______ of LM Act provides Declarations on pre-packaged commodities

a. Sec 20
b. Sec 25
c. Sec 18
d. Sec 27

56. Rule_______ of the LM Rules read with ________Schedule provides for standard quantities in which various commodities should be packed.

a. rule 6 and fourth schedule
b. rule 5 and second schedule
c. rule 6 and second schedule
d. None of the above

57. Declarations to be made on every package are given in

a. Rule 5
b. Rule 7
c. Rule 8
d. Rule 6

58. The height of letters in the declaration shall not be less than ___mm height

a. 0.5
b. 1
c. 0.1
d. 2

59. Section 36 of the LM Act provides

a. Penalty for selling of non-standard packages
b. Penalty for non-production of documents
c. Compounding of offences
d. Penalty for alteration of weight and measure

60. Chapter ____ of LM Act is related to Offences and Penalties

a. IV
b. II
c. V
d. VI

61. The height of letters in the declaration when blown, formed, molded, embossed or perforated, the height of letters shall not be less than ____mm

a. 1
b. 3
c. 2
d. 1.5

62. A person by whom the business is carried on or owned and is responsible for ensuring the compliance is?

a. FSM
b. FBO
c. PRP
d. All of the above

63. AGMARK logo with blend A is for?

a. Admixture of any two refined edible oil except Rice bran oil
b. Blend of only Refined edible oil
c. Blend of only Rice bran oil
d. None of the above

64. In year 1986 the important Act has been enacted called as ________

a. Export act
b. Essential commodities act
c. Consumer Protection act
d. None of the above

65. Declaration of quantity in relation to commodities (sold by weight or volume) which may be qualified by the words "When Packed"
   a. Second Schedule
   b. Third Schedule
   c. Fourth Schedule
   d. First Schedule

66. Commodities to be packed in specified quantities is provided in which Schedule
   a. First Schedule
   b. Third Schedule
   c. Second Schedule
   d. Fourth Schedule

67. ASCI Stands for
   a. The Advertising Standards Council of India
   b. The Advertising State Council of India
   c. The Advertising Standards Code of India
   d. None of the above

68. Which of the following is not a fundamental Principles of ASCI
   a. To ensure the truthfulness and honesty
   b. To ensure the advertisements are not offensive
   c. Complaint procedure
   d. None of the above

69. Non-conformance of product is analyzed by?
   a. Control chart
   b. Pareto analysis
   c. Affinity diagram
   d. All of the above

70. A summons issued by a court must be in
   a. Duplicate
   b. Triplicate
   c. Writing and Duplicate
   d. Writing and Triplicate

71. Code of Criminal Procedure was enacted in the year
   a. 1974
   b. 1961
   c. 1973
   d. 1986

72. Under which section of Cr.P.C. the Assistant Public Prosecutor is appointed
   a. Sec 20
   b. Sec 24
   c. Sec 13
   d. Sec 25

73. Section 304 of Cr.P.C. deal with
   a. Protection to accused against double prosecution for the same offence
   b. Withdrawal from prosecution
   c. Legal aid to the accused at state expenses
   d. Order to release on probation of good conduct

74. An Executive Magistrate is empowered to grant remand under section 167, Cr.P.C. for a maximum period of

a. 15 days b. 7 days

c. 60 days d. 90 days

75. Under which Section of Cr.P.C. a person who is avoiding execution of a warrant may be proclaimed absconder

a. Section 81 b. Section 83

c. Section 82 d. Section 84

76. Under which of the following sections of the Code of Criminal Procedure, police can arrest an accused without warrant?

a. Section 42 b. Section 39

c. Section 41 d. Section 45

77. Point out the incorrect statement

a. In a cognizable offence any police officer may without any order from a Magistrate and without a warrant arrest any person

b. A private person may arrest or cause to be arrested any person committing a cognizable offence

c. An Executive Magistrate may arrest offender when any offence is committed in his presence and within his jurisdiction

d. None of the above is correct

78. Object of investigation is

a. To punish accused b. To acquit accused

c. To collect evidence d. To convict accused

79. An order of life imprisonment may be passed by

a. A Chief Judicial Magistrate b. A Sessions Judge

c. A Metropolitan Magistrate d. Any Magistrate of first class

80. Under which Section of Cr. P.C. an accused person can himself be a competent witness?

a. Section 315 b. Section 300

c. Section 313 d. Section 317

81. When accused does not have sufficient means to engage pleader, the Session Court may assign pleader for defence at expense of the state, it is insured by which section of Cr. P.C?

a. Section 301 b. Section 304

c. Section 306 d. Section 305

82. When a person who would otherwise be competent, to compound an offence under section 320 of Cr. P.C. is dead, then?
    a. Offence cannot be compounded
    b. Offence can be compounded by an eye witness
    c. Offence can be compounded by legal representative of such person without consent of the Court
    d. Legal representative of such person can compound offence with consent of the Court

83. Three years period of limitation is prescribed for taking cognizance of offence punishable with imprisonment for a term not exceeding
    a. One year
    b. Three year
    c. Five year
    d. Seven year

84. When can a trial court release an accused on bail under section 389(3) of Cr. P.C. after conviction?
    a. Where accused is on bail, and imprisonment is not exceeding 3 years
    b. Where accused is on bail, and imprisonment is not exceeding 5 years
    c. Where accused is on bail, and imprisonment is not exceeding 7 years
    d. Where offence is exclusively bailable whether accused is on bail or not

85. Which section of the Code of Criminal Procedure provides that public prosecutor inchagre of a case may with consent of court at any time before judgment is pronounced withdraw from prosecution of any person in respect of any offence for which he is tried?
    a. Section 304
    b. Section 306
    c. Section 321
    d. Section 313

86. Which section of the Code of Criminal Procedure provide for trial before a Court of Session?
    a. Section 225 to Section 237
    b. Section 238 to Section 243
    c. Section 251 to Section 259
    d. Section 260 to Section 265

87. In a first information an offence is cognizable and other is non-cognizable, whole case shall be deemed to be
    a. Cognizable
    b. Non-cognizable
    c. It is to be seen whether
    d. None of these

88. In reference to information relating to commission of cognizable offence which of following statement is not correct?
    a. It may be given orally to officer incharge of police station
    b. It is reduced to writing by or under direction of officer incharge of police station
    c. Information reduced to writing is to be signed by person giving it
    d. Copy of information cannot be given free of cost to informant

89. A conditional order for removal of public nuisance under section 133 Cr. P.C. may be passed by
    a. The District Magistrate only
    b. The Sub-Divisional Magistrate only
    c. The Executive Magistrate only
    d. Any of above Magistrates

90. In proceeding under section 107 of the Code of Criminal Procedure an Executive Magistrate may require to execute a bond for keeping peace for such period not exceeding ________ as Magistrate thinks fit.
    a. One year
    b. Two years
    c. Three years
    d. Six months

91. Technical Barriers to Trade (TBC) emerged from the
    a. Ceylon round of WTO
    b. Tokyo round of WTO
    c. European round of WTO
    d. None of the above.

92. Quality council of India was set up in the year
    a. 1998
    b. 1996
    c. 1997
    d. 1990

93. BAP (Best Aquaculture Practices) is
    a. Comprehensive and proven third-party aquaculture
    b. Best methods to producing aquaculture
    c. Both a and b
    d. None of these

94. Commodity containing more than 25 kg or 25 litres (50 in case cement and fertilizers) are ________ from specific requirement of retail packages.
    a. Not exempted
    b. Exempted
    c. May be or not
    d. None

ANSWERS

1. Fundamentals of Chemistry

Q. No.	*Ans*	*Q. No.*	*Ans*	*Q. No.*	*Ans*	*Q. No.*	*Ans*	*Q. No.*	*Ans*
1	c.	41	d.	81	c.	121	d.	161	c.
2	b.	42	a.	82	c.	122	d.	162	c.
3	b.	43	c.	83	d.	123	a.	163	b.
4	b.	44	b.	84	c.	124	c.	164	b.
5	a.	45	d.	85	c.	125	b.	165	d.
6	c.	46	c.	86	c.	126	a.	166	d.
7	b.	47	a.	87	c.	127	c.	167	b.
8	c.	48	c.	88	b	128	a.	168	c.
9	d.	49	a.	89	c.	129	c.	169	d.
10	a.	50	b.	90	c.	130	b.	170	a.
11	c.	51	c.	91	d.	131	a.	171	d.
12	a.	52	d.	92	c.	132	a.	172	c.
13	a.	53	b.	93	d.	133	d.	173	c.
14	d.	54	c.	94	d.	134	c.	174	c.
15	d.	55	b.	95	a.	135	d.	175	d.
16	b.	56	c.	96	b.	136	c.	176	a.
17	d.	57	a.	97	a.	137	a.	177	b.
18	c.	58	d.	98	c.	138	b.	178	d.
19	a.	59	a.	99	b.	139	b.	179	a.
20	d.	60	a.	100	d.	140	a.	180	a.
21	b.	61	c.	101	a.	141	d.	181	c.
22	a.	62	c.	102	c.	141	b.	182	d.
23	c.	63	c.	103	b.	143	d.	183	a.
24	b.	64	b.	104	b.	144	c.	184	c.
25	c.	65	d.	105	c.	145	c.	185	b.
26	a.	66	d.	106	a.	146	d.	186	d.
27	c.	67	a.	107	b.	147	c.	187	a.
28	a.	68	c.	108	b.	148	c.	188	b.
29	d.	69	a.	109	a.	149	c.	189	c.
30	b.	70	b.	110	c.	150	a.	190	b.
31	c.	71	b.	111	b.	151	b.	191	b.
32	c.	72	c.	112	c.	152	b.	192	c.
33	d.	73	d.	113	b.	153	d.	193	c.
34	b.	74	a.	114	c.	154	b.	194	c.
35	c.	75	c.	115	b.	155	d.	195	a.
36	d.	76	a.	116	b.	156	c.	196	b
37	c.	77	a.	117	a.	157	a.	197	c.
38	d.	78	d.	118	c.	158	b.	198	a.
39	c.	79	b.	119	d.	159	b.	199	d.
40	a.	80	b.	120	d.	160	c.	200	a.

2. Fundamentals of Food Science and Nutrition

Q. No.	Ans	Q. No.	Ans	Q. No.	Ans	Q. No.	Ans	Q. No.	Ans
1	c.	41	c.	81	b.	121	b.	161	b.
2	b.	42	b.	82	a.	122	b.	162	c.
3	d.	43	d.	83	b.	123	a.	163	b.
4	b.	44	b.	84	c.	124	b.	164	b.
5	c.	45	c.	85	b.	125	c.	165	a.
6	b.	46	a.	86	c.	126	d.	166	a.
7	b.	47	d.	87	d.	127	c.	167	d.
8	c.	48	a.	88	b.	128	a.	168	d.
9	b.	49	c.	89	d.	129	b.	169	c.
10	d.	50	c.	90	a.	130	b.	170	a.
11	b.	51	a.	91	b.	131	d.	171	a.
12	c.	52	a.	92	b.	132	a.	172	a.
13	a	53	c.	93	a.	133	a.	173	b.
14	b.	54	a.	94	d.	134	d.	174	c.
15	d.	55	d.	95	a.	135	b.	175	c.
16	d.	56	a.	96	a.	136	b.	176	b.
17	c.	57	c.	97	b.	137	a.	177	d.
18	b.	58	b.	98	b.	138	b.	178	d.
19	a.	59	a.	99	c.	139	a.	179	b.
20	c.	60	d.	100	b.	140	b.	180	a.
21	b.	61	c.	101	b.	141	a.	181	b.
22	a.	62	d.	102	c.	141	d.	182	b.
23	b.	63	a.	103	a.	143	b.	183	d.
24	b.	64	a.	104	b.	144	c.	184	b.
25	a.	65	d.	105	d.	145	b.	185	c.
26	c	66	b	106	b.	146	a.	186	c.
27	c	67	d.	107	a.	147	a.	187	d.
28	b.	68	c.	108	b.	148	c.	188	a.
29	b.	69	d.	109	b.	149	b.	189	c.
30	a.	70	b.	110	d.	150	a.	190	d.
31	b.	71	b.	111	a.	151	a.	191	c.
32	b.	72	b.	112	b.	152	d.	192	c.
33	d.	73	d.	113	a.	153	c.	193	b.
34	c.	74	d.	114	b.	154	a.	194	b.
35	a.	75	b.	115	b.	155	b.	195	b.
36	b.	76	a.	116	b.	156	b.	196	a.
37	b.	77	c.	117	b.	157	b.	197	d.
38	d.	78	b.	118	b.	158	a.	198	b.
39	c	79	a.	119	d.	159	a.	199	a.
40	d.	80	a.	120	a.	160	b.	200	d.

3. Fundamentals of Food Processing and Technology

Q. No.	Ans	Q. No.	Ans	Q. No.	Ans	Q. No.	Ans	Q. No.	Ans
1	a.	41	a.	81	c.	121	d.	161	a.
2	b.	42	a.	82	b.	122	b.	162	b.
3	c.	43	b.	83	d.	123	a.	163	b.
4	c.	44	b.	84	d.	124	b.	164	c.
5	c.	45	a.	85	a.	125	b.	165	b.
6	a.	46	a.	86	d.	126	a.	166	b.
7	d.	47	c.	87	b.	127	c.	167	c.
8	c.	48	d.	88	d.	128	c.	168	b.
9	c.	49	d.	89	c.	129	d.	169	b.
10	d.	50	d.	90	c.	130	d.	170	d.
11	c.	51	b.	91	a.	131	b.	171	c.
12	a.	52	b.	92	d.	132	a.	172	a.
13	d.	53	c.	93	b.	133	a.	173	b.
14	c.	54	c.	94	c.	134	a.	174	b.
15	a.	55	c.	95	c.	135	d.	175	d.
16	c.	56	a.	96	c.	136	c.	176	c.
17	b.	57	b.	97	d.	137	c.	177	b.
18	a.	58	c.	98	c.	138	a.	178	a.
19	d.	59	b.	99	b.	139	b.	179	d.
20	c.	60	b.	100	b.	140	d.	180	c.
21	a.	61	b.	101	a.	141	c.	181	b.
22	b.	62	b.	102	c.	142	a.	182	b.
23	a.	63	a.	103	c.	143	c.	183	c.
24	a.	64	b.	104	a.	144	a.	184	b.
25	c.	65	b.	105	c.	145	a.	185	b.
26	b.	66	d.	106	a.	146	a.	186	a.
27	d.	67	d.	107	b	147	b.	187	b.
28	a.	68	a.	108	c.	148	d.	188	b.
29	c.	69	a.	109	b.	149	c.	189	a.
30	b.	70	b.	110	a.	150	b.	190	d.
31	c.	71	b.	111	d.	151	d.	191	a.
32	a.	72	c.	112	b.	152	b.	192	c.
33	a.	73	b.	113	b.	153	d.	193	d.
34	c.	74	b.	114	d.	154	b.	194	a.
35	b.	75	a.	115	b.	155	a.	195	a.
36	b.	76	a.	116	b.	156	a.	196	b.
37	b.	77	c.	117	b.	157	d.	197	d.
38	b.	78	b.	118	c.	158	a.	198	c.
39	a.	79	b.	119	c.	159	b.	199	d.
40	a.	80	c.	120	a.	160	b.	200	a.

Q. No.	Ans	Q. No.	Ans	Q. No.	Ans	Q. No.	Ans	Q. No.	Ans
201	d.	221	c.	241	b.	261	a.	281	a.
202	c.	222	d.	242	a.	262	b.	282	a.
203	b.	223	c.	243	c.	263	b.	283	c.
204	a.	224	a.	244	d.	264	a.	284	b.
205	b.	225	c.	245	c.	265	b.	285	d.
206	b.	226	d.	246	d.	266	d.	286	c.
207	d.	227	d.	247	d.	267	d.	287	b.
208	a.	228	a.	248	b.	268	c.	288	c.
209	a.	229	b.	249	d.	269	a.	289	a.
210	d.	230	b.	250	b.	270	d.	290	c.
211	b.	231	c.	251	a.	271	c.	291	d.
212	c.	232	b.	252	c.	272	a.	292	d.
213	b.	233	b.	253	b.	273	c.	293	d.
214	b.	234	c.	254	d.	274	a.	294	b.
215	b.	235	b.	255	b.	275	b.	295	c.
216	b.	236	c.	256	b.	276	a.	296	c.
217	c.	237	b.	257	d.	277	b.	297	b.
218	d.	238	c.	258	a.	278	a.	298	c.
219	a.	239	a.	259	d.	279	d.	299	b.
220	a.	240	b.	260	d.	280	d.	300	c.

4. Advances in Food Science and Technology

Q. No.	Ans	Q. No.	Ans	Q. No.	Ans	Q. No.	Ans	Q. No.	Ans
1	b.	21	d.	41	c.	61	c.	81	d.
2	d.	22	a.	42	d.	62	c.	82	a.
3	a.	23	d.	43	b.	63	d.	83	b.
4	d.	24	b.	44	b.	64	d.	84	c.
5	a.	25	d.	45	a	65	a.	85	d.
6	c	26	c.	46	d.	66	b.	86	a.
7	d.	27	d.	47	b.	67	c.	87	b.
8	c.	28	c.	48	d.	68	c.	88	c.
9	d.	29	d.	49	a.	69	a.	89	c.
10	d.	30	d.	50	a.	70	d.	90	a.
11	a.	31	a.	51	d.	71	c.	91	d.
12	d.	32	c.	52	d.	72	b.	92	d.
13	b.	33	b.	53	b.	73	d.	93	d.
14	c	34	d.	54	d.	74	d.	94	b.
15	a.	35	d.	55	d.	75	d.	95	b.
16	a.	36	c.	56	b.	76	a.	96	c.
17	d.	37	d.	57	b.	77	d.	97	a.
18	d.	38	d.	58	c.	78	d.	98	c.
19	c.	39	a.	59	d.	79	c.	99	b.
20	d.	40	d.	60	d.	80	c.	100	b.

5. Fundamentals of Food Safety

Q.No.	Ans	Q. No.	Ans	Q. No.	Ans	Q. No.	Ans	Q. No.	Ans	Q. No.	Ans	Q.No.	Ans
1	a	21	c	41	d	61	c	81	a	101	b	121	b
2	d	22	d	42	a	62	b	82	d	102	a	122	a
3	a	23	a	43	d	63	d	83	b	103	b	123	c
4	c	24	c	44	a	64	d	84	a	104	c		
5	a	25	d	45	c	65	d	85	d	105	a		
6	a	26	a	46	a	66	a	86	c	106	d		
7	a	27	a	47	b	67	b	87	d	107	a, c		
8	b	28	d	48	d	68	b	88	d	108	b		
9	d	29	b	49	a	69	c	89	a	109	a		
10	a	30	c	50	a	70	a	90	a	110	c		
11	a	31	c	51	b	71	a	91	b	111	d		
12	b	32	b	52	c	72	c	92	a	112	b		
13	a	33	c	53	b	73	c	93	d	113	d		
14	b	34	a	54	b	74	c	94	a	114	c		
15	d	35	b	55	c	75	d	95	a	115	b		
16	c	36	d	56	a	76	c	96	c	116	d		
17	b	37	c	57	c	77	b	97	d	117	c		
18	b	38	c	58	a	78	d	98	a	118	a		
19	d	39	c	59	d	79	b	99	a	119	d		
20	d	40	c	60	b	80	c	100	b	120	a		

6. Introduction to Food Safety and Standard Act, 2006

Q.No.	Ans	Q. No.	Ans	Q. No.	Ans	Q. No.	Ans	Q. No.	Ans	Q. No.	Ans	Q.No.	Ans	Q.No.	Ans
1	c	21	a	41	d	61	d	81	b	101	b	121	d	141	a
2	b	22	b	42	b	62	a	82	a	102	c	122	d	142	c
3	a	23	a	43	b	63	c	83	c	103	b	123	a	143	d
4	d	24	d	44	d	64	a	84	a	104	a	124	c	144	d
5	d	25	c	45	b	65	c	85	b	105	c	125	b	145	b
6	b	26	b	46	d	66	a	86	c	106	b	126	c	146	c
7	b	27	d	47	a	67	d	87	c	107	b	127	d	147	c
8	b	28	a	48	b	68	c	88	c	108	a	128	d	148	d
9	a	29	a	49	b	69	b	89	a	109	b	129	a	149	b
10	c	30	b	50	a	70	b	90	c	110	a	130	b	150	b
11	c	31	a	51	b	71	c	91	b	111	d	131	a	151	c
12	a	32	b	52	c	72	d	92	a	112	c	132	a	152	b
13	d	33	c	53	b	73	d	93	c	113	d	133	b	153	d
14	a	34	c	54	d	74	d	94	a	114	b	134	b	154	c
15	d	35	c	55	c	75	c	95	b	115	b	135	c	155	b
16	b	36	d	56	b	76	d	96	c	116	c	136	c	156	a
17	c	37	b	57	c	77	c	97	c	117	c	137	c	157	c
18	c	38	a	58	d	78	b	98	b	118	b	138	a	158	a
19	b	39	b	59	d	79	b	99	c	119	a	139	d	159	c
20	d	40	d	60	a	80	c	100	b	120	c	140	b	160	a

Q.No. Ans	Q. No. Ans	Q. No. Ans	Q. No. Ans	Q. No. Ans	Q. No. Ans	Q.No. Ans
161 c	181 d	201 c	221 a	241 c		
162 c	182 d	202 b	222 c	242 c		
163 b	183 c	203 a	223 a	243 a		
164 a	184 d	204 d	224 b	244 d		
165 b	185 a	205 b	225 a	245 c		
166 c	186 d	206 a	226 c	246 a		
167 d	187 b	207 b	227 a	247 d		
168 b	188 b	208 a	228 d	248 a		
169 b	189 a	209 a	229 a	249 a		
170 c	190 c	210 b	230 c	250 c		
171 d	191 a	211 c	231 b			
172 c	192 b	212 a	232 c			
173 d	193 a	213 b	233 a			
174 a	194 c	214 d	234 c			
175 b	195 b	215 d	235 a			
176 c	196 a	216 c	236 c			
177 a	197 d	217 b	237 a			
178 b	198 c	218 d	238 d			
179 b	199 b	219 a	239 c			
180 a	200 d	220 c	240 c			

7. Introduction to Codex Alimentarius

Q. No.	Ans	Q. No.	Ans	Q. No.	Ans	Q. No.	Ans	Q. No.	Ans.
1	a	11	b	21	b	31	b	41	a
2	d	12	d	22	d	32	b	42	c
3	a	13	a	23	c	33	b	43	b
4	d	14	c	24	a	34	c	44	b
5	b	15	d	25	a	35	d	45	a
6	d	16	a	26	b	36	a	46	d
7	b	17	d	27	d	37	a	47	c
8	c	18	a	28	a	38	d	48	c
9	b	19	c	29	a	39	a	49	a
10	c	20	c	30	c	40	c	50	d

8. Miscellaneous Laws-

Q. No.	Ans	Q. No.	Ans	Q. No.	Ans	Q. No.	Ans	Q. No.	Ans
1	a	21	a	41	c	61	c	81	b
2	d	22	b	42	b	62	b	82	d
3	d	23	c	43	b	63	a	83	b
4	a	24	c	44	b	64	c	84	a
5	a	25	c	45	a	65	b	85	c
6	b	26	c	46	c	66	c	86	a
7	d	27	c	47	c	67	a	87	a
8	a	28	b	48	d	68	c	88	d
9	c	29	c	49	c	69	d	89	d
10	a	30	d	50	a	70	c	90	a
11	b	31	a	51	c	71	c	91	b
12	d	32	d	52	a	72	d	92	c
13	a	33	c	53	b	73	c	93	a
14	a	34	b	54	c	74	b	94	b
15	c	35	c	55	c	75	c		
16	a	36	b	56	b	76	c		
17	d	37	b	57	d	77	d		
18	d	38	a	58	b	78	c		
19	c	39	a	59	a	79	b		
20	b	40	a	60	c	80	a		

Assistant Commissioner (Food) cum Designated Officer Examination – Maharashtra

Exam Date: 30 November 2014

We are thankful to Syed Imran Hashmi for contributing this section (question and answer). He is Senior Research Assistant at College of Food Technology, Vasantrao Naik Marathwada Krishi Vidyapeeth, Parbhani.

Time: 1 hr **Total Questions: 100** **Total Marks: 200**

1. Who was awarded the' International Environment Goldman Prize' considered as' Green Nobel' in April 2014?

   A) Ramesh Agrawal B) Sundarlal Bahuguna
   C) Rajendha Singh D) Megha Patkar

2. Which Pharmaceutical Company has taken over Ranbaxy Laboratories Limited?

   A) Glaxo B) Sun Pharma
   C) Pfizer D) Merck

3. Which of the following IT companies has been awarded the international Ashden Award in 2014 for energy conservation?

   A) WIPRO B) TCS
   C) Infosys D) Tech-Mahindra

4. Consider the following statements:

   (a) Brazil has won the World Cup the highest number of times, Five, till June 2014.
   (b) It is the only team to have played in the final round in all the football World Cups, till June 2014.

   A) only (a) B) only (b)
   C) (a) and (b) D) None of these

5. Match the following

Column A	Column B
a) Padma Vibhushan (2013)	(i) Pandit Bhimsen Joshi
b) Padma Bhushan (2013)	(ii) Prof. Yash Pal
c) Padma Shri (2013)	(iii) Rahul Dravid
d) Bharat Ratna (2009)	(iv) Dr. Sudarshan Agrawal

Match of Correct pair:

A) (i) (ii) (iii) (iv) B) (ii) (iii) (iv) (i)

C) (iii) (ii) (iv) (i) D) (iv) (iii) (ii) (i)

6. ________ has been appointed as a Brand Ambassador or for awareness in women regarding Vyasan Mukti Programme (Addiction Free Programme).

A) Sadhana Amte B) Rani Bang

C) Sindhutai Sapkal D) Sonali Bendre

7. Select the correct statement/statements:

(a) Maharashtra has 5,983 km of railway route which is 9.2 percent of total railway route in the country.

(b) There are 3 international and 5 domestic airports in Maharashtra.

Answer Options:

A) Statement (a) is correct, statement (b) is incorrect

B) Statement (a) is incorrect, statement (b) is correct

C) Both the statements (a) and (b) are correct

D) Both the statements (a) and (b) are incorrect

8. The Fifth BRICS summit was hosted by ________ in ________

A) India, March 2012 B) Brazil, March 2013

C) South Africa, March 2013 D) Indonesia, March 2012

9. What was the name of the totally indigenous surface to air missile successfully test fired in May 2014?

A) Agni B) Akash

C) Astra D) Prithvi

10. Election Commission of India appointed __________ and __________ as the National Icons to help promote voter participation in India.

A) Saina Nehwaland Sania Mirza B) Rahul Dravid and Sachin Tedulkar

C) Mary Komand Priyanka Chopra D) Saina Nehwal and Mary Kom

11. Which amongst the given images is the correct mirror image of the given question image?

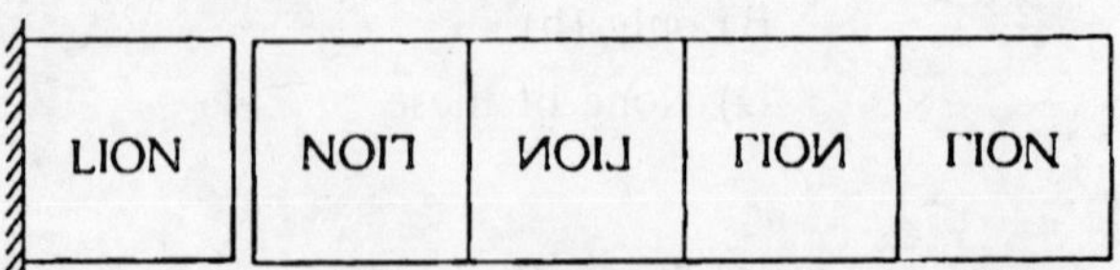

(A) (B) (C) (D)

A) A B) B

C) C D) D

12. Which one of the cubes given below is not obtained by folding accompanying paper cutout?

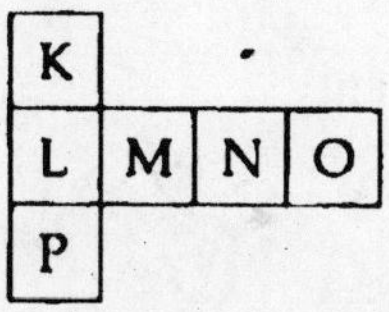

(1) 

(2) 

(3) 

(4) 

A) (1) B) (2)
C) (3) D) (4)

13. Study the pattern and select an appropriate option for the question mark:

91|13|117
147|21|189
203|29|261
119|??|153

A) 11 B) 23
C) 17 D) 16

14. Which option given below does not belong to following grid?

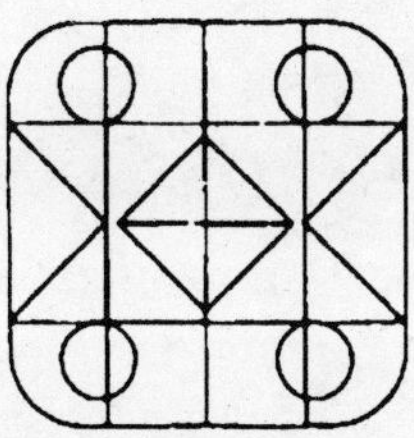

(1) 
(2) 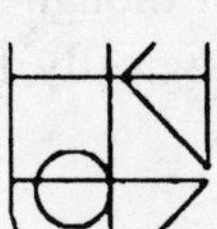
(3) 
(4) 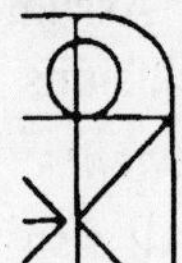

A) (1) B) (2)
C) (3) D) (4)

15. In a symbolic language, if 'POSSIBLE' word is written as 'SLVPLYOB' then in the same symbolic language how will the word 'FREEZE' be written?

A) IOBBWB B) COHCBH
C) COBSWH D) IOHBCB

16. If it were two hours later, it would be half as long until mid night if it were one hour later. What time is it now?

A) 18.30 B) 20.00

C) 21.0 D) Data is in sufficient

17. Which option is identical with the accompanying solid?

(1) 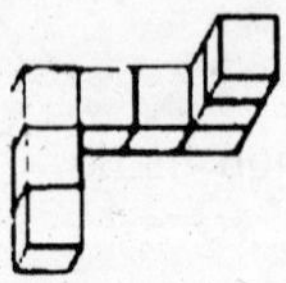 (2) 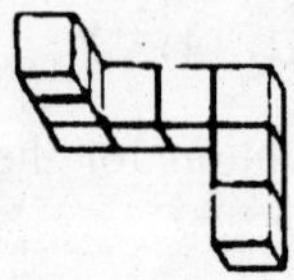 (3) 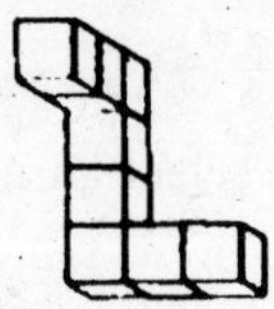 (4) 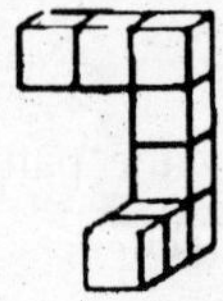

A) (1) B) (2)

C) (3) D) (4)

18. How many triangles are therein the given figure?

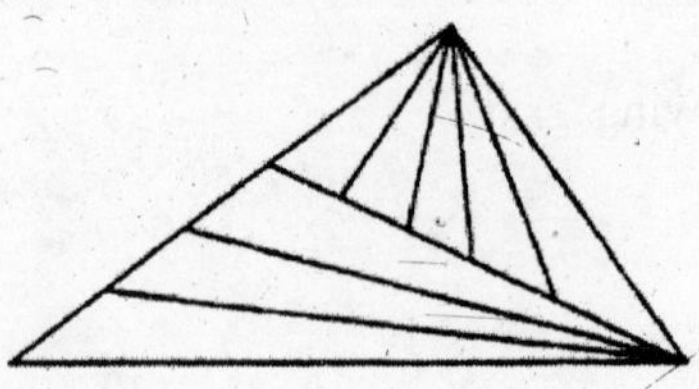

A) 24 B) 22

C) 20 D) 25

19. Below are given three statements followed by four conclusions numbered (I), (II), (III) and (IV). Assume that all statements are true even though they appear to be absurd. Read all conclusions and then decide which of them logically follow from the given statements.

Statements:

(a) All fish are birds

(b) All bacteria are birds

(c) Some birds are viruses

Conclusions:

(I) Some fish are bacteria (II) Some bacteria are viruses

(III) Some viruses are fish (IV) Some viruses are fish

A) None follows B) Only (I) follows

C) Only (I) and (II) follow D) Only (II) and (IV) follow

20. Which numbere dimage should be replaced by another image to make series logically consistent?

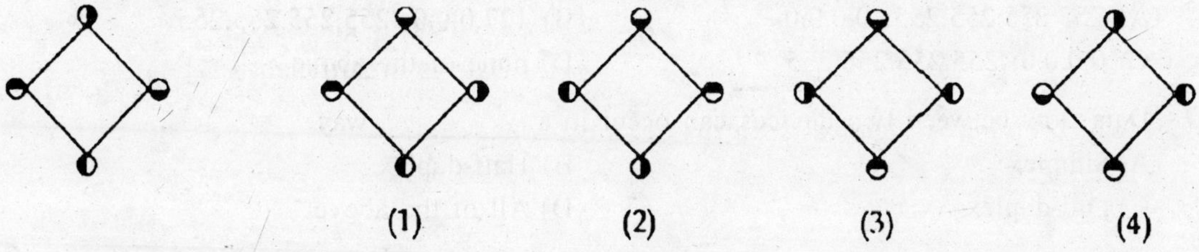

A) (1) B) (2)
C) (3) D) (4)

21. Consider the following statements:

a. The Governor of a state is part of the state legislature; head dresses the legislature and can send messages to it.

b. The legislative council cannot delay the non-money bill more than six months.

Which of the statements given above is/are correct?

A) Only (a) B) Only (b)
C) (a) and (b) D) None of the two

22. ______, ____and ______were elected from Mumbai province in the Constituent Assembly.

(a) Dr. B.R. Ambedkar (b) Sardar Vallabhbhai Patel
(c) Mrs. Hansa Mehta (d) Shyama Prasad Mukherjee

A) Only (a), (b) and (d) B) Only (a), (c) and(d)
C) Only (b), (c) and (d) D) Only (a), (b) and (c)

23. Match the pairs (Directive Principles):

(A)	(B)
(a) Local Self Government	(i) Article 40
(b) Right to Work	(ii) Article 41
(c) Uniform Civil Code	(iii) Article 44
(d) Prohibition of Slaughter of Cows	(iv) Article 48

A) (i) (iii) (iv) (ii) B) (iv) (ii) (iii) (i)
C) (ii) (i) (iii) (iv) D) (i) (ii) (iii) (iv)

24. According to which Constitutional Amendment, it is binding on the President to act according to the advice of the Council of Ministers?

A) 44th B) 52nd
C) 42nd D) 24th

25. In which of the following states, the Vidhan Parishad does not exist?

A) Jammu and Kashmir B) Maharashtra
C) Bihar D) Madhya Pradesh

26. A host can get its IP address from its DHCP server by using ___________ as source address and as the destination address.
A) 255.255.255.255; 0.0.0.0
B) 127.0.0.0; 255.255.255.255
C) 0.0.0.0; 255.255.255.255
D) none of the above

27. Data flow between two devices can occur in a __________ way.
A) Simplex
B) Half-duplex
C) Full-duplex
D) All of the above

28. "Sahayika", (one of the media lab Asia projects) is __________.
A) Ontology building and management Tool
B) Web portal for empowering of disabled
C) An assessment for mentally retarded children
D) None of the above

29. 127.0.0.1 is a
A) limited broadcast address
B) direct broadcast address
C) multicast address
D) loopback address

30. Which one of the following is an error reporting protocol?
A) ARP
B) TCP
C) UDP
D) ICMP

31. IS 22000 is for:
A) FSMS
B) HACCP
C) FSSC
D) BRC

32. Can a corporation or association of persons apply for information under RTI.
A) No they cannot apply
B) Yes they can apply
C) Yes, as corporation and firms are treated as persons, they can apply
D) No, corporation and firms are not treated as persons

33. Consider the following statements with reference to water:
(a) According to WHO report, 3900 children die every day of water borne diseases.
(b) 1.1 billion people live without clean drinking water.
(c) 1.8 million people die every year from diarrhoeal diseases.
Which of the statements given above are correct?
A) (a) and (b)
B) (b) and (c)
C) (a) and (c)
D) (a), (b) and (c)

34. Which of the following is not an object of the Right to Information Act 2005?
A) Curtail Corruption
B) Promote transparency in the working of every public authority
C) Keep all the citizens informed of everything
D) Promote accountability in the working of every public authority

35. Which of the following courts has authority to entertain an appeal against the order passed under Right to Information Act?

A) District Court
B) High Court
C) Sessions Court
D) None of the above

36. Which of the following statements is/are correct?

(a) Human Rights are based on international consensus.

(b) They apply not only to countries that have recognized these rights in their legal institutions, but virtually to all the countries.

A) (a) only
B) (b) only
C) Both (a) and (b)
D) Neither (a) nor (b)

37. Which case out of the following is the landmark judgment to protect working women's rights to human dignity against sexual harassment?

A) C. B. Muthamma Vs Union of India
B) Maneka Gandhi Vs Union of India
C) Vishakaand others Vs State of Rajasthan
D) Harla Vs State of Rajasthan

38. Which court has jurisdiction to grant protection order and other order sunder the protection of women from Domestic Violence Act, 2005?

A) Sessions Court
B) Judicial Magistrate of the First Class
C) Judicial Magistrate of the Second Class
D) None of the above

39. Which of the following, women cannot claim protection under the provisions of protection of women from Domestic Violence Act presuming that they are staying with the abuser in the same house?

(a) Adopted daughter
(b) Woman staying with him in live-in-relationship
(c) Wife of unlawful second marriage
(d) Mother

Answer options:

A) (a) and (d)
B) (b) only
C) (b) and (c)
D) All can claim

40. Which day is observed as the foundation day of the National Human Rights Commission?

A) 10th October
B) 11th October
C) 12th October
D) 13th October

41. The wavelength range in nm of microwave radiation is (in m):

A) 10^5-10^7
B) 10^4-10^6
C) 10^3-10^5
D) None of the above

42. The IUPAC Name for

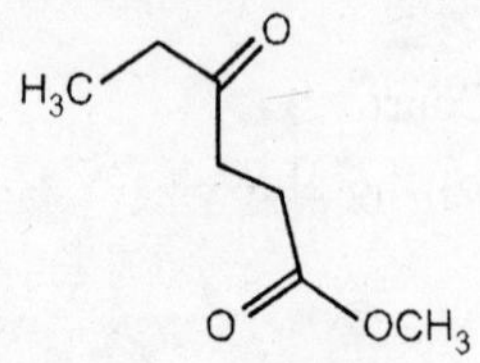

A) Ethyl-4-oxoheptonate B) Methyl-4-oxoheptonate
C) Ethyl-4-oxohexonate D) Methyl-4-oxohexonate

43. Out of the following, which is not the method of preparation of transuranic elements?
A) Heavy ion bombardment B) Ion-exchange
C) Neutron bombardment D) Highvoltage nuclei

44. When solid melts, there is:
A) An increase in enthalpy B) No change in enthalpy
C) A decrease in enthalpy D) Decrease in internal energy

45. Among the following, which is the least acidic?
A Phenol B) o-cresol
C) p-nitrophenol D) P-chlorophenol

46. Following reaction is an example of

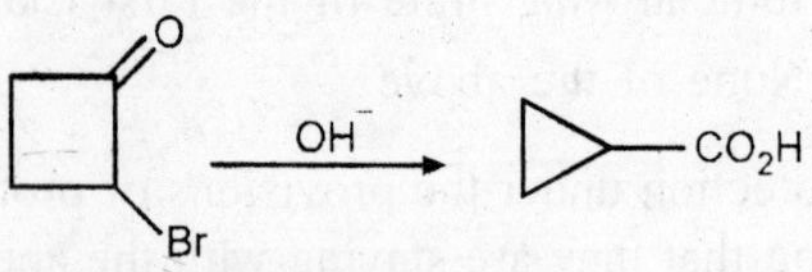

A) Wolf rearrangement C) Semibenzilic mechanism
C) Steven's rearrangement D) Wahner-Meerwin rearrangement

47. Which Molecule has greatest dipole moment?
A) HCl B) HF
C) HI D) HBr

48. Thermo gravimetric analysis is not concerned with:
A) Time B) Temperature
C) Weight D) Reagent of precipitation

49. What can be said about the spontaneity of reaction when:
A) "H and" S are both positive B) "Hand" S are both negative
C) "H is positive and" S negative D) "H is negative and "S positive

50. Which of the following is a thermosetting plastic?
A) Polyethylene B) Bakelite
C) Polystyrene D) None of these

51. ___________ are present in onions

A) Cellulose B) Galactans

C) Pectins D) Fructosans

52. The change in texture, colour and physical state which occurs when starch is heated in water is known as___________.

A) Flavonoids B) coagulation

C) Gelatinization D) Keratinisation

53. Heat cramps are due to deficiency of:

A) NaCl B) $KMnO_4$

C) Iron D) Ca:P

54. The Adult human body synthesizes daily about ___________mg cholesterol.

A) 1000 B) 2000

C) 3000 D) 500

55. Dals adulterated with Kesari dal is identified by:

A) Adding alcoholic potash and water and boil for 15 min

B) Iodine test

C) Physical examination

D) HCl test

56. Food contaminants means :

A) They are intentionally added to food for processing.

B) Substances not intentionally added to food but are present due to processing/treatment/ packaging etc.

C) presence of harmful chemicals and micro organisms

D) none of the above

57. Vitamin_________ is necessary for blood coagulation.

A) E B) B12

C) B6 D) K

58. _________ is the reserve carbohydrate found in liver and muscle.

A) Glucose B) Glycogen

C) Starch D) Dextins

59. The level of aflatoxinin staple food stuff has been found to be positively correlated to incidence of:

A) Lung cancer B) Stomach cancer

C) Liver cancer D) Oralsubmucousfibrosis

60. The energy value of food can be expressed in terms of ________.

A) Kcal
B) MJ
C) kilo Joules
D) All are correct

61. Food may contain naturally occurring toxic agents or toxic substances formed in cookıng that, are more harmful than the small amounts of pesticides that lingerin the food weeat. Can you identify the food that contains nitrosoamines formed by the reaction of nitrates and nitrites with amino acids?

A) Cooked preserved meats
B) Bananas artificially ripened in an atmosphere of ethylene
C) Mushrooms cooked inaluminiumpots
D) Cheese aged over 6 months

62. Cold plasma is a:

A) Solid state of matter
B) Liquid state of matter
C) Gaseous state of matter
D) None of the above

63. Fractional sterilization means:

A) Radiationsterilization
B) Incineration
C) Membrane filtration
D) Tyndallisation

64. Which of the following is considered as a non-thermal process?

A) Sterilization
B) Pulse delectric field
C) Induction cooking
D) Conduction

65. CAP and MAP stand for:

A) Controlled Automated Packaging and Modified Automated Packaging
B) Controlled Aseptic Packaging and Modified Aseptic Packaging
C) Controlled Atmosphere Packaging and Modified Atmosphere Packaging
D) Controlled Aesthetic Packaging and Modified Aesthetic Packaging

66. Codex Alimentarious Commission's Secretariat is at:

A) Rome
B) Delhi
C) Paris
D) Berlin

67. India has been member of Codex Alimentarious Commission since

A) 1954
B) 1964
C) 1966
D) 1947

68. In codex Alimentarious there are _______ co-ordinating members.

A) 2
B) 4
C) 6
D) 8

69. In India NCCP (National Codex Contact Point) is with

(a) MOHFW (b) FDAMah (c) FSSAI (d) NIFTEM

A) (a) only B) (c)only

C) (b) and (d) D) (d)

70. Ad hoc inter-governmental task force is codex committee for:

(a) Full term (b) Fixed Period (c) Permanent (d) None of Above

A) (a) Only B) (a) and (b)

C) (b) only D) (d) only

71. Nano technology and nano science involve the study of phenomena and materials and the manipulation of structures, devices and systems that exist at the nano scale less than nanometres (nm) in size.

A) 150 B) 200

C) 100 D) 300

72. Which are the main safety concerns for Genetically modified foods?

A) Food Poisoning/Low yield and Out crossing

B) Contamination/Gene transfer and colour change

C) Contamination/DNA transfer and colour change

D) Allergenicity/Gene transfer and Outcrossing

73. Foods for special dietary uses or functional foods or nutraceuticals or health supplements is defined in which section under FSS Act:

A) Section 22 B) Section 26

C) Section 16 D) Section 23

74. Genetically Modified Organisms (GMOs) can be defined as organisms:

A) In which the genetic material (DNA) has been altered in a way that does not occur naturally,

B) In which the genetic material (DNA) has been removed and does not occur naturally.

C) In which the complete genetic material (DNA) has been replaced.

D) None of the above.

75. Organic food refers to crop or livestock that are grown on the farm without the application of:

A) Synthetic fertilizers or pesticides B) Natural fertilizers or pesticides

C) Harmful fertilizers or pesticides D) New fertilizers or pesticides

76. Mustard seeds are adulterated generally with :

A) Papaya seeds B) Poppy seeds

C) Argemone seeds D) Onion seeds

77. The dose of radiation measured in the SI unit is known as :

A) Ray (Ry)
B) Gray (Gy)
C) Gram (Gm)
D) Microgram (Mg)

78. Which country has allowed GM food legally?

A) India
B) USA
C) EU
D) Dubai

79. Japan is the only country which has formulated dregulated system for functional food called as :

A) Foods for Special Health Use (FOSHU)
B) Fruits for Specified Health Use (FOSHU)
C) Foods for Specified Health Use (FOSHU)
D) None of the above

80. The preservative that destroys thiamine is :

A) Benzoic acid
B) Sulphur dioxide
C) Acetic acid
D) Propionic acid

81. Who will notify the Adjudicating Officer for the State?

A) The Central Government
B) The State Government
C) Food Safety Authority
D) Legal Ministry

82. During Sampling FSO will divide the food product in how many parts?

A) 4
B) 5
C) 3
D) 2

83. Which part of schedule 4 is applicable to Milk and Milk product industry?

A) Part I
B) Part III
C) Part IV
D) Part V

84. What is sub-standard food?

A) An article of food shall be deemed to be sub-standard if it does not meet the specified regulations but does not render the food unsafe.
B) An article of food shall be deemed to be sub-standard if it does not meet the specified standards but does not render the food unsafe.
C) An article of food shall be deemed to be sub-standard if it meets the specified standards but renders the food unsafe.
D) An article of food shall be deemed to be sub-standard if it does meet the specified standards but does not render adulteration.

85. Who is a food business operator?

A) Means any undertaking, whether for profit ornotand whether publicorprivate, carrying out any of the activities related to any stage of manufacture, processing, packaging, storage, transportation, distribution of food, import and includes food services, catering services, sale of food or food ingredients.

B) Means any undertaking who does the food business.

C) Means any undertaking, for profit and whether publicorprivate, carrying out any of the activities related to any stage of manufacture, processing, packaging, storage, transportation, distribution of food, import and includes food services, catering services, sale of food or food ingredients.

D) None of the above

86. ________ is part of quality management focused on providing confidence that quality requirements will be fulfilled.

A) Quality management B) Quality

C) Quality Assurance D) Updating

87. There are ________ HACCP principles.

A) 5 B) 7

C) 8 D) 10

88. HACCP has been defined by

A) Codex B) US FDA

C) ISO D) FDA MS

89. IS16021 : 2012 is for:

B) HACCP B) GMP

C) ISO D) GHP

90. The GMP may be treated as generic pre-requisite to ________

A) HACCP B) GHP

C) Food Audit D) ISO

91. ________ is the first HACCP principle.

A) Establish critical limit B) Conduct hazards analysis

C) Determine CCPs D) Establish corrective action

92. IS16020 : 2012 is for ________

A) GMP B) HACCP

C) ISO D) GHP

93. HACCP based on standards operating procedures are developed by

A) NFSMI B) FICCI

C) FSSAI D) NIFTEM

94. The removal of soil, food residue, dirt, grease or other objectionable matter is

A) Disinfection B) Fumigation
C) Cleaning D) Irradiation

95. There are ______ hygiene specific requirements.

A) 4 B) 6
C) 8 D) 10

96. Which order is not repealed by FSSA?

A) Cold Storage Order 1980
B) Fruit Products Order 1955
C) Solvent Extracted Oil, De-oiled Meal and Edible Flour Control Order1967
D) Vegetable Products Control Order 1967 FPO

97. Which agency is responsible for operation of Export (Quality Control and Inspection) Act 1963?

A) Codex B) The Export Inspection Council
C) The Export Quality Inspection D) Export house

98. Which BIS standard is compulsory for Packaged drinking water?

A) IS 14243 B) IS 13543
C) IS 14543 D) IS 14534

99. General Conference of Weights and Measures (CGPM) and the International Organization of Legal Metrology (OIML) supports the following Act/Rules:

A) FSSA B) AGMARK
C) Legal Metrology D) VOP

100. AGMARK certification is compulsory for the following food product:

A) Milk B) Fruit juices
C) Water D) Blended edible oil

ANSWERS

Q. No.	*Answer*	*Justification*
1	A.	With a small internet cafe as his headquarters, Ramesh Agrawal organized villagers to demand their right to information about industrial development projects and succeeded in shutting down one of the largest proposed coal mines in Chhattisgarh. Hence awarded International Goldman Environmental Prize in 2014 [Reference:http://www.goldmanprize.org/recipient/ramesh-agrawal]
2.	B.	In 2014, Sun Pharma acquired the entire 63.4% share of Ranbaxy making the conglomerate world's fifth largest special tygeneric pharma company [Reference: http://en.wikipedia.org/wiki/Ranbaxy_Laboratories]
3	C.	Ashdenisa London-based charity that works in the field of sustainable energy and development. Its work includes the annual Ashden Awards, advocacy and research in the field of sustainable energy, and mentoring and practical support for award winners. Infosys has cut its energy bills by a staggering $80 million since 2008. Hence, awarded International Ashden Award. [Reference: http://www.ashden.org/awards/2014]
4	A.	The 20 World Cup tournaments have been won by eight different national teams. Brazil have won five times, and they are the only team to have played in every tournament. However, in June 2014 Final Match was played between Argentina and Germany
5	B.	
6	C	Sindhutai Sapkal (she is a social worker & social activist known for her work in raising orphaned children in India [Reference: http://www.hindustantimes.com/india-news/a-unique-literary-meet-in-pune-on-anti-addiction/article1-928220.aspx]
7	A.	Statement (a) is correct while Maharashtra has only two International Airports (Mumbai and Nagpur) and 23 domestic airports
8	C.	Fifth BRICS Summit was organized on 26-27 March 2013 in Durban, South Africa [Reference:http://www.brics5.co.za]
9	C.	It seems to be wrong question because out of given sample only Akash is Surface to air missile which was test fired in 2013 while in 2014 on Astra was test fired which is air to air missile
10	D.	The Election Commission (EC) of India on 22 January 2013 announced Saina Nehwal and Mary Kom as the National Icons to help promote, voter participation in India. Saina Nehwal and Mary Kom, both are Olympic Bronze Medal lists in the London Olympics 2012, in Badminton and Boxing respectively.

Q. No.	Answer	Justification
11	B.	Image (B) can be directly imposed with given Image.
12	C.	If we fold the above image then Letter N should be on Opposite side of Letter L and hence N cannot be a side to L. Hence Answer 3 image cannot be obtained.
13	C.	In all three equations, we can establish a relation as follows: a | b | c, b = (c – a)/2 Hence: First = (117– 91) / 2 =13 Second = (189 – 147)/ 2 = 21 Third = (261 – 203)/ 2 =29 Fourth = (153– 119) / 2 = 17
14	A.	Above given figure do not contain any triangle with half circle in a box.
15	D.	
16	A.	
17	B.	If we rotate the given image to right by 90 degree with as light upward twist, we will obtain image (2)
18	C.	
19	C.	
20	B.	
21	C.	Both statements are correct
22	D.	Dr. Shama Prasad Mukherjee was elected from Bengal in constitutional assembly.
23	D.	DIRECTIVE PRINCIPLES OF STATE POLICY
		Organization of village panchayats.
		Right to work, to education and to public assistance in certain cases.
		44. Uniform civil code for the citizens.
		48. Organisation of agriculture and animal husbandry.
		48A. Protection and improvement of environment and safe guarding of forests and wild life.
24	C.	Before 42th Amendment, 1976, it was not, constitutionally, mandatory for the president to act according to the advice of the council of ministers. However, the 42nd amendment made it binding on the president to act according to the advice of the Councils of Ministers
25	D.	Vidhan Parishad is the upper House of the State Legislature. It is not in existence in very State. Very few States have bicameral Legislature that means having two Houses. At present five states viz. Utter Pradesh, Bihar, Karnataka, Maharashtra and Jammu & Kashmir have Vidhan Parishad while, remaining 23 States have one House, *i.e.* Vidhan Sabha.

Q. No.	*Answer*	*Justification*
26	B.	
27	D.	Data flow between two devices can occur in one of three ways: simplex, half-duplex, or full-duplex.
28	D.	Sahayika: The Knowledge Network - The project has been taken up with IIT kharagpur. Sahayika is a system that aims at supplementing the knowledge requirement of the school students, based on the prescribed curriculum. The objective of the software is to provide school children with a knowledge network through which they can perform concept based as well as topic based navigation of contents and to provide the knowledge workers with the facility of building the structure for a particular subject.
29	D.	The IP address 127.0.0.1 is a special purpose address reserved for use on each computer. 127.0.0.1 is conventionally a computer's loopback address.
30	D.	Internet Control Message Protocol (ICMP) is an error reporting and diagnostic utility and is considered a required part of any IP implementation. Understanding ICMP and knowing what can possibly generate a specific type of ICMP is useful in diagnosing network problems.
31	A.	IS 22000 is a Food Safety Management System
32	A.	The RTI Act, 2005 gives the right to information only to the citizens of India. It does not make provision for giving information to Corporations, Associations, Companies etc. which are legal entities/persons, but not citizens. However, if an application is made by an employee or office-bearer of any Corporation, Association, Company, NGO etc. indicating his name and such employee/office bearer is a citizen of India, information may be supplied to him/her. In such cases, it would be presumed that a citizen has sought information at the address of the Corporation etc.
33	D.	All statements are correct
34	C.	It is not the objective of RTI to inform everything to every citizen
35	D.	According to RTI, No court shall entertain any suit, application or other proceeding in respect of any order made under this Act and no such order shall be called in question otherwise than by way of an appeal under this Act.
36	C.	Both statements are correct as per UDHR.
37	C.	The Vishaka Guidelines were a set of procedural guidelines for use in India in cases of sexual harassment. They were promulgated by the Indian Supreme Court in 1997 and were superseded in 2013 by the Sexual Harassment of Women at Workplace (Prevention, Prohibition and Redressal) Act.
38	B.	See, The Protection Of Women From Domestic Violence Act, 2005 For details.

Q. No.	Answer	Justification
39	C.	
40	C.	12th Oct., 1993 (constituted under the protection of human right ordinance of 28 Sept., 1993)
41	D.	The above values should be in negatives *i.e.* 10^{-5} and 10^{-7}
42	D.	One methyl group(-CH_3) is attached while other total carbons in molecule are 6. Hence IUPAC name should be Methyl-4-oxohexonate.
43	B.	Transuranic elements preparation involves bombardment of high energy which does not involve ion exchange.
44	A.	Enthalpy is total energy of system, when solid melts there is increase in enthalpy.
45	B.	
46		This reaction seems to be Kulinkovich Reaction, which is not given in option.
47	B.	Amongst different halogens (F, Cl, Br, and I), Fluorine has highest electron gativity, hence pulls up electron from hydrogen atom in covalent bond and responsible for possessing greater dipole movement.
48	D.	Thermo gravimetric analysis or thermal gravimetric analysis (TGA) is a method of thermal analysis in which changes in physical and chemical properties of materials are measured as a function of increasing temperature (with constant heating rate), or as a function of time (with constant temperature and/or constant mass loss). And does not include reagent of precipitation
49	D.	
50	B.	Bakelite is an early plastic. It is a thermosetting phenol formaldehyde resin, formed from an elimination reaction of phenol with formaldehyde.
51	A.	No Justification
52	C.	Starch gelatinization is a process that breaks down the intermolecular bonds of starch molecules in the presence of water and heat, allowing the hydrogen bonding sites (the hydroxyl hydrogen and oxygen) to engage more water.
53	A.	Heat cramps are involuntary muscle spasms or jerk; They are caused by deficiency of water and sodium;
54	B.	One of the major uses of cholesterol is the synthesis of bile acids. These are synthesized in the liver from cholesterol and are secreted in the bile. They are essential for the absorption of fat from the contents of the intestine. A clue to the importance of cholesterol is that more than 90% of the bile acids are not lost in the feçes but are reabsorbed from the lower intestine and recycled to the liver. There is some loss, however, and to compensate for this and to meet other needs, the liver synthesizes some 1500–2000 mg of new cholesterol each day. It synthesizes cholesterol from the products of fat metabolism.

Q. No.	*Answer*	*Justification*
55		Kesari dal is wedge shaped, with a slant on one side and a square face on the other side which is a physical test while it can also be used by using HCl as follows:
		Put a sample in dilute hydrochloric acid. Pink color develops indicating the presence of kesari dal. Put a sample in dilute hydrochloric acid. Pink color develops indicating the presence of kesari dal.
56	B.	Definition of Food contaminants as given by FSSAI Training Manual.
57	D.	Vitamin K (quinone) is necessary for clouting of blood.
58	B.	We cant find justification for such a complicated question.
59	C.	Aflatoxin has potential to lead to liver disease in dogs; hence may be correlated to incidence.of liver cancer.
60	C.	Kilo Joules is an international unit of metabolic energy as recommended by WHO, while Cal is also generally used which means kcal. KCal and MJ units were never reported by any scientist for measurement of metabolic energy.
61	A.	
62	C	In a generic sense, plasma is a fourth state of matter. While cold plasma is experimentally obtained in gaseous state of matter. Both C and D could be correct.
63	D.	In the years before the development of the autoclave, liquids and other objects were sterilized by exposure to free flowing steam at 100oC for 30 minutes on each of 3 successive days, with incubation periods between the steaming. The method was called fractional sterilization because a fraction was accomplished on each day. It was also called tydallization after its developer, John Tyndall.
64	B.	Pulsed electric field (PEF) processing is a non-thermal method of food preservation that uses short bursts of electricity for microbial inactivation and causes minimal or no detrimental effect on food quality attributes.
65	C.	
66	A.	CAC is situated Rome, Italy
67	B.	India has been member of Codex Alimentarious Commission since 1964
68	C.	in CAC, there are Six Regional Coordinating Committees I. Asia (CCASIA) (Chair: Malaysia) Coordinating Committee for Asia II. Africa (CCAFRICA) (Chair: Uganda) III. Europe (CCEurope) Note: India is not a member of the other Regional (Chair: Slovak Republic) Committees but is entitled to participate in the meetings

Q. No.	*Answer*	*Justification*
		IV. Latin America and the Caribbean as an observer (CCLAC) (Chair: Dominican Republic) V. Near East (CCNEA) (Chair: Egypt) VI. North America and the South West Pacific (CCNASWP) (Chair: Canada)
69	A.	National Codex Contact Point and All other codex related activities are handled by Ministry of Health and Family Welfare
70	C.	Ad hoc Intergovernmental Task Forces: In 1999, the Commission realized that its rather inflexible committee structure was not able to cope with the demand for standards and guidelines across an ever-widening range of subjects. It decided to create a third type of subsidiary body called a Codex ad hoc Intergovernmental Task Force, which is a Codex Committee with very limited terms of reference established for a fixed period of time.
71	C.	Nanotechnology and nanoscience involve the study of phenomena and materials, and the manipulation of structures, devices and systems that exist at the nanoscale, < 100 nanometres (nm) in size
72	D.	Main issues of concern for human health are allergenicity, gene transfer and outcrossing.
73	A.	
74	A.	Standard definition of GMO.
75	A.	Organic food refers to crops or livestock that are grown on the farm without the application of synthetic fertilizers or pesticides, and without using genetically modified organisms.
76	C.	Argemone seeds have a rough surface with a little tail at one end. Mustard seeds are smooth. Upon pressing, mustard seeds are yellow inside while argemone seeds are white.
77	B.	
78	B.	
79	C.	Japan is the only country that has formulated a specific regulatory approval process for functional foods. Known as Foods for Specified Health Use (FOSHU), these foods are eligible to bear a seal of approval from the Japanese Ministry of Health and Welfare. Currently, 100 products are licensed as FOSHU foods in Japan.
80	B.	
81	B.	
82	A.	

Q. No.	*Answer*	*Justification*
83	B.	Schedule 4 of FSSA is ? General Hygienic and Sanitary practices to be followed by Food Business operators? in which Part III deals with ? Specific Hygienic and Sanitary Practices to be followed by Food Business Operators engaged in manufacture, processing, storing & selling of Milk and Milk Products?
84	B.	It is the definition of sub-standard food as per section(3) – zx of FSSA, 2006
85	A.	Definition as per FSSA
86	C.	Generally accepted definition of quality assurance
87	B.	
88	A.	
89	B.	IS 16021:2012 is Indian Standard ?GOOD MANUFACTURING PRACTICES (GMP) — REQUIREMENTS FOR ORGANIZATIONS IN THE FOOD PROCESSING SECTOR?
90	A.	
91	B.	
92	A\D.	16020:2012 is Indian Standard ?FOOD SAFETY MANAGEMENT—REQUIREMENTS FOR GOOD HYGIENE PRACTICES?
93	A.	Foodservice SOPs are written practices and procedures and are the basic ingredient to producing safe food. It is essential to train employees and emphasize the importance of following the procedures. The National Food Service Management Institute (NFSMI) has developed food safety SOPs in conjunction with USDA and FDA.
94	C.	it's a general definition of cleaning
95	C.	there are eight hygiene specific requirements
96	A.	The following Acts/Orders mentioned in second schedule of the Act are going to be repealed in Food Safety and Standards Act, 2006: I. Prevention of Food Adulteration Act, 1954 II. Fruit Products Order, 1955 III. Meat Food Products Order, 1973 IV. Vegetable Oil Products (Control) Order, 1947 V. Edible Oils Packaging (Regulation) Order, 1998 VI. Solvent Extracted Oil, De oiled Meal, and Edible Flour (Control) Order, 1967 VII. Milk and Milk Products Order, 1992 Any other order under Essential Commodities Act, 1955 relating to food excluding Cold Storage Order

Q. No.	*Answer*	*Justification*
97	B.	Export Inspection Council was established under above act.
98	C.	IS 14543 is Indian Standard for PACKAGED DRINKING WATER
		(OTHER THAN PACKAGED NATURAL MINERAL WATER SPECIFICATION? which is compulsory)
99	C.	Uniform standards and weights measures were established based on metric system. This act was based on international system of units as recognized by the (CGPM) and the International organization of legal metrology (OIML).
100	D.	Notwithstanding the provisions of 2.7 of labelling and packaging regulations, no person shall either by himself or by any servant or agent sell blended edible oil.

Delhi Subordinate Services Selection Board

Food Safety Officer Exam–2017

Q1. Red colour of processed meat products is due to

a) Nitrohemoglobin
b) Nitrosylmyoglobin
c) Oxyxanthine
d) All of the above

Q2. Which vitamin is used for fortifying milk?

a) Vitamin B_6
b) Vitamin B_2
c) Vitamin C
d) Vitamin D

Q3. Butyl hydroxyanisole (BHA) is a

a) Sweetener
b) Leavening agent
c) Anti-caking agent
d) Antioxidant

Q4. Mono sodium glutamate is used as

a) Natural flavour
b) Preservative
c) Stabilizer
d) Flavour enhancer

Q5. Bacteriostatic enzyme found in honey is

a) Pectinase
b) Carboxy peptidase
c) Lipase
d) Lysozyme

Q6. In a controlled atmosphere storage system

a) CO_2 is increased and nitrogen is reduced
b) CO_2 is reduced and oxygen is increased
c) CO_2 is increased and oxygen is reduced
d) High pressure oxygen is used

Q7. Limiting amino acids in cereals are

a) Lysine and threonine
b) Arginine
c) Tyrosine and tryptophan
d) All of the above

Q8. Basal metabolism is most closely related with

a) Body height
b) Body surface area
c) Body weight
d) Sex

Q9. If an animal is rested before slaughter, the keeping quality of meat is improved due to increased levels of.......... in muscles.

a) Lactose
b) Lactic acid
c) Protein
d) Fats

Q10. A dipolar ion with spatially separated positive and negative charges is called

a) Isoion
b) Zwitterion
c) Ionophore
d) Zwitterphore

Q11. As per the food standards and safety regulations, sterilized milk should not spoil at room temperature for at least

a) 2 days
b) 7 days
c) 10 days
d) 15 days

Q12. TSS for ready to serve fruit beverage should not be less than

a) 5%
b) 10%
c) 15%
d) 20%

Q13. Addition of BHT to oils can prevent
a) Hydrolytic rancidity
b) Oxidative rancidity
c) High temperature damage
d) Bacterial action

Q14. There are several cases of poisoning due to contaminated honey. While two persons died, others show symptoms of blurred vision, paralysis, breathing trouble and vomiting, the poisoning is likely caused by
a) Shigellosis
b) Enteritis
c) Botulism
d) Salmonellosis

Q15. Sample taken by the FSO should generally be divided into
a) 2 parts
b) 3 parts
c) 4 parts
d) Kept as whole

Q16. *Aspergillus niger* is used in production of
a) Lactose
b) Citric acid
c) Malic acid
d) Acetic acid

Q17. Eggs are selected for storage by
a) Oiling
b) Waxing
c) Candling
d) None of the above

Q18. Preserving action of salt is due to
a) High osmotic pressure
b) Chloride ion being harmful to microbes
c) Interference with proteolytic enzymes
d) All of the above

Q19. Food authority in India consists of a chairman and
a) 8 members
b) 14 members
c) 22 members
d) 28 members

Q20. Who can prescribe the permissible limit of food additives for food to be sold in local shops?
a) Food authority
b) Commissioner for food safety
c) Local health authority
d) Food safety officer

Q21. Phytate in legume seeds mainly decreases the availability of
a) Proteins
b) Fats
c) Vitamins
d) Minerals

Q22. Which milk adulterant can be detected by iodine?
a) Starch
b) Formaldehyde
c) Boric acid
d) Sodium bicarbonate

Q23. Coloured juices are preserved using
a) Potassium metabisulphite
b) Sodium benzoate
c) Sorbic acid
d) Malic acid

Q24. PFA act is regulated by
a) Ministry of health and family welfare
b) Ministry of agriculture
c) Ministry of food processing
d) Ministry of chemicals

Q25. Which of the following vitamin is water soluble?
a) Thiamine
b) Retinal
c) Tocopherol
d) Calciferol

Q26. *Clostridium botulinum* is inhibited by
a) pH less than 6
b) pH less than 4.5
c) pH greater than 7.0
d) none of the above is true

Q27. After pasteurization, milk must be immediately cooled to below
a) 0° C
b) 4° C
c) 10° C
d) 15° C

Q28. Degumming of vegetable oil is done by
a) Phosphoric acid
b) Citric acid
c) Lactic acid
d) Both a & b

Q29. Minimum milk solids percentage in double toned milk is
a) 7.5%
b) 8%
c) 9%
d) 10%

Q30. Tea drinking may cause.........deficiency which may be counteracted by adding milk.
a) Iron
b) Iodine
c) Calcium
d) None of the above

Q31. Food preservative permitted in alcoholic wines is
a) Nisin
b) Sulfur dioxide
c) Benzoic acid
d) Sorbic acid

Q32. Which of the following is not a disaccharide?
a) Galactose
b) Sucrose
c) Lactose
d) Maltose

Q33. Maillard browning causes loss of which amino acid?
a) Lysine
b) Tryptophan
c) Histidine
d) All of the above

Q34. Which is not an aromatic amino acid?
a) Phenylalanine
b) Histidine
c) Tryptophan
d) Tyrosine

Q35. Which is an essential fatty acid?
a) Stearic acid
b) Linoleic acid
c) Palmitic acid
d) All of the above

Q36. Final acceptor of electron in mitrochondrial oxidation is
a) NAD
b) NADP
c) $FADH_2$
d) Oxygen

Q37. In mitochondria, fatty acids are oxidized to
a) Oxaloacetate
b) Pyruvate
c) Acetyl CoA
d) Malate

Q38. Specific dynamic action (SDA) is highest for
a) Carbohydrates
b) Proteins
c) Fats
d) All have same SDA

Q39. Botulinum toxin is a
a) Cytotoxin
b) Ototoxin
c) Neurotoxin
d) Enterotoxin

Q40. Green rot in eggs is caused by

a) *P. fluoroscens* b) *P. graveolens*
c) *A. perolens* d) *C.tetani*

Q41. Compound commonly used for solvent extraction of fats is

a) Ethanol b) N-hexane
c) Benzyl ester d) M-xylene

Q42. Corn syrup mainly contains

a) Glucose b) Sucrose
c) Galactose d) Fructose

Q43. Butyric acid fermentation of milk is caused by

a) *Streptococci* b) *Enterococci*
c) Yeast species d) *Clostridium* species

Q44. High iodine number of Fat indicates

a) Higher degree of unsaturation b) Higher degree of saturation
c) Higher degree of oxidation d) Higher molecular weight

Q45. Hydrolytic rancidity of fats

a) Requires oxygen b) Produces free fatty acids
c) Increase at low temperature d) All of the above are true

Q46. Amino acid which is used in gluconeogenesis is

a) Alanine b) Histidine
c) Tryptophan d) Arginine

Q47. Common organism which produces enterotoxin is

a) *Clostridium tetani* b) *Clostridium botulinum*
c) *Escherichia coli* d) *Strep. pyogens*

Q48. Which fungus is used in production of soya sauce?

a) *Lactobacillus* b) *Saccharomyces*
c) *Aspergillus* d) *Penicillium*

Q49. Development of most grain pests is inhibited if grain moisture content is below

a) 25% b) 15%
c) 10% d) 2%

Q50. Minimum temperature for use of phosphine as fumigant is

a) 35° C b) 22° C
c) 15° C d) 0° C

Q51. Peroxisomes are associated with which process in C_3 plants but not in C_4 plants?

a) Chemiosmosis b) Krebs cycle
c) Photorespiration d) Photosynthesis

Q52. Basic material used for preparing rasgulla is

a) Khoya b) Curd
c) Rabri d) Chhana

Q53. Khapra beetle is a serious pest of stored
a) Mango
b) Wheat
c) Potatoes
d) Apples

Q54. Which has the lowest R.Q.?
a) Monosaccharides
b) Disaccharides
c) Proteins
d) Fats

Q55. A food poisoning incidence during a religious fair in which patients show copious watery stools, extreme dehydration and collapse is likely to be a case of
a) Salmonellosis
b) Botulism
c) Cholera
d) Streptococcal infection

Q56. Commissioner of food safety can prohibit sale of any article of food for a maximum period of
a) Permanently
b) One month
c) Six months
d) One year

Q57. Packaged honey, which is labelled as produced in the Himalayas, but is actually produced near Delhi, is an instance of
a) Spurious food
b) Misbranded food
c) Sub-standard food
d) Adulterated food

Q58. Bacteria which are most useful in genetic engineering are
a) *Escherichia, Agrobacterium*
b) *Rhizobium, Azobacter*
c) *Rhizobium, Diplococcus*
d) *Nitrosomonas, Klebsiella*

Q59. Transposon is also known as
a) S-element
b) Jumping gene
c) Flipping gene
d) Travelling gene

Q60. Which growth hormone produces apical dominance?
a) Ethylene
b) Cytokinin
c) Gibberellin
d) Auxin

Q61. If a person stores an adulterant, he is liable for a maximum penalty of
a) 1 lakh
b) 2 lakhs
c) 5 lakhs
d) 10 lakhs

Q62. All are powers of food safety officer, except
a) Entry and inspection of food outlets
b) Taking food samples
c) Seizure of food articles
d) Sanctioning prosecution

Q63. Pepsin is an example for the class of enzyme
a) Oxidoreductase
b) Transferase
c) Hydrolase
d) Ligase

Q64. In TCA cycle, isomerization of citrate occurs by
a) Oxidoreductase
b) Transferase
c) Hydrolase
d) Lyase

Q 65. Sprouting on onion during storage is inhibited by using
a) Calcium nitrate
b) Malic hydrazide
c) Calcium sorbate
d) GA

Q66. Which is not true of homogenized milk?
a) Does not show creaming
b) Has whiter colour
c) Is more stable to light
d) All of the above are true

Q67. During production of yoghurt, protease activity is exhibited by
a) Lactobacillus
b) Strep. thermophillus
c) Both
d) None

Q68. Who can impose emergency prohibitory orders under the Food safety and standards act 2006?
a) The designated officer
b) Commissioner of food safety
c) Food safety officer
d) Both a and b

Q69. Naturally acting toxin found in cabbage is
a) Prussic acid
b) Oxalic acid
c) Goitrogen
d) Solanine

Q70. Effect of enzymes upon activation energy of the reaction is to
a) Increase the activation energy
b) Decrease the activation energy
c) No change in activation energy
d) Depends on type of enzyme

Q71. A dry, wine means one that
a) Has higher alcohol content
b) Contains less water
c) Made from dried raw material
d) Virtually free from sugar

Q72. Which enzyme is involved in browning of cut surfaces of fruits and vegetables?
a) Amino acid oxidase
b) Polyphenol oxidase
c) Catalase
d) Peroxidase

Q73. Which is widely used to control enzymatic browning in fruits and vegetables during processing and drying?
a) Acetic acid
b) Potassium metabisulphite
c) Sucrose
d) Potassium permanganate

Q74. Main purpose of blanching of fruits and vegetables before preservation is
a) To remove tissue gases
b) To soften tissues
c) To sterilize
d) To inactivate enzymes

Q75. In C_4 photosynthesis pathway, which compound traps atmosphere CO_2?
a) RuBP
b) Oxaloacetate
c) Phosphoenol pyruvate
d) Malate

Q76. A major anti-nutritional factor present in mustard is
a) Oleic acid
b) Erucic acid
c) Elagic acid
d) Bentic acid

Q77. Which compound is extensively used in baking to improve dough properties?
a) Potassium chloride
b) Potassium sulfate
c) Potassium carbonate
d) Potassium bromate

Q78. What percent of total milk protein is casein?
a) 50% b) 60%
c) 80% d) 100%

Q79. In a cell cycle, RNA and protein growth takes place during
a) G1 phase b) G2 phase
c) S phase d) None of the above

Q80. When an F1 organism is crossed with a genotype identical with the dominant parent it is called
a) Test cross b) Poly cross
c) Mendel cross d) Back cross

Q81. Probiotics are
a) Cancer inducing microbes b) Safe antibiotics
c) Food allergens d) Live microbial food supplements

Q82. Function of porin protein is
a) Cytoskeleton formation b) Transport
c) Structural d) Immunological

Q83. Temperature dependent bacterial death rate follows
a) Sigmoid curve b) Linear curve
c) Log curve d) None of the above

Q84. Punishment for selling unsafe food which has resulted in death is imprisonment
a) Upto 2 years b) Upto 5 years
c) Upto 7 years d) From 7 years to life imprisonment

Q85. Central licensing is required for dairy units processing milk more than
a) 10000 litres per day b) 50000 litres per day
c) 100000 litres per day d) 250000 litres per day

Q86. Over polishing of rice will make it deficient in
a) Vit. B_{12} b) Vit. B_1
c) Vit. C d) Vit. A

Q87. Which fungus is used in production of Roquefort cheese?
a) *Saccharomyces* b) *Candida*
c) *Penicillium* d) *Aspergillus*

Q88. Which distilled liquor is produced from molasses?
a) Whisky b) Rum
c) Brandy d) Vodka

Q89. Which gas is used as a medium for preservation of foods?
a) Oxygen b) Hydrogen
c) Nitrogen d) Chlorine

Q90. If a strained tomato juice has not less than 25% salt free tomato solids, it is called
a) Tomato ketchup b) Tomato juice
c) Tomato puree d) Tomato paste

Q91. Low level irradiation can be used upon fresh fruits to
a) Kill insects b) Kill molds
c) Inhibit bacteria d) None of the above

Q92. Percentage of TSS in a fruit jam should not be less than
a) 42.5% b) 55%
c) 65% d) 75%

Q93. Presence of which enzyme indicates inadequate pasteurization ?
a) Acid phosphatase b) Protease
c) Alkaline phosphatase d) All of the above

Q94. HTST pasteurization is done at
a) 63 °C for 90 sec b) 72 °C for 15 sec
c) 85 °C for 15 sec d) None of the above

Q95. Which of the following is a non reducing sugar?
a) Glucose b) Fructose
c) Maltose d) Sucrose

Q96. Which antibiotic is allowed for surface treatment of cheese?
a) Tetracycline b) Rifampicin
c) Bacitracin d) Natamycin

Q97. Which is not an anti-oxidant?
a) Lecithin b) Sorbic acid
c) Ascorbic acid d) Tocopherol

Q98. According to the food safety and standards regulations, which artificial sweetener is permitted in jams & jellies?
a) Saccharine b) Acesulfame
c) Sucralose d) Neotame

Q99. Hazen unit is a measure of
a) Turbidity b) Salinity
c) Softness d) Colour

Q100. Allostearic regulation of glycolysis mainly occurs at the level of
a) Glucokinase b) Phosphofructokinase
c) Aldolase d) Pyruvate kinase

ANSWERS

1. b.	14. c.	27. c.	40. a.	53. b.	66. c.	79. a.	92. c.
2. d.	15. c.	28. a.	41. b	54. d.	67. a.	80. d	93. c.
3. d.	16. b.	29. c.	42. a.	55. c.	68. a	81. d.	94. b.
4. d.	17. c.	30. a.	43. d.	56. d.	69. c.	82. b.	95. d.
5. d.	18. d.	31. b.	44. a.	57. b.	70. b.	83. c.	96. d.
6. c.	19. c	32. a.	45. b.	58. a.	71. d.	84. d.	97. b.
7. a.	20. b.	33. d.	46. a.	59. b.	72. b.	85. b.	98. c.
8. c.	21. d.	34. b.	47. d.	60. d.	73. b.	86. a.	99. d.
9. b.	22. a.	35. b.	48. c.	61. d.	74. d.	87. c.	100. d.
10. b.	23. b.	36. d.	49. b.	62. d.	75. a.	88. b	
11. d.	24. a.	37. c.	50. c.	63. c.	76. b	89. c.	
12. b.	25. a.	38. b.	51. c	64. d.	77. d.	90. c.	
13. b.	26. b.	39. c.	52. d.	65. b.	78. c.	91. a.	

41.(*b*) N-hexane is non polar solvent that is highly effective in dissolving fats and oils and is also non polar.

Appendix–

Tables for quick reference

Index of table

TABLE 1:
Classification of carbohydrates based on molecular size

Carbohydrates	*Example*	*Sugar unit/s*	*Source*
Monosaccharide (single sugar unit)	Glucose	Glucose	Fruits, starch
	Galactose	Galactose	Milk (as lactose)
	Fructose	Fructose	Fruit
Oligosaccharide			
Disaccharide	Sucrose	Glucose + Fructose	Sugar cane, beet
(2 sugar units)	Lactose	Glucose + Galactose	Milk
Trisaccharide	Isomaltotriose	Glucose + Glucose + Glucose	Degradation product of starch
(3 sugar units)	Gentianose	Glucose + Glucose + fructose	Gentian rhizome
Polysaccharide (more than 10 sugar units)	Starch	Glucose	Cereals, tubers
	Cellulose	Glucose	Plant stem
	Pectin	Galacturonic acid	Fruits
	Alginic acids	Monouronic acid + guluronic acid	Brown seaweeds
	Carrageenans	Galactose	Red seaweed

TABLE 2:
Dietary fiber functions and benefits

Type of fiber	*Functions*	*Benefits*
Soluble	• It adds bulk to our diet, • It has high satiety value • It attracts water and gets converted to gel during digestion. The gel traps carbohydrates thus slowing absorption of glucose • It balances intestinal pH and stimulates intestinal fermentation production of short-chain fatty acids	• Lowers blood sugar levels • Reduce risk of colorectal cancer
Insoluble fiber	• It adds bulk to our diet, • It has high satiety value • It lowers total and LDL cholesterol • It regulates blood sugar • It increases the passage of foods through the digestive system • It adds bulk to the stool	• It reduces risk of heart disease • It may reduce onset risk or symptoms of metabolic syndrome and diabetes • It facilitates regularity • It alleviates constipation

TABLE 3:
Types of amino acids

Essential amino acids	*Non-essential amino acids*
Leucine	Glycine
Valine	Alanine
Isoleucine	Proline
Phenylalanine	Serine
Tryptophan	Cysteine
Methionine	Tyrosine
Threonine	Asparagine
Histidne (essential for infants)	Glutamine
Lysine	Aspartic acid
Arginine (semi-essential)**	Glutamic acid

** Arginine is a semi-essential amino acid for humans. It appears to be required under certain metabolic conditions.

TABLE 4:
Commonly occurring saturated fatty acid

Name	*# of carbon*	*Occurrence*
Lauric acid	12:0	Coconut oil, palm kernel oil, breast milk
Myristic acid	14:0	Nutmeg butter, palm kernel oil
Palmitic acid	16:0	Palm oil, meat
Stearic acid	18:0	Meat, cocoa butter
Arachidic acid	20:0	Peanut oil, corn oil

TABLE 5:
Commonly occurring unsaturated fatty acid

Name	*# of carbon*	*Occurrence*
Name	# of carbon	Occurrence
Palmitoleic acid	16:1 (n-7)	Macadamia oil, sea buckthorn oil, liver
Oleic acid	18:1 (n-9)	Pecan oil, canola oil, peanut oil, macadamia oil
Linoleic acid	18:2 (n-9, 12)	Safflower oil, sunflower oil, wheat germ oil
Arachidonic acid	20:4 (ω-6)	Phospholipids of cell membrane
Eicosapentaenoic acid	20:5 (ω-3)	Fish oil, cod liver oil, seaweed
Docosahexaenoic acid	22:6 (ω-3)	Sea fish, *Crypthecodiniumcohnii*

TABLE 6: Major vitamin sources and their deficiency diseases

Vitamin	*Source*	*Deficiency disease*
Vitamin A	Breast milk, green-yellow vegetables such as carrots, kale, broccoli, and sweet potatoes, or reddish-yellow fruits like apricots, papaya, and peaches.	Night blindness, Toad skin disease
Vitamin B1 (Thiamine)	Yeast, cereal grains, oatmeal, flax, sunflower seeds, cauliflowers, potatoes, oranges, brown rice, asparagus, legumes, water melons	Beri-beri
Vitamin B2 (Riboflavin)	Avocados, asparagus, banana, okra, cheese, leafy green vegetables, legumes, lover, kidney, mushrooms, almonds, tomatoes, yeast	Ariboflavinosis
Vitamin B3 (Niacin)	Liver, chicken, beef, fish, cereals, peanuts, legumes, avocados, dates, tomatoes, cabbage, asparagus, nuts, legumes, leaf vegetables, broccoli, carrots	Pellagra
Vitamin B5 (Pantothenic acid)	Avocado, whole grain cereals, legumes, eggs, meats, royal jelly, yoghurt, avocado, broccoli, peanut meal, molasses, mushroom, rice, wheat bran, yeast	Paresthesia
Vitamin B7 (Biotin)	Raw egg yolk, liver, green leafy vegetables	Neurological disorder
Vitamin B9 (Folate)	Dark green leafy vegetables, fruits and fruit juices, nuts, beans, peas, dairy products, poultry and meat, eggs, seafood, grains, avocado, spinach, liver, asparagus, Brussels sprout	Macrocytic anemia
Vitamin B12 (Cobalamin)	Shellfish, liver, cheese, egg	Pernicious anemia
Vitamin C (Ascorbic acid	Chilli pepper, guava, kiwi, parsley, broccoli, papaya, strawberry, orange, lemon, pineapple, melon, kale, cauliflower, cabbage, lime, mango, spinach, tomato	Scurvy
Vitamin D	Fish liver oil	Rickets, osteomalacia
Vitamin E	Wheat germ oil, sunflower oil, almond oil, safflower oil, palm oil, olive oil, green leafy vegetables, avocados	Neural disorder, Sterility

TABLE 7: Major mineral sources and their deficiency diseases

Mineral	*Source*	*Deficiency disease*
Calcium	Dairy products, eggs, canned fish, green leafy vegetables, nuts,	Osteoporosis
Chlorine	Table salt	Hypochloremia
Chromium	Broccoli, cereals, lean meat, organ meats, cheese, mushrooms, asparagus, green beans, potatoes, prunes, bananas, nuts and molasses	Neural disorder, Peripheral neuropathy
Copper	Mushroom, spinach, greens, seeds, raw cashews, raw walnuts, barley	Menkes disease Leukopenia, Neutropenia

Contd....

Mineral	Source	Deficiency disease
Iodine	Sea vegetables, iodized salt, eggs, yoghurt, milk, fish, shellfish, strawberries	Goiter
Iron	Red meat, fish, grains, dry beans, eggs, spinach, turmeric, cumin, parsley, lentil, tofu, asparagus, leafy vegetables, soybean, shrimps, beans, tomatoes, olives, dried fruits	Anemia
Magnesium	Raw nuts, soybean, cocoa mass, spinach, sea vegetables, tomato, beans, ginger, cumin, cloves	Hypomagnesaemia
Manganese	Spelt grain, brown rice, beans, spinach, pineapple, rye, soybean, thyme, raspberries, strawberries, garlic, squash, eggplant, cloves, cinnamon, turmeric	Osteoporosis, Schizophrenia
Molybdenum	Tomatoes, onion, carrots	Esophegal squamous cell carcinoma
Phosphorus	Red meat, dairy foods, fish, poultry, bread, rice, oats	Hypophosphatemia
Potassium	Legumes, potato skin, tomatoes, banana, papaya, lentils, whole grains, dry beans, avocado, yam, soybean, spinach, sweet potato, turmeric	Hypokalemia
Selenium	Brazil nuts, mustard, mushrooms, barley, cheese, garlic, tofu seeds, cold water fish (cod, salmon)	Keshan disease
Sodium	Table salt, sea vegetables, milk, spinach	Hyponatremia
Zinc	Eggs, dry beans, mushroom, spinach, asparagus, red meat, green peas, yoghurt, seeds, oats	Hypozincemia

TABLE 8:
Some anti-nutritional factors and their source

Anti-nutritional factors	Source
Cyanogenic glycoside	Lima bean
DOPA	Broad bean, lathyrus
Favism factor	Fababean
Goitrogen	Soybean and peanut
Lectins	Soybean and common bean
Phytic acid	Cereals and pulses
Protease inhibitors	Soybean, lima bean and chickpea
Saponins	Common bean and cowpea

TABLE 9:

Water activity and growth of microorganisms in food

Range of a_w	*Microorganisms generally inhibited by lowest a_w in this range*	*Foods generally within this range*
1.00–0.95	*Pseudomonas, Escherichia, Proteus, Shigella, Klebsiella, Bacillus, Clostridium perfringens*, some yeasts	Highly perishable (fresh) foods and canned fruits, vegetables, meat, fish, milk, and beverages.
0.95–091	*Salmonella, Vibrioparahaemolyticus, C. botulinum, Serratia, Lactobacillus, Pediococcus*, some molds, yeasts (*Rhodotorula, Pichia*)	Some cheeses (Cheddar, Swiss, Muenster, Provolone), cured meat (ham), bread, tortillas
0.91–0.87	Many yeasts (*Candida*, Torulopsis, *Hansenula*), Micrococcus.	Fermented sausage (salami), sponge cakes, dry cheeses, margarine
0.87–0.80	Most molds (mycotoxigenic penicillia), *Staphyloccocus aureus*, most *Saccharomyces* spp.	Most fruit juice concentrates, sweetened condensed milk, syrups, jams, jellies, soft pet food
0.80–0.75	Most halophilic bacteria, mycotoxigenic *Aspergilli*	Marmalade, marzipan, glacé fruits, beef jerky
0.75–0.65	Xerophilic molds *Aspergillus chevalieri, A. candidus, Wallemia sebi), Saccharomyces bisporus*	Molasses, raw cane sugar, some dried fruits, nuts, snack bars, snack cakes
0.65–0.60	Osmophilic yeasts (*Saccharomyces rouxii*), few molds (*Aspergillus echinulatus, Monascus bisporus*)	Dried fruits containing 15-20% moisture; some toffees and caramels; honey, candies
0.60–0.50	No microbial proliferation	Dry pasta, spices, rice, confections, wheat
0.50–0.40	No microbial proliferation	Whole egg powder, chewing gum, flour, dry beans.
0.40–0.30	No microbial proliferation	Cookies, crackers, bread crusts, breakfast cereals, dry pet food, peanut butter
0.30–0.20	No microbial proliferation	Whole milk powder, dried vegetables, freeze dried corn.

Adapted from L.R. Beuchat, Cereal Foods World, 26:345 (1981)

TABLE 10 :
Spoilage of some common foods

Products	*Spoilage*	*Causative Microorganism*
Bread	Mouldiness	*Rhizopus stolonifer*
	Ropiness	*Bacillus subtilis,*
	Red crumb	*Geotrichum aurantiacum*
	Red bread	*Serratia marcescens*
	Chalky bread	*Endomycopsis fibuligera*
Macaroni	Gas formation	*Enterobacter cloacae*
Milk	Gas production	*Clostridium* and *Bacillus* spp
	Proteolysis	*Pseudomonas fluorescens*
	Ropiness	*Alcaligens viscolactis*
	Alkali production	*Pseudomonas fluorescens,*
	Sour or acid flavour	*Streptocossus lactis*
	Caramel flavour	*Streptocossus lactis*
	Barny flavour	*Enterobacter oxytocum*
	Turnip flavour	*Escherichia coli*
	Fruity flavour	*Pseudomonas fragi*
	Blue milk	*Pseudomonas syncyanea*
	Yellow milk	*Pseudomonas synxantha*
	Red milk	*Serratia marcescens,*
	Brown milk	*Pseudomonas putrifaciens*
Unsweetened evaporated milk	Coagulation	*Bacillus subtilis, B. coagulans*
Sweetened condensed milk	Buttons	*Aspergillus repens*
Butter	Cheesiness	*Lactobacillus* spp
	Malty flavour	*Streptocossus lactis*
	Surface taint	*Pseudomonas putrifaciens*
	Fishiness	*Aeromonas hydrophila*
	Skunklike flavour	*Pseudomonas mephitica*
	Reddish-pink colour	*Fusarium culmorum*
Meat	Surface slime	*Pseudomonas* spp, *Bacillus* spp,
	Phosphorescence	*Photobacterium* spp
	Red spot	*Serratia marcescens*
	Whiskers	*Thamnidium elegans,*
	Black spot	*Cladosporium herbarum*
	Green patches	*Penicillium expansum*
	White spot	*Sportrichum carnis*
Fish	Greenish yellow	*Pseudomonas fluorescens*
Egg	Black rot	*Proteus melanovogenes*
	Colourless rot	*Pseudomonas* spp.
	Green rot	*Pseudomonas fluorescens*
	Pink rot	*Pseudomonas* spp.
	Red rot	*Serratia* spp.
Sugar cane juice	Sliminess	*Leuconostoc mesenteroides*
Maple sap	Ropiness	*Enterobacter aerogenes*
	Cloudiness	*Pseudomonas flurescens*
	Red sap	*Micrococcus roseus*
Honey	Fermentation	*Zygosachharomyces mellis*
Carbonated beverage	Fermentation	*Torulopsis* spp

TABLE 11:
Some common spoilage of fruits and vegetable products

Types of spoilage	*Causative organism*
Alternaria rot	*Alternaria tenuis*
Anthracnose	*Colletotrichum lindemuthianum*
Bacterial soft rot	*Erwinia carotovora*
Black mold rot	*Aspergillus niger*
Blue mold rot	*Penicillium digitatum*
Brown rot	*Monilinia fructicola*
Downy mildew	*Phytophthora* spp.
Green mold rot	*Cladosporium* spp., *Trichoderma* spp.
Gray mold rot	*Botrytis cinerea*
Pink mold rot	*Trichothesium roseum*
Watery soft rot	*Sclerotinia sclerotiorum*

TABLE 12:
Spoilage of thermally processed foods

Spoilage	*Causative organisms*
Flat sour of acidic products	*Bacillus coagulans,*
TA spoilage (thermophilic-anaerobic)	*Clostridium thermosaccharolyticum*
Sulphide or sulphur stinker	*Desulfotomaculum nigrificans*

TABLE 13:
Some bacteria leading to food-borne infections

anism	*Symptoms*	*Foods involved*
illus cereus	Nausea, abdominal cramps, diarrohea, vomiting	Custard, cereal products, sauces, meat
stridium botulinum	Paralysis of involuntary muscles of body. Earlier symptoms of botulism are indigestion, nausea and vomiting.	Canned foods
herichia coli	Illness, fever, headache, abdominal cramp, diarrhoea, vomiting	Coffee, cheese, water
ella sonnei,	Abdominal cramps, fever, diarrhoea, blood in stool, headache, prostration	Milk, beans, potato, fish
hylococcus aureus	Salivation, nausea, vomiting, abdominal cramping and diarrhoea	Custard and cream-filled bakery foods, ham and poultry
o parahaemolyticus	Abdominal pain, diarrhoea, watery stool, blood and mucus in stool, nausea, vomiting	Raw marine foods, marine fish, shellfish
nia dotuberculosis	Abdominal pain, headache, diarrhoea, nausea, vomiting	Pork, meat, raw milk

TABLE 14:
Some common mycotoxins present in food

Mycotoxin	*Source*	*Foods isolated from*
Aflatoxin	*Aspergillus flavus* and *A. parasiticus*	Peanut
Alimentary toxic aleukia (ATA)	*Cladosporium, Penicillium, Fusarium* spp.	Grain
Deoxynivalenol (DON	*Fusarium graminearum, F. culmorum*	Wheat, corn, barley, oats, rice, rye
Fumonisins	*Fusarium verticillioides, F. proliferatum*	Corn, sorghum, rice, navy beans,
Luteoskyrin	*Penicillium islandicum*	Rice flour
Ochratoxin	*Aspergillus ochraceus, A. ostianus, Penicillium cyclopium, P. viridcatum*	Corn, wheat, barley, peanuts
Patulin	*Penicillium expansum, P. patulum, Aspergillus clavatus, A. giganteus*	Rotten apple, apple cider, apple juice
Penicillic acid	*Penicillium puberulum, P. cyclopium, P. thomii*	Dried beans, tobacco
Roquefortine	*Penicillium roqueforti*	Blue cheese, Roqueforti cheese
Sterigmatocystin	*Aspergillus regulosus, A. Nidulans, A. versicolor*	Wheat, oats
Zearalenone	*Fusarium graminearum, F. culmorum*	Corn and corn products, oats, barley, rye, wheat, soybeans, rice, sorghum, walnuts

TABLE 15:
Different types of malt beverages

Malt beverages (Beer)					
Top fermented			**Bottom fermented**		
Brewed with strains of *Saccharomyces cerevisiae*			Brewed with strains of *Saccharomyces uvarum* (formerly *Saccharomyces carlsbergensis*)		
Types	*Alcohol content*	*Properties*	*Types*	*Alcohol content*	*Properties*
Ale	4.0–5.0	Pale, highly hopped	Pilsener	3.0-3.8	Pale, medium hop taste
Porter	5.0	Dark-brown, heavy bodied, high foaming, less hops	Dortmund	3.0-3.8	Pale, less bitter than pilsener, contains less hops
Stout	5.0-6.5	Very dark, heavily bodied and highly hopped with a strong malt aroma.	Munich beer	2.0-5.0	Dark, aromatic and full-bodied with a slightly sweet taste with slight hops

** Alcohol content expressed in % w/v

TABLE 16:
Some common alcoholic beverages

Beverages	*Nature*	*Substrate*	*Culture*
Wine	Un-distilled	Grapes	*Saccharomyces cerevisiae* var. *ellipsoideus*
Rum	Distilled	Sugarcane juice	*Saccharomyces cerevisiae* var. *ellipsoideus*
Whiskeys	Distilled	Grain mashes	*Saccharomyces cerevisiae* var. *ellipsoideus*
Brandy	Distilled	Grapes	*Saccharomyces cerevisiae* var. *ellipsoideus*
Champagne	Sparkling	Grapes	*Saccharomyces cerevisiae*
Mead	Un-distilled	Honey	———

TABLE 17:
Some common fermented food products

Product	*Substrate*	*Culture*
Vinegar	Sugary and starchy substrate	*Saccharomyces cerevisiae var. ellipsoideus; Glucanobacter*
Sauerkraut	Cabbage	*Enterobacter cloacae; Leuconostoc mesenteroides*
Tea	Tea (Camellia sinensis)	*Aspergillus, Penicillium and Rhizopus*
Coffee	Coffee	*Leuconostoc mesenteroides; Lactobacillus brevis; Streptococcus faecalis*
Cocoa	Cocoa	*Candida krusei*
Soya sauce	Soybean	*Aspergillus oryzae; Bacillus spp.*
Miso	Soybean	*Aspergillus oryzae; Saccharomyces rouxii Zygosaccharomyces spp.*
Tempeh	Soybean	*Rhizopus stolonifer, R. oryzae*
Ang-khak	Rice	*Monascus purpureus*
Natto	Soybean	*Bacillus natto*
Minchin	Wheat gluten	------
Tofu	Soybean	*Mucor spp.*
Idli	Rice	*Leuconostoc mesenteroides; Streptococcus faecalis Pediococcus cerevisiae*
Poi	Corn	*Lactobacillus pastorianus*

TABLE 18:
Some fermented dairy products

Dairy products	*Culture*
Yoghurt	*Lactobacillus delbrueckii* subsp. *bulgaricus; Streptococcus thermophillus*
Bulgarian buttermilk	*Lactobacillus delbrueckii* subsp. *bulgaricus*
Kefir	*Lactobacillus brevis*
Kumiss	*Streptococcus lactis*
Taette	*Streptococcus lactis*
Skyr	*Streptococcus thermophillus*

TABLE 19:
Some common industrial products from microorganisms

Products	*Source*
Amylase	*Aspergillus niger; Bacillus subtilis*
Cellulase	*Aspergillus niger, Trichoderma viride*
Invertase	*Saccharomyces cerevisiae*
Lipase	*Aspergillus niger*
Protease	*Aspergillus oryzae*
Lactic acid	*Lactobacillus delbrueckii* subsp. *bulgaricus;*
Dextran	*Leuconostoc mesenteroides*
Citric acid	*Aspergillus niger, Penicillium luteum*
Single cell protein	*Spirulina maxima; Candida utilis*

TABLE 20:
FSSAI parameters for milk

Dairy products	*Milk fat%*	*MSNF*
Cow milk (Punjab, Haryana)	4.0 %	8.5 %
Cow milk (AP, Assam, Bihar)	3.5 %	8.5 %
Buffalo milk (Assam, Bihar)	6.0 %	9.0 %
Buffalo milk (AP, J&K, TN)	5.0 %	9.0 %
Toned milk	3.0 %	8.5 %
Double toned milk	1.5 %	9.0 %
Skim milk	< 0.5 %	8.7 %
Full cream milk	6.0 %	9.0 %

TABLE 21:
FSSAI parameters for some dairy products

Dairy products	*Milk fat%*	*Moisture*	*MSNF*
Cream powder	Min 42 %	Max 5.0 %	> 34 %
Chhanna / Paneer	Max 15 % (dw)	Max 70 %	—
Cheddar cheese	Min 40 % (dw)	Max 47 %	—
Processed cheese	Min 40 % (dw)	Max 47 %	
Whole milk powder	Min 26 %	Max 4.0 %	> 34 %
Partially skim milk powder	1.5 % – 26 %	Max 5.0 %	> 34 %
Skim milk powder	Max 1.5 %	Max 5.0 %	> 34 %
Sweetened condensed milk	Min 9 %		>34 %

** dw = dry weight basis

TABLE 22:
Types of cheese

Cheese type	*Moisture*	*Milk fat % (dw)*
Hard pressed cheese	Max 39 %	Min 48 %
Semi hard cheese	Max 45 %	Min 40 %
Semi soft cheese	Max 52 %	Min 45 %
Soft cheese	Max 80 %	Min 20 %
Mozzarella cheese	Max 60 %	Min 35 %
Pizza cheese	Max 54 %	Min 35 %

TABLE 23:
FSSAI parameters for Ice cream and frozen desserts

Product	*Wt vol (gm/l)*	*Milk fat % (dw)*	*Total solids*	*Protein*
Ice cream				
Ice cream	Min 525	Min 10	Min 36	Min 3.5
Medium fat ice cream	Min 475	2.5 to 10	Min 30	Min 3.5
Low fat ice cream	Min 475	Max 2.5	Min 26	Min 3.0
Frozen dessert				
Frozen dessert	Min 525	Min 10	Min 36	Min 3.5
Medium fat frozen dessert	Min 475	2.5 to 10	Min 30	Min 3.5
Low fat frozen dessert	Min 475	Max 2.5	Min 26	Min 3.0

TABLE 24:
FSSAI parameters for F&V

Fruit product	*TSS*	*Juice %*
Tomato paste	25%	____
Tomato puree	9 %	____
Tomato ketchup/sauce	25 %	____
Tomato juice	5 %	____
Fruit squash	40 %	25 %
Fruit crush	55 %	25 %
Fruit syrup	65 %	25 %
Fruit cordial	30 %	25 %
Fruit nectar	15 %	20 %
Fruit jam	65 %	____
Fruit jelly	65 %	____
Fruit juice	10 %	____
- Grape fruit juice	9 %	____
- Lime juice	6 %	____
- Grape juice	15 %	____

TABLE 25:
Different analytical testing

Analytical method	*Objective (for the determination of)*
Saponification value OR Koettstorfer number	Average molecular weight of fatty acids
Hehner value	Insoluble fatty acids
Anisidine value	Rancidity of oil
Barfoed test	Monosaccharide sugars
Benedict's test	Reducing sugars
Bial's test	Pentose sugars
Biurett test	Protein
Dubois method	Sugar
Ehrlich's reagent	Indole nucleus in amino acids
Fiske and Subbarow method	Phosphorus
Folin Lowry test/Lowry test	Protein
Kirschner value OR Reichert value OR Polenske value	Volatile fatty acids
Kjeldahl method	Crude protein
Lea method	Rancidity of oil
Molisch test	Carbohydrates
Nelson – Somogyi method	Reducing sugar
Seliwanoff's test	Difference between ketose and aldose
Soxhlet method	Crude fat
Thiobarbituric acid (TBA) test	Rancidity of oil
Totox method	Rancidity of oil
Wong method	Iron
Xanthoproteic test	Aromatic amino acids

TABLE 26:
Different classes of food additives

Food additives	*Examples*
Acidulants	Acetic acid, citric acid, malic acid, phosphoric acid, lactic acid
Anti-blooming agent	Sodium tristearate
Anticaking agent	Tricalcium phosphate, Aluminium silicate
Antifoaming agent	Dimethyl polysiloxane
Antimicrobial agent	Ca propionate, Na benzoate, Potassium sorbate
Antioxidant	Butylated hydroxyanisole, Tertiary butylhydroquinone (TBHQ), Propyl gallate
Bread improvers	Potassium bromate, sodium bisulphate
Colorant	Tartrazine, Carmosine, Bixin, Curcumin,
Emulsifier	Lecithin, Polyglycerol polyricinoleate (PGPR), Ammonium phosphatides
Flavour enhancers	Mono sodium glutamate
Glazing agents	Beewax, candelilla wax, carnauba wax, shellac
Humectants	Propylene glycol, hexylene glycol, butylene glycol, glyceryl triacetate
Thickening agent	Xanthan gum, Na alginate, pectin, carboxymethyl cellulose

TABLE 27:
Different thickening and stabilizing agents and their source

Polysaccharides	*Source*
Agar	Seaweeds
Alginic acids	Seaweeds
Amylopectin	Plant
Amylose	Plant
Carrageenan	Seaweeds
Cellulose	Plant
Guar gum	Plant gums
Gum arabic	Exudates
Locust bean gum	Plant gums
Pectin	Plant
Xanthan	Microbes

TABLE 28:
Some typical operations and the food product

Unit operation	*Product*
Blanching	Vegetables
Churning	Butter
Conching	Chocolate
Curing	Meat
Degumming	Oil
Malting	Beer
Pearling	Sorghum
Proofing	Bread
Refining	Chocolate
Rolling	Tea
Smoking	Meat
Winnowing	Cocoa
Withering	Tea

TABLE 29:
Spice and condiments and their principal components

Spice and condiments	*Principal components*
Basil	Linalool, 1, 8-cineol
Cardamom	1, 8- Cineol
Cinnamon	Eugenol, Linalool
Clove	Eugenol, eugenyl acetate
Coriander	*d*-linalool, α-pinene
Cumin	Cuminic aldehyde, terpinene
Curry leaves (Kari leaves)	Sabinene, α-pinene
Dill	Carvone, limonene
Fennel	Anethole, fenchone
Fenugreek	3-hydroxy-4,5-dimethyl-oxolane-2-furanone.
Lemongrass	Citral, myrcene
Mint	Menthol, menthone
Nutmeg	1,8-cineol, borneol
Pepper, black	Sabinene, α-pinene,
Saffron	Safranal, pinenes
Star anise	Anethole, α-pinene
Turmeric	Turmerone, dihydrotumerone
Vanilla	Vainllin

TABLE 30:
Hot and pungent non-volatile components in spices

Spice and condiments	*Principal components*
Black or white pepper	Piperine, chavicine
Garlic	Diallylsulfide
Ginger	Zingiberene, curcumene
Mustard	Allyl isothiocyanate
Onion	Diallylsulfide
Chili, red	Capsaicin,

TABLE 31:
Some spices with their antimicrobial components

Spices	*Antimicrobial component*	*Effective against*
Chile pepper	Capsaicin	Molds, bacteria
Clove	Eugenol	*Escherichia coli, Staphylococcus aureus, Aspergillus*
Coriander	Dodecenal	*Salmonella*
Garlic	Allicin	*Salmonella typhii, Shigella dysenteriae,* molds, yeasts
Ginger	Gingerone, gingerol	*Escherichia coli, Bacillus subtilis*
Mustard	Allyl isothiocyanate	*Escherichia coli, Pseudomonas, Staphylococcus aureus, Saccharomyces cerevisiae*

TABLE 32:
Institutions/Organization/Acts/Law, establishment date and their head quarters

	Institutions/Organization/Acts /Law	*Establishment*	*HQ*
BIS	Bureau of Indian Standards	1986	New Delhi
CFTRI	Central Food Technological Research Institute	1950	Mysore
DFRL	Defense Food Research Laboratory	1961	Mysore
FAO	Food and Agriculture Organization	1945	Rome
FPO	Fruit Products Order	1955	New Delhi
FSSAI	Food Safety and Standards Authority of India	2011	New Delhi
ISO	International Organization for Standardization	1947	Geneva
NDDB	National Dairy Development Board	1965	Anand
NDRI	National Dairy Research Institute	1923	Karnal
NIFTEM	National Institute of Food Technology Entrepreneurship and Management	2006	Sonepat
NIN	National Institute of Nutrition	1958	Hyderabad
PFA	Prevention of Food Adulteration	1954	New Delhi
WHO	World Health Organization	1948	Geneva
WTO	World Trade Organization	1995	Geneva

TABLE 33:
Highlights of FSS Act

Section	*Main points*
16	Duties and function of food authority
18	General principles to be followed in administration of the Act
19	Use of food additives or processing aid
20	Contaminants, naturally occurring toxic substances,heavy metals etc.
21	Pesticides, veterinary drugs residues,antibiotics residues and micro count
22	Genetically modified foods, organic foods,functional foods and Proprietary foods
23	Packaging and labelling of foods
24	Restrictions of advertisement and prohibition as to unfair trade practices
25	Import of foods
26	Responsibility of food business operators
27	Liability of manufacture,packer,wholesaler,distributor
28	Food recall process
29	Authorities responsible for enforcement of Act
30	Commissioner of food safety of the states
31	Licensing and registration of food business
32	Improvement
33	Prohibition of orders
34	Emergency prohibition,notices and order
35	Notification of food poisoning
36	Designated officer
37	Food safety officer
38	Power of food safety officers
39	Liability of food safety officers in certain cases
40	Purchasers may have food analyzed
42	Procedure for launching prosecutions
43	Recognization and accreditation of laboratories
44	Recognization of organization or agency for food safety audit
47	Sampling and analysis
48	General Provisions related to offence
49	General provisions related to penalty
50	Penalty for selling food not of the nature or substances or quality demanded
51	Penalty for sub-standard foods
52	Penalty for mis-brandined food
53	Penalty for misleading advertisement
54	Penalty for food containing extraneous matter

Contd...

Section	*Main points*
55	Penalty for failure to comply with directives of food safety officer
56	Penalty for unhygienic processing
57	Penalty for processing adulterant
59	Punishment for unsafe food
60	Punishment for interfering with seized items
61	Punishment for false information
63	Punishment for carrying out business without license
65	Compensation in case of injury or death of consumer
66	Offenses by companies
68	Adjudication
69	Power to compound offense
91	Power of central government to make rules
92	Power of food authority to make regulations
93	Laying of rules and regulations before parliament
94	Power of stategovernment to make rules
97	Repeal and saving
98	Transitory provisions for food standards

TABLE 34:
Functional classes, definitions and Technical purposes as in FSSAI

Sr.No.	Functional classes	Definition	Technical purpose
1.	Acidity regulator	A food additive, which controls the acidity or alkalinity of a food.	Acidity regulator, acid, acidifier, alkali, base, buffer, buffering agent, pH adjusting agent
2.	Anticaking agent	A food additive, which reduces the tendency of components of food to adhere to one another.	Anticaking agent, anti-stick agent, drying agent, dusting agent
3.	Antifoaming agent	A food additive, which prevents or reduces foaming.	Antifoaming agent, de-foaming agent
4.	Antioxidant	A food additive, which prolongs the shelf-life of foods by protecting against deterioration caused by oxidation.	Antioxidant, antioxidant synergist, anti browning agent
5	Bleaching agent	A food additive (non-flour use) used to decolorize food. Bleaching agents do not include pigments.	Bleaching agent
6.	Bulking agent	A food additive, which contributes to the bulk of a food without contributing significantly to its available energy value.	Bulking agent, filler
7	Carbonating agent	A food additive used to provide carbonation in a food.	Carbonating agent
8	Carrier	A food additive used to dissolve, dilute, disperse or otherwise physically modify a food additive or nutrient without altering its function (and without exerting any technological effect itself) in order to facilitate its handling, application or use of the food additive or nutrient.	Carrier, carrier solvent, nutrient carrier, diluent for other food additives, encapsulating agent
9.	Colour	A food additive, which adds or restores colour in a food.	Colour, decorative pigment, surface colourant
10.	Colour retention agent	A food additive, which stabilizes, retains or intensifies the colour of a food	Colour retention agent, colour fixative, colour stabilizer, colour adjunct
11.	Emulsifier	A food additive, which forms or maintains a uniform emulsion of two or more phases in a food.	Emulsifier, plasticizer, dispersing agent, surface active agent, crystallization inhibitor, density adjustment agent (flavouring oils in beverages), suspension agent, clouding agent

12.	Emulsifying salt	A food additive, which, in the manufacture of processed food, rearranges proteins in order to prevent fat separation.	Emulsifying salt, melding salt
13.	Firming agent	A food additive, which makes or keeps tissues of fruit or vegetables firm and crisp, or interacts with gelling agents to produce or strengthen a gel.	Firming agent
14.	Flavour enhancer	A food additive, which enhances the existing taste and/or odour of a food.	Flavour enhancer, flavour synergist
15.	Flour treatment agent	A food additive, which is added to flour ordough to improve its baking quality or colour.	Flour treatment agent, flour bleaching agent, flour improver, dough conditioner, dough strengthening agent
16.	Foaming agent	A food additive, which makes it possible to form or maintain a uniform dispersion of a gaseous phase in a liquid or solid food.	Foaming agent, whipping agent, aerating agent
17.	Gelling agent	A food additive, which gives a food texture through formation of a gel.	Gelling agent
18.	Glazing agent	A food additive, which when applied to the external surface of a food, imparts a shiny appearance or provides a protective coating.	Glazing agent, sealing agent, coating agent, surface-finishing agent, polishing agent, film-forming agent
19.	Humectant	A food additive, which prevents food from drying out by counteracting the effect of a dry atmosphere.	Humectant, moisture retention agent, wetting agent
20.	Packaging gas	A food additive gas, which is introduced into a container before, during or after filling with food with the intention to protect the food, for example, from oxidation or spoilage.	Packaging gas
21.	Preservative	Afood additive, which prolongs the shelf-life of a food by protecting against deterioration caused by microorganisms.	Preservative, antimicrobial preservative, antimycotic agent, bacteriophage control agent, fungistatic agent, antimould and antirope agent, antimicrobial synergist
22.	Propellant	Afood additive gas, which expels a food from a container	Propellant

23.	Raising agent	A food additive ora combination of food additives, which liberate(s) gas and thereby increase(s) the volume of a dough or batter.	Raising agent
24.	Sequestrant	A food additive, which controls the availability of a cation.	Sequestrant
25.	Stabilizer	A food additive, which makes it possible to maintain a uniform dispersion of two or more components.	Stabilizer, foam stabilizer, colloidal stabilizer, emulsion stabilizer
26.	Sweetener	A food additive (other than a mono-or disaccharide sugar), which imparts a sweet taste to a food.	Sweetener, intense sweetener, bulk sweetener
27.	Thickener	A food additive, which increases the viscosity of a food.	Thickener, bodying agent, binder, texturizing agent

TABLE 35:
List of prebiotics approved by FSSAI

S.No.	Prebiotic Compounds
1.	Polydextrose
2.	Soybean oligosaccharides
3.	Isomalto-oligosaccharides
4.	Fructo-oligosaccharides
5.	Gluco-oligosaccharides
6.	Xylo-oligosaccharides
7.	Inulin
8.	Isomaltulose
9.	Gentio-oligosaccharides
10.	Lactulose
11.	Lactoferrin
12.	Sugar alcohols such as lactitol, sorbitol, maltitol, inositol, isomalt.
13.	Galacto-oligosaccharides.

TABLE 36:
List of strains of probiotics as approved by FSSAI

S. No.	Name of the Microorganism
1.	*Lactobacillus acidophilus*
2.	*Lactobacillus plantarum*
3.	*Lactobacillus reuteri*
4.	*Lactobacillus rhamnosus*
5.	*Lactobacillus salivarius*
6.	*Lactobacillus casei*
7.	*Lactobasillus brevis*
8.	*Lactobacillus johnsonii*
9.	*Lactobacillus delbrueckii* sub-sp. *bulgaricus*
10.	*Bacillus coagulans*
11.	*Lactobacillus fermentum*
12.	*Lactobacillus caucasicus*
13.	*Lactobacillus helveticus*
14.	*Lactobacillus lactis*
15.	*Lactobacillus amylovorus*
16.	*Lactobacillus gallinarum*
17.	*Lactobacillus delbrueckii*
18.	*Bifidobacterium bifidum*
19.	*Bifdobacterium lactis*
20.	*Bifidobacterium breve*
21.	*Bifidobacterium longum*
22.	*Bifidobacterium animalis*
23.	*Bifidobacterium infantis*
24.	*Streptococcus thermophilus*
25.	*Saccharomyces boulardii*
26.	*Saccharomyces cerevisiae*
27.	*Lactobacillus paracasei*
28.	*Lactobacillus gasseri*

Note: These organisms may be used either singly or in combination but shall be declared on the label with full information and has to be Non-GMO.

Also read

Objective Food Science

By Sanjeev Sharma and Harshad Kalwit

Salient features

- ✓ *4000 + multiple choice questions*
- ✓ *Glossary of about 1500 technical terms*
- ✓ *Dedicated section for CFTRI entrance exam*
- ✓ *Numerical type problems for GATE exam*
- ✓ *Matching type questions for ICAR and GATE exam*
- ✓ *Collection of previous CFTRI, ICAR NET, ICAR PG entrance exam papers (solved and unsolved)*
- ✓ *Solved paper of GATE papers since 2008*

To buy the book

Contact Jain Brothers Publisher: 011- 23618426; 011-45097398

Log on to : www.amazon.in; www.thejainbrothers.com

Learn and Practice
Food Science and Food Safetyat
Maniavarsity App
MANIA VARSITY
Download today at
ANDROID APP ON
Google play

Gujarat Designated Officer, Food and Drugs Control Administration, 2019-20 [Solved]

Exam Date: 05-01-2020

Note: ***Question 1 to 100 are from General Studies which is out of scope of this book. Question 101 to 300 are from the concerned subject i.e. Food Technology***

101. A Sample for testing to Accredited Laboratory is sent by
(A) Food Business operator (B) Food Safety Officers
(C) Designated Officers (D) None of the Above

102. When a sample has been taken by food safety officers he will send to food analyst on
(A) On Same day itself (B) Next Day
(C) Succeeding working day (D) Next 2 days

103. In case of Imported food Articles the Food Analyst shall send the report with in period of
(A) 2 days (B) 5 days
(C) 7 days (D) 14 days

104. The penalty for selling food not of the nature or substances of quality demanded is
(A) Not Exceeding Rs. 5 Lakhs (B) Not Exceeding Rs. 3 Lakhs
(C) Minimum 3 Lakhs (D) Minimum 5 Lakhs

105. All proceeding before Adjudicating Officer are deemed to be
(A) Non Judicial proceedings (B) Judicial proceedings
(C) Quasi-Judicial Proceedings (D) None of the above

106. Any Civil Court is empowered to grant injunctions in respect of any action or any suit under FSSA ACT.
(A) Only Adjudicating Officer is Empowered (B) Only in Appellate Tribunal
(C) Both of the above (D) None of the above

107. Any person aggrieved by any decision or order of the tribunal may file appeal to high court within period of
(A) 15 Days (B) 30 Days
(C) 45 Days (D) 60 Days

108. Under Repeal & Savings of FSSA, a license issued under any such enactment or order, Which are in force of the date of commencement of FSSA ACT shall continue to be in force till
(A) For 6 months (B) For 3 months
(C) Till date of expiry (D) Not more than 1 year

109. The Food Safety & Standard Rules, 2011 came into force from
(A) 5th August 2011. (B) 20th January 2011
(C) 23rd August 2011. (D) 5th May 2011

110. The Food Analyst issue the report in
(A) Form VA (B) Form VI
(C) Form VIA (D) Form VIIA

111. The Food Safety Officers when draw the sample for surveillance issues
(A) Form VA (B) Form VI
(C) Both of the above (D) None of the above

112. Total _________ Manuals have been issued by DGHS, New Delhi for analyzing the sample of Food Articles
(A) 13 (B) 11
(C) 09 (D) 07

113. A Food business operator in Palanpur (Gujarat), Notifies Food Safety officers and send the sample for testing under Rule 2.4.5. The Food safety officers may send same to accredited laboratory situated in
(A) Delhi (B) Kolkata
(C) Mumbai (D) Chennai

114. The Appeal by Food Business operator to designated officer against the report of Food Analyst is to be made within
(A) 30 Days (B) 15 Days
(C) 14 Days (D) 7 Days

115. Every Appeal, Petition or application made by the appellant or petitioner before Appellate Tribunal shall be in
(A) One Copy (B) Two Copies
(C) Three Copies (D) Four Copies

116. The amount of fees payable for an appeal in appellate tribunal on Rs. 10 lakhs of Penalty imposed shall be
(A) Rs. 10000 (B) Rs. 7500
(C) Rs. 5000 (D) Rs. 15000

117. A food Business operator having cereals, Pulses milling units with installed capacity of 5 MT/ per day will have to obtain license from
(A) State Licensing Authority (B) Central Licensing Authority
(C) Both State & Central (D) Only Registration with Central

118. Any food Articles delivered to consumer by E-commerce FBO, shall have shelf life of _________ before Expiry at the time of delivery toconsumer
(A) 30% or 15 Days (B) 40% or 30 Days
(C) 30% or 45 Days (D) 45% or 30 Days

119. To get a copy of duplicate license for the canteen of Shri Laxmanbhai Bimjibhai Trust Kelavani Mandal has to pay Fees of

(A) Rs.200 (B) Rs. 500
(C) Rs.100 (D) Rs. 300

120. A raw milk is brought to a dairy plant by a producer or farmer within _______ of Milking

(A) 3 Hours (B) 4 hours
(C) 5 hours (D) 6 hours

121. "Warm Meat" meant for immediate sale has to be stored at

(A) Cool Condition (B) between 0 - 2 degree Centigrade
(C) between 0 - 4 degree Centigrade (D) need not be in cool condition

122. Every person Employed for meat handling at meat shop shall be medically examined annually for

(A) Sputum and X-Ray of Chest (B) Stool for Protozoal
(C) Presence of Entro Pathogenics (D) All of the above

123. Once thawed the pre-prepared food

(A) Shall not be refreezed for future use
(B) Can be used after refreeze at 4 degree C for 10 minutes
(C) Can be used after refreeze at 0 degree C for 15 minutes
(D) Can be used after refreeze at 4 degree C for 30 minutes

124. On Container or Label of any infant food shall have

(A) A picture of Infant (B) A picture of woman
(C) A picture of both (D) None of the Above

125. The label of An Infant food /Infant Milk Subsitute shall have words printed

(A) Complete Food (B) Health Food
(C) Both of the above (D) None of the above

126. The word "Not for Phenyl Ketoneurics" shall be displayed on product containing

(A) Acesul fame Potassium (B) Aspartame (Methyl ester)
(C) Neotame (D) Sucralose & Saccharin Sod.

127. The label of any Food product may have words _______

(A) As a recommended by Medical Profession (B) As suggested by Medical Practitioner
(C) As approved by Medical Practitioner (D) None of the above

128. The requirement of list of ingredients, Lot No., Nutrional Information may not be on package label

(A) Less than 100 sq.cm (B) More than 100 sq.cm
(C) More than 150 sq.cm (D) All of the above

129. A food business operator shall comply with the provisions of the Food Safety &Standards (packaging) regulations 2018 by

(A) 24th December 2018 (B) 19th march 2018

(C) 1st July 2019 (D) 24th July 2019

130. Maximum permitted amount of Non-volatile substance released from material or article into food simulants is

(A) Specific Migration Limit (B) Over - All Migration Limit

(C) Compounded Migration Limit (D) None of the above

131. Printing inks for use on food packages shall confirm to

(A) IS:12247 (B) IS:13576

(C) IS:15495 (D) IS:13601

132. Chipped enamelled containers can be used for

(A) Preparation of Food (B) Packaging of Food

(C) Storing of Food (D) None of the above

133. The Wax used for coating paper or board for packaging of food shall be

(A) White Bees Wax (B) Yellow Bees Wax

(C) Paraffin Wax (D) Carnauba Wax

134. The suggested packaging materials for Milk & Milk products under Sch-IV of FSS (Packaging) Regulations 2018 is

(A) Wax Coated paper butter wrappers (B) Mud or Clay Pots

(C) Tin Plate container (D) All of the above

135. Condensed Milk sweetened, Milk Powder, skimmed milk powder, shall not be sold except

(A) Under BIS certification mark (B) under ISI certification mark

(C) Both of the above (D) None of the above

136. Flavoured Tea shall be sold only by those manufacturer registered with

(A) Tea Board (B) Spices & Condiments Board

(C) National Milk Products Board (D) Agriculture Produce Board

137. Imported coconut oil, Olive oil can be sold for human consumption

(A) As such without any process (B) Only after refining

(C) Only after double refining (D) For other purpose except cooking

138. ________ is the solvent permitted to be used in extraction of cocoa butter, Oils & Fats, and edible soyaflour

(A) *n*-butane (B) *n*-hexane

(C) *n*-isopropane (D) *n*-cyclopentane

139. Methyl Mercury (Calculated as element) as contaminant in food can be for maximum 0.25 PPM in

(A) Beverages (B) Meat & Fish Products

(C) Sugar Confactionary & Veg Oils (D) All Foods

140. Aflatoxin is

(A) a crop contaminant

(B) Naturally occurring toxic substance

(C) Residual contaminant

(D) Toxic substance as a result of contact with hazardous chemicals

141. Micronutrients are vital parts of

(A) Fortified Food (B) Neutraceutical Food

(C) Dietary Food (D) Health Supplements

142. _______ shall not be used in any form in any article of food as IRON source

(A) Heme Iron (B) Non-Heme Iron

(C) Both of the above (D) None of the above

143. Every manufacturer & packer of fortified food shall give undertaking on quality assurance

(A) Every monthly (B) Every quarterly

(C) Twice in a Year (D) Once in a year

144. Milk & Vegetable oil shall be fortified with following micronutrients

(A) Vitamin A&D (B) Vitamin B12

(C) Vitamin B1, B2, B3 & B6. (D) All of the above

145. The source nutrient for iron fortification in double fortified salt is

(A) Ferrous Citrate (B) Ferrous sulphate

(C) Ferric Pyrophosphate (D) Ferrous Bisglycinate

146. "People with Thalassemia may take under medical supervision" statement appears in package of

(A) Fortified Milk (B) Fortified Oil

(C) Double Iodised Salt (D) Iodised Salt

147. The tag line on package of Fortified Food is

(A) Swasth Poshan Sampoorna Jeevan (B) Sampoorna Poshan Swasth Jeevan

(C) Swasth Poshan Swasth Jeevan (D) Sampoorna Poshan Sampoorna Jeevan

148. Food that contains non viable food components that confer health benefits to the consumer by modulation of gut microbiota are food:

(A) with probiotic ingredients (B) with prebiotic ingredients

(C) with special dietary use (D) for special medical purpose

149. __________ are not defined under section 22 of FSSA Act 2006

(A) Functional Food (B) Novel Food

(C) Staple Food (D) Organic Food

150. Vitamins, Minerals & Amino acids specified in Schedule-I & Schedule-II of FSS (Health Supplements –Nutraceuticals) regulations, 2016 means

(A) nutritional ingredients (B) nutrient ingredients

(C) micro nutrient (D) premixes

151. The general quality requirements & standards as specified in Indian pharmacopeia has to be fulfilled for health supplements in

(A) Tablets (B) Capsules

(C) Syrups (D) All of the above

152. The minimally processed Amla Juice is a

(A) Health Supplement (B) Nutraceutical Food

(C) Food for special Dietary use (D) None of the above

153. The RDA of nutrients added to article of food are specified by

(A) Indian Pharmacopeia (B) Indian Council of Medical Research

(C) Bureau of Indian Standards (D) None of the above

154. Health supplements shall use additives mentioned under

(A) Schedule-VA (B) Schedule-VE

(C) Schedule-VF (D) All of the above

155. The International Food Standard Body is

(A) Indian Council of Medical Research (B) Codex Alimentarius

(C) Codex Alimentarius commission (D) FAO of United Nations

156. Enzymes only under Schedule-VI can be used as ingredients for

(A) Nutraceuticals (B) Health Supplements

(C) Food for special diatary use (D) All of the above

157. A statement that product is not to be used by pregnant, nursing & lactating women or by infants, elderly except when medically advised is applicable for

(A) Nutraceuticals (B) Health Supplements

(C) Food for special diatary use (D) Food for Special Medical Purpose

158. No FBO shall use additives in prebiotic/probiotic preparation except those specified in

(A) Schedule-VI (B) Schedule-VII

(C) Schedule-VIII (D) Schedule V A to VF

159. RDA means
(A) Recommended Daily Average
(B) Regular Daily Average
(C) Recommended Dietary Allowance
(D) Recommended Daily Allowance

160. The time limit for chemical testing of samples by Referral laboratories fixed by FSSAI is
(A) Within 5 working days
(B) Within 7 working days
(C) Within 10 working days
(D) Within 15 working days

161. Investigation for the purpose of fixation of standard of any article of food is one of the function of
(A) Referral Laboratory
(B) Notified Laboratory for import
(C) Accredited Laboratory
(D) NABL approved Laboratory

162. The approx quantity of sample of prepared food to be sent to Food Analyst is
(A) 200 gm
(B) 250gm
(C) 400 gm
(D) 500gm

163. The certificate of analysis issued by Referral Food Laboratory is in
(A) Form B
(B) Form A
(C) Form VIA
(D) Form VII A

164. For the purpose of import license from Central Licensing Authority, the food importer has to
(A) Obtain license from state authority
(B) Registration under FSSA
(C) Register with Director of Foreign trade
(D) None of the above

165. For the imported food article to be cleared by custom, the valid shelf life of article shall be
(A) Not less than 60%
(B) 3 months before expiry
(C) Both of the above
(D) None of the above

166. The objective of Food recall procedure is
(A) To ensure removal of food from all stage of food chain
(B) to ensure dissemination of information to concerned stake holders
(C) to ensure retrieval, destruction or reprocessing of food under recall
(D) All of the above

167. An up-to date food recall plan is required for FBO'S engaged in
(A) Manufacture
(B) Import
(C) Wholesale
(D) All of the above

168. Main objective of Food Safety & Standard Act, 2006 are
(A) Ensure safe & wholesome food
(B) Consolidate different laws of food
(C) Regulate manufacture, storage, distribution, sale & import of food
(D) All of the above

169. Designated Officer means officer appointed under __________ of FSSA

(A) Section 30 (B) Section 36

(C) Section 37 (D) Section 45

170. License means a license granted under ________ of FSSA

(A) Section 31 (B) Section 32

(C) Section 33 (D) Section 43

171. In case of contravention punishable with imprisonment the Designation Officer will send his recommendation to Commissioner of Food Safety for sanctioning prosecution within

(A) 30 Days (B) 15 Days

(C) 14 Days (D) 7 Days

172. In case where special court are established, the offences punishable with imprisonment years are tried within

(A) 3 years (B) more than 3 years

(C) 5 years (D) More than 5 years

173. The procedure for launching prosecution are in

(A) Section 42 of FSS Act (B) Section 38 of FSS Act

(C) Rule 2.1.3.4 of FSS Rules (D) Rule 2.4.1. of FSS Rules

174. Among the four parts of sample drawn by Food Safety Officer

(A) 2 Parts are kept by FSO (B) 2 parts are sent to Food Analyst

(C) 2 parts are sent to designated officer (D) None of the above

175. The penalty for possessing adulterant injurious to health is

(A) Not exceeding 1 Lakh Rupees (B) Not exceeding 3 Lakh Rupees

(C) Not exceeding 5 Lakh Rupees (D) Not exceeding 10 Lakh Rupees

176. The punishment for carrying out a business with out license, except those exempted is

(A) Imprisonment upto 6 months & fine upto 5 Lakh Rupees

(B) Imprisonment upto 3 months & fine upto 3 Lakh Rupees

(C) Imprisonment upto 3 months only

(D) Fine upto 3 Lakh Rupees only

177. The minimum qualification for appointment of Presiding Officer of Food Appellate Tribunal is

(A) Judicial Magistrate First Class (B) Additional District Magistrate

(C) District Judge (D) Retired Food Safety Commissioner

178. When a sample is drawn from open container another sample from container in original condition

(A) is mandatorily required (B) only if such container is available

(C) shall avoid sampling from open container (D) None of the above

179. Residues of veterinary drugs in food includes
(A) Parent compound
(B) Metabolites of compound
(C) Associated impurities of compound
(D) All of the above

180. E-Commerce FBO's shall obtain registration and license from
(A) Central Registration Authority Only
(B) State Licensing Authority Only
(C) Central Licensing Authority Only
(D) Concerned registration & Licensing Authority

181. The Annual return for businesses other than milk & milk Products is in
(A) Form C
(B) Form D-1
(C) Form D-2
(D) Form E

182. _________ did not became part of the Acts/Orders repealed under section 97 of FSSA
(A) The Edible oils packaging (Regulation) order,1998
(B) The Infant Milk Substitutes, Feeding bottles & Infant Food Act, 1992
(C) The Solvent Extracted Oil, De-oiled Meal and Edible flour (Control) order, 1967
(D) The Milk & Milk products order, 1992

183. Food Additive means
(A) Added substances for improving nutritional qualities
(B) Normally consumed as a food
(C) Added for technological or organoleptic purpose
(D) None of the above

184. Food Article if injurious to health can be
(A) only unsafe food
(B) only substandard
(C) only misbranded
(D) None of the above

185. Tenure of Chair Person of Food Authority is
(A) 1 year
(B) 2 years
(C) 3 years
(D) 5 years

186. The Chief Executive Officer of Food Authority is appointed by
(A) Chairman of Food Authority
(B) Selection Committee of Food Authority
(C) Central Government
(D) All of the above

187. Scientific panels are established by
(A) Food Authority
(B) Selection Committee of Food Authority
(C) Chairman of Food Authority
(D) CEO of Food Authority

188. Designated Officer sanctions or launch prosecution in case of contravention for
(A) substandard food
(B) a mis-branded food
(C) unhygienic manufacturing of food
(D) All of the above

189. Under FSS Rules no person shall either himself or by any servant or agent sell
(A) Dahi prepared from sterilized milk
(B) Turmeric containing any foreign substance
(C) Admixture of edible vegetable oils by NDDB
(D) Mixture of Coffee with Chicory

190. It is mandatory to have BIS Certification for products
(A) Partly skimmed powder
(B) Follow up formula
(C) Packaged drinking water
(D) All of the above

191. In hydrogenated vegetable oil, colour of ghee
(A) can be added
(B) can be added if authorized by Food Authority
(C) cannot be added
(D) None of the Above

192. In pasteurization, every particle of milk is
(A) heated at 60 degree C holding at least 30 minutes
(B) heated at 72 degree C holding at least 15 seconds
(C) Both of the above
(D) None of the above

193. In Ultra high temperature sterilization for milk products, it is heated upto
(A) 135 degree C for 1 minute
(B) 130 degree C for 5 minutes
(C) 130 degree C for 5 seconds
(D) 135 degree C for 1 second

194. ______________ is composite milk products
(A) Shrikh and with fruit
(B) Ice-cream with fruit
(C) Flavoured fermented milk
(D) All of the above

195. Homogenous & no deposition of solids shall take place on standing
(A) Full cream milk
(B) Standardised milk
(C) Skimmed milk
(D) All of the above

196. Pasteurized cream is used mandatorily to make .
(A) White butter
(B) Table Butter
(C) Cooking Butter
(D) All of the above

197. Use of the flavouring agent is prohibited in any articles of food
(A) Coumarin
(B) p-Propylanisole
(C) Dihydrocoumarin
(D) All of the above

198. ______________ composite the sweetening property of natural sweetener, stevia leaves
(A) Stevioside
(B) Rebaudioside A
(C) Both of the above
(D) None of the above

199. As per FSS regulation, solution of Annatto colour in oil is for use in

(A) Cheese (B) Butter

(C) Both of the above (D) None of the above

200. A proprietary food means standards are not specified but does not include

(A) functional foods (B) Nutraceuticals

(C) Health supplements (D) All of the above

201. ________ are packed in clean & sterile containers

(A) Natural mineral water (B) Packaged drinking water

(C) Drinking water (D) All of the above

202. Vanaspati means, any refined edible vegetable oil or oils subjected to a process of

(A) Dehydrogenation (B) Hydrogenation

(C) Oxidation (D) Sublimation

203. Inter-esterification of an edible fatty material will change physical property

(A) Viscocity (B) Specific gravity

(C) Melting point (D) All of the above

204. "Khoa" or "Mawa" does not contain

(A) milk & milk powder (B) cream and cream powder

(C) added starch or sugar (D) milk fat products

205. ______ is a fermented concentrated milk product

(A) Dahi (B) Chakka

(C) Yogurt (D) Lassi

206. The frozen dessert may contain

(A) Vegetable oils & fats with M. P < 37 degree C

(B) Vegetable proteins products

(C) Milk and/or Milk products

(D) All of the above

207. Cheddar cheese is

(A) unripened, soft cheese (B) from cultures other than lactic acid

(C) White to light cream colour (D) None of the above

208. A license of FBO may be suspended by Designated Officer if

(A) the FBO has failed to comply with regulations

(B) failed to comply with improvement notice

(C) failed to inform on unsafe/substandard food

(D) All of the above

209. FBO's are not included under requirement of FSMS guidelines
(A) Petty FBO's for registration
(B) Street food vendors
(C) Catering & Food Service operators
(D) None of the above

210. For checking the misuse of non edible ice as edible ice it is required to add colour
(A) Indigo carmine
(B) Sunset Yellow
(C) Ponceau 4R
(D) Malachite Green

211. Lipoproteins are water soluble & can be separated into protein & lipid moieties by
(A) extraction with suitable solvents
(B) filtration using 0.2 micron filter pads
(C) distillation in column
(D) by evaporation

212. Gluten is
(A) synonymous of protein in wheat
(B) constituent of wheat kernel
(C) combination of wheat proteins on kneading
(D) formed when washed with water

213. It is also called as vapour phase chromatography
(A) Gas Chromatography
(B) High Pressure liquid Chromatography
(C) Gas Liquid Chromatography
(D) Thin Liquid Chromatography

214. As compared with TLC, in HPTLC, the chromatography layer
(A) are slightly thinner than conventional
(B) have smaller grain size
(C) better separation performance
(D) All of the above

215. The value to determine the water insoluble fatty acids present in fat is
(A) R.M. Value
(B) Polenske Value
(C) Both of the above
(D) None of the above

216. The B. R. reading for detection of foreign fats/Oil in milk means
(A) Butyro-Reichert Reading
(B) Baudin-Refractometer reading
(C) Butyro-Refractometer reading
(D) Baudin-Reichert Reading

217. In Urease enzyme test for detection of Urea in milk, the indicator is
(A) Phenol Red
(B) Alizarin Green
(C) Methyl Red
(D) Bromocresol Green

218. The important effect of micro organisms where one organism makes condition favourable for growth of the second is
(A) Symbiotic
(B) Synergetic
(C) Metabiotic
(D) Antibiotic

219. Spoilage in foods may be due to
(A) insects
(B) physical Changes
(C) growth & activities of microorganisms
(D) All of the above

220. Streptococcus Lactiscauses
(A) color change in milk
(B) no color change in milk
(C) no spoilage of milk
(D) production of antibiotics

221. Meat, Fish, etc are grouped under
(A) low-acid Foods
(B) medium-acid foods
(C) acid foods
(D) high-acid foods

222. Enamel coating in cans containing zinc oxide cannot be used to store.
(A) berries
(B) beets
(C) meat
(D) corn

223. The fungus known as bread mold is
(A) Mucor
(B) Penicillium
(C) Rhizopus
(D) Aspergillus

224. Red Pigmentation on spoilt food is caused by
(A) Psedomonas
(B) Clostridium
(C) Salmonella
(D) Serratia

225. The rapid slowing of chemical and enzymatic reactions in foods is achieved by
(A) quick freezing
(B) sharp freezing
(C) dehydro freezing
(D) None of the above

226. Which of the following are easily subjected to deterioration?
(A) raw cane juice
(B) sucrose
(C) honey
(D) molasses

227. Coliform bacteria are present in
(A) fresh fruit juices
(B) frozen fruit juices
(C) Both of the above
(D) None of the above

228. Packaging films for meat with poor gas penetration encourage the growth of
(A) Bacillus
(B) Lactic acid bacteria
(C) Clostridium
(D) Mucor

229. What is germicidal ice?
(A) Ice with chemical preservative
(B) Ice which is crushed
(C) Ice with Antiseptic Solution
(D) None of the above

230. The centrifugal procedure used for removing bacteria from milk is
(A) centrifugation
(B) bactofugation
(C) separation
(D) None of the above

231. Spoilage of drink is evidenced by
(A) rancidity and sourness
(B) offensive odor and taste
(C) cloudiness and ropiness
(D) discoloration & clarity

232. _______ are harmless probiotics & currently used in preparations
(A) Lactobacilli (B) Bifido bacteria
(C) Streptococcus Thermophilus (D) All of the above

233. ______ enzymes used in confectionary industry
(A) Amylase (B) Invertase
(C) Protease (D) Pectinase

234. The classification of acids or base on the basis of Arrhenius theory is on
(A) Protons (B) Ions
(C) Electronpair (D) All of the above

235. Chloroform, Carbon tetrachloride, Benzene are
(A) Amphoteric solvents (B) Protogenic solvents
(C) Protophylic Solvents (D) Aprotic solvents

236. Non-aqeuous titration is preferred for compound which are
(A) insufficient acidic (B) insufficient basic
(C) Both of the above (D) None of the above

237. The amount of unsaturation present in fats/oil is determined by
(A) Iodine Number (B) R.M. Number
(C) Polenske Number (D) Saponification Number

238. The rancidity in fats/oils is due to
(A) Hydrogenation (B) Oxidation
(C) Esterification (D) Polymorphism

239. The common tests for ranicidity
(A) Peroxide Value (B) TBA test
(C) Determination of carbonyl (D) All of the above

240. Rendering, Pressing & Solvent Extraction are principal methods for extraction of
(A) Edible fats & oils from veg tissues (B) Edible fats & oils from animal tissues
(C) Both of the above (D) None of the above

241. Sucrose is
(A) Monosaccharide (B) Oligosaccharide
(C) Homopolysaccharide (D) Heteropolysachharide

242. ________ is not found naturally but by commercial extract from Barley Malt
(A) Alphaamylase (B) Betaamylase
(C) Diastase (D) None of the above

243. The Molisch reaction is the test for identification of
(A) Protein (B) Fats
(C) Carbohydrates (D) Lipids

244. Amino acids in human are source of
(A) Protein
(B) Fats
(C) Carbohydrates
(D) Lipids

245. _______ is the method used for determination of nitrogen in foods
(A) Clerjet method
(B) TBA test
(C) Molisch Reaction
(D) Kjeldahl method

246. The "Amphoterism" property of protein is due to
(A) Free Carboxyl group
(B) Free Amino Group
(C) Both of the above
(D) None of the above

247. The state of water in Lactose Monohydrate is
(A) Freewater
(B) Adsorbed water
(C) Water of hydration
(D) All of the above

248. _______ is for measuring specific gravity
(A) Pycnometer
(B) Hydrometer
(C) Westphal Balance
(D) All of the above

249. In UV-V is Spectroscopy, the UV spectrum wavelength range is
(A) 200-350 nm
(B) 200-700 nm
(C) 350-700 nm
(D) None of the above

250. The common radiation source for measurement in UV range is
(A) Tungsten filament lamp
(B) Deuterium electric discharge lamp
(C) Nernst filament
(D) Nichrome wire

251. The wavelength range of 2.5-15 micrometer applies to
(A) near IR
(B) mid IR
(C) far IR
(D) None of the above

252. Following detector is not use for Gas Chromatography
(A) Thermal Conductivity Detector (TCD)
(B) Photo Diode Array Detector (PDA)
(C) Photo Ionisation Detector (PID)
(D) Electron Capture Detector (ECD)

253. Wijis method is used to determine
(A) Peroxide value
(B) Acid Value
(C) Iodine Value
(D) Saponification Value

254. _______ is a chemical substance used for "Control of Wavelength" calibration in UV Spectroscopy
(A) Potassium chloride
(B) Potassium Dichromate
(C) Holmium Perchlorate
(D) Sodium perchlorate

255. Fats are hydrolyzed by
(A) hydrolases
(B) oxidases
(C) microbiallipase
(D) pectinases

256. RUCO means

(A) Re Used Cooking Oil
(B) Repacked Unused Cooking Oil
(C) Repurpose Used Cooking Oil
(D) Repeatly Used Cooking Oil

257. The vegetable oil used for frying should have

(A) TPC< 20%
(B) TPC < 25%
(C) TPC 20% & above
(D) TPC 25% & Above

258. Diseases like hypertension, Alzheimer, atherosclerosis are associated in toxicity of

(A) blend of vegetable oils
(B) Oils with higher TPC
(C) Palmolein mixed with sesame oil
(D) Use of unsatuarated oil

259. ITCFSAN means

(A) Institute for Training of Consumers, Food Suppliers And Nutrition
(B) Indian Training Centre for Food Safety and Nutrition
(C) International Training Centre for Food Safety & Applied Nutrition
(D) International Training Centre for Food Safety And Nutrition

260. ITCFSAN is partnership between

(A) Ministry of Commerce & World Bank
(B) Ministry of Health & United Nation
(C) Ministry of Human Resource & WHO
(D) Ministry of Food & World Bank

261. The corner stones of ITCFSAN

(A) Training with impact
(B) Teaching to manage risk
(C) Supporting towards self compliance
(D) All of the above

262. The online portal for food licensing by FSSAI is

(A) Food Registration & License system
(B) Food Licensing & Registration System
(C) Food Licensing & Renewal System
(D) Food Registration & Laboratory System

263. FSKAN means

(A) Food Safety Knowledge And Network
(B) Food Standardisation, Knowledge And Network
(C) Food Safety Knowledge Assimilation Network
(D) Food Standardisation knowledge Assimilation Network

264. The initiative by FSSAI as mandated under section 16, 3 (e) of FSSA Act is

(A) FOSTAC
(B) Info Lnet
(C) FSKAN
(D) ITCFSAN

265. FOSTAC means

(A) Food Officers Safety Training & Certification
(B) Food Standardisation And Training Centre
(C) Food Safety Training And Certification
(D) Food Suppliers Training Certification

266. The initiative by FSSAI to prevent Food waste & food loss is

(A) ISFO (B) IFSA

(C) ISFS (D) IFSSA

267. "Aajse Thoda Kam" is a tag line under

(A) Health India Movement (B) Fit India Movement

(C) Eat Right India Movement (D) All of the above

268. Under Swasth Bharat Yatra the theme Eat Right India encompasses

(A) Eating Healthy, Safe & Fortified Food (B) No Food Wastage

(C) Cycling & Brisk walking (D) All of the above

269. The FSSAI Publication on Safe &Nutrition Food on Food Adulteration is

(A) Pink Book (B) Dart Book

(C) Yellow Book (D) Orange Book

270. The core activities of BIS

(A) Standards formulation (B) Product & System certification

(C) Hall marking (D) All of the above

271. AGMARK is a certification mark confirming to

(A) Standards of directorate of Marketing & Inspection (DMI)

(B) ISI standards

(C) Products under BIS

(D) Standards under FSSA for veg oils & fats

272. _______ items, under FSS regulation has fewer conditional restriction for AGMARK

(A) Honey Dew (B) Tea

(C) Ghee (D) All of the above

273. While framing standards under AGMARK, existing standards of following are considered

(A) FSSA (B) Codex Alimentarius

(C) International Organisation for Standards (D) All of the above

274. The Orange Book of FSSAI publication is

(A) SNF at work place (B) SNF at schools

(C) SNF at homes (D) SNF at religious place

275. FSSAI initiated "Diet4life" programme for

(A) Safe & Sustainable Diet

(B) Comprehensive platform towards IEM management

(C) Healthy Diet for adolescences

(D) Diet for school children

276. FSSAI is authority under
(A) Ministry of Consumer Affairs, Food & Public Distribution
(B) Ministry of Health &Family Welfare
(C) Ministry of Food Procarine Industries
(D) Ministry of Women & Child Development

277. The Global Food Safety Partnership (GFSP) of FSSAI is
(A) Public-Private initiative
(B) Promoting global co-operation for food safety capacity building
(C) Work is focussed on low & middle income countries
(D) All of the above

278. CPGRAMS means
(A) Centre of Public Governance Rights And Monitoring Society
(B) Centralized Public Grievance Redress And Monitoring System
(C) Centre of Puplic Grievance, Rights And Monitoring System
(D) Centralized Public Grievance Redressal Management System

279. The "Food Safety Connect" is the online portal of FSSAI for
(A) Standards of Food
(B) Act & Rules of Food Safety
(C) Consumer Grievance Redressal Mechanism
(D) Information on unsafe, substandard Food

280. A unique reference number is provided to consumer on registering at online grievance via
(A) Mail (B) SMS
(C) Both of the above (D) None of the above

281. ______ has been declared as the India's first fully organic state
(A) Gujarat (B) Punjab
(C) Sikkim (D) Assam

282. _______ has been awarded as a country's first Clean Street Food Hub
(A) Kankaria Ahmedabad (B) Juhu Chowpatty, Mumbai
(C) Girgam Chowpatty, Mumbai (D)Chandni Chowk, Delhi

283. For quick detection of Argemon seeds in mustard seeds, when pressed, the mustard seeds inside is_______colour & Argemon Seeds inside is colour respectively
(A) Yellow, Black (B) Black, White
(C) Yellow, White (D) White, Yellow

284. In quick detection of Chickory in Coffee, powder when added to glass of water
(A) Coffee powder will sink (B) Chickory will sink
(C) Chickory will be on surface (D) None of the above

285. When 2-3 drops tincture of iodine is added to Ghee/Butter the blue color indicates adulteration of

(A) Rhodamine B (B) Starch
(C)Turmeric (D) Artificial Flavour

286. "Jaivik Bharat" is the logo for

(A) Organic foods imported to India (B) Organic & Non organic food from India
(C) Organic Foods from India (D) All of the above

287. The web based real time inspection platform for food safety, inspection & sampling is

(A) FoSCoRIS (B) FPAS
(C) IFSQA (D) FosTaC

288. The Food Safety supervisor course & certification is undertaken by

(A) ITGFSAN (B) FoSCoRIS
(C) FosTaC (D) All of the above

289. The Agriculture & Processed Food Products Export Development Authority (APEDA) monitors products

(A) Fruits, Vegetables Cereals, Dairy Products (B)Alcoholic Beverages
(C) Fluoriculture (D) All of the above

290. The APEDA functions includes

(A) providing financial assistance (B) approving packaging of products
(C) as a agent between buyers & sellers (D) All of the above

291. GAMA means

(A) Goods And Marketing Agency
(B) Grievances Against Marketing & Advertisement
(C) Grievances Against Misleading Advertisement
(D) None of the above

292. GAMA is portal by

(A) Department of the Consumer Affairs (B) Department of Food & Public distribution
(C) Department of Health (D) Department of information

293. GAMA is online portal for

(A) Complaints on quality of foods (B) Approving online advertisement
(C) Complaints on misleading advertisements (D) All of the above

294. ______ are the key sectors under GAMA

(A) Food & Agriculture (B) Health, Education & Real Estate
(C) Transport & Financial services (D) All of the above

295. The 3-tier redressal machinery under Consumer Protection Act is

(A) Judicial (B) Quasi Judicial
(C) Both of the above (D) None of the above

296. The scope of complaint under Consumer Protection Act is for a product or service

(A) Paid (B) Promised

(C) Partly Paid or Promised (D) All of the above

297. Every year the National Consumer Day is celebrated on

(A) 15th March (B) 20th June

(C) 24th December (D) 18th March

298. The World Consumer Day 2019 theme is

(A) Trusted Smart Products (B) Making Digital Market Place Fairer

(C) Timely Disposal of Consumer Complaints (D) Alternate Consumer Dispute Redressal

299. The International agency with India that works on sustainable development of agriculture as well as on food & nutrition security is

(A) WHO (B) FAO

(C)IFAD (D)WFP

300. Food Smart Consumer portal highlights

(A) Claims /Myth Busters (B) Consumer rights & Smart Buying guides

(C) Popular Publications of FSSAI (D)All of the above

ANSWERS

Gujarat Designated Officer, Food and Drugs Control Administration, 2019

101. B	141. A	181. B	221. A	261. D
102. C	142. A	182. B	222. C	262. B
103. B	143. C	183. C	223. C	263. C
104. A	144. A	184. A	224. D	264. C
105. B	145. B	185. C	225. A	265. C
106. D	146. C	186. C	226. A	266. B
107. D	147. B	187. A	227. C	267. C
108. C	148. B	188. D	228. B	268. D
109. A	149. C	189. B	229. A	269. B
110. D	150. B	190. D	230. B	270. D
111. D	151. D	191. C	231. C	271. C
112. B	152. D	192. C	232. D	272. D
113. C	153. B	193. D	233. B	273. D
114. A	154. D	194. D	234. B	274. A

115. C	155. C	195. D	235. D	275. B
116. C	156. B	196. B	236. C	276. B
117. A	157. C	197. D	237. A	277. D
118. C	158. D	198. C	238. B	278. B
119. A	159. D	199. B	239. D	279. C
120. B	160. A	200. D	240. B	280. B
121. D	161. A	201. A	241. B	281. C
122. D	162. D	202. B	242. C	282. D
123. A	163. B	203. D	243. C	283. C
124. D	164. C	204. C	244. A	284. B
125. D	165. C	205. B	245. D	285. B
126. B	166. D	206. D	246. C	286. C
127. D	167. D	207. D	247. C	287. A
128. A	168. D	208. B	248. D	288. C
129. C	169. B	209. D	249. A	289. D
130. B	170. A	210. A	250. B	290. A
131. C	171. C	211. A	251. B	291. C
132. D	172. B	212. C	252. B	292. A
133. C	173. A	213. C	253. C	293. C
134. D	174. C	214. D	254. B	294. D
135. B	175. D	215. B	255. C	295. B
136. A	176. A	216. C	256. C	296. D
137. A	177. C	217. A	257. B	297. C
138. B	178. B	218. C	258. B	298. A
139. D	179. D	219. D	259. D	299. B
140. A	180. D	220. B	260. A	300. D

Kerala Food Safety Officer Exam, 2015

[Unsolved]

Maximum marks: 100

Total Time: 1 hr 15 min

1. Consumption of raw soybeans can be harmful to health because of the presence of following anti-nutritional factor:
(A) Phytic acid
(B) Tannins
(C) Oxalates
(D) Trypsin inhibitor

2. In a standard fruit jam preparation the content of total soluble solids should not be less than:
(A) 68% W/W
(B) 45% W/W
(C) 65% W/W
(D) 70% W/W

3. The safe level of irradiation for foods, which presents no toxicological hazard is:
(A) 5.0 kGy
(B) 10.0 kGy
(C) 7.0 kGy
(D) 25.0 kGy

4. Subjecting rice to higher degree of polishing is associated with following:
(A) Better nutritional density and easy digestibility
(B) Better glycemic index and suitability for diabetics
(C) Lowered nutritional and better cooking characteristics
(D) Higher bioavailable nutrients and lowered sensory quality

5. The browning occurring in cut apples on aeration is due to the presence of:
(A) Polyphenolases
(B) Oxidoreductases
(C) Polymeric oxidases
(D) Polyhydrogenases

6. FSSAI stands for:
(A) Fire Safety and Security Association of India
(B) Food Safety and Standards Authority of India
(C) Fire Safety and Standards Arrangements Incorporation
(D) Food Safety and Security Association of India

7. Identify the correct group of stimulating constituents present in tea :
(A) Theobromine, triphylline, catechol
(B) Caffein, tricantenol, trimethylamine
(C) Theonitrile, caffeicol, theophylline
(D) Caffeine, theobromine, theophylline

8. Acceptable daily intake level of additives is derived from following :
(A) No observed adverse effect level of compound and uncertainty factor
(B) Level at which toxicity may not occur in humans
(C) Levels likely to be used in foods
(D) Chemical nature of the compound

9. Identify the cluster of essential fatty acids for humans from the following :
   (A) Myristic, arachidonic and capric acids
   (B) Linolenic, linoleic and arachidonic acid
   (C) Stearic, malic and acetic acid
   (D) Linolenic, stearic and cholic acid

10. Aseptic packaging refers to :
    (A) Use of sterile packaging containers
    (B) Heating the food to make it sterile and then pack
    (C) Packaging sterile food in sterile atmosphere in sterile packaging
    (D) Using ultra high temperature for processing

11. The latest indicator organism for proper pasteurisation is :
    (A) Coxiella burnetti (B) Mycobacterium tuberculosis
    (C) Bacillus anthrasis (D) FMD virus

12. Rasagolla is prepared using :
    (A) Paneer (B) Channa
    (C) Khoa (D) Condensed Milk

13. Aseptic packaging is used after which among the following processing method?
    (A) Pasteurisation (B) UHT Pasteurisation
    (C) Freezing (D) Drying

14. The water percentage of cow milk is approximately :
    (A) 80% (B) 90%
    (C) 87% (D) 50%

15. Which among the following practice reduces the occurrence of Mastitis?
    (A) Feeding concentrate (B) Urea molasses lick
    (C) Teat dipping (D) Automatic water bowl

16. Which among the following is used to test fat in milk?
    (A) Lactometer (B) Anemometer
    (C) CRO (D) Milkotester

17. The bacterial culture used to prepare Yoghurt contains Streptococcus thermophilus and
    (A) Lactobacillus bulagaricus (B) Yersinia enterocolitica
    (C) Alcaligenes viscolactis (D) Escherichia coli

18. Which among the following is used to sterilize milk cans in dairies?
    (A) Steam (B) Iodophore solution
    (C) Autoclaving (D) All the above

19. The base material for preparing Shrikhand is :
(A) Chakka (B) Channa
(C) Curd (D) Cheese

20. 'Outlines of Dairy Technology' is written by :
(A) Jagadish Prasad (B) N.S.R. Shastry
(C) Sukumar De (D) Tufail Ahamed

21. The pink colour characteristic of cured meat is due to :
(A) Myoglobin (B) Nitrosyl myoglobin
(C) Haemoglobin (D) Nitrosyl haemochromogen

22. Natural casing for sausage preparation is derived from :
(A) Intestinal submucosa (B) Collagen
(C) Intestinal mucosa (D) Cellulose

23. PSE condition of pork is caused due to :
(A) Short term pre-slaughter stress (B) Chronic stress
(C) Rapid decline of muscle pH (D) Both (A) and (C)

24. The vitamin which is ABSENT in chicken egg :
(A) Vitamin C (B) Vitamin B_{12}
(C) Vitamin A (D) Vitamin E

25. The bacterium known as "terror of the deep" due to the sea food poisoning it causes with the highest fatality rate of any food borne bacterium :
(A) *Salmonella enteritidis* (B) *Vibrio vulnificus*
(C) *Vibrio parahaemolyticus* (D) *Clostridium botulinum*

26. The stunning method recommended for slaughter of adult cattle :
(A) Electric stunning (B) Penetrative captive bolt pistol
(C) Carbon dioxide gas stunning (D) All of the above

27. The dressing percentage for pigs is approximately :
(A) 53% (B) 65%
(C) 75% (D) 88%

28. _________ is used for testing the effectiveness of bleeding of carcass.
(A) Sodium nitrate (B) Malachite green
(C) Sodium ascorbate (D) All of the above

29. The larval nematode worm seen in striated muscle of pigs infecting human beings after ingestion of such infected pork is :
(A) *Trichinella spiralis* (B) *Toxoplasma gondii*
(C) *Tichuristrichiura* (D) *Taenia solium*

30. Pick out the WRONG statement:
(A) The first transgenic cow, "Rosie", produced human protein-enriched milk
(B) Green rot in eggs is mainly caused by *Pseudomonas fluorescens*
(C) Bloom is the term used for preservation of meat using salt
(D) Pork and poultry meat are more susceptible to rancidity as they are richer in unsaturated fatty acids than other meats

31. In a complaint against several accused, if the complainant withdraws his complaint against one accused, the Magistrate can :
(A) Convict that particular accused
(B) Acquit all the accused
(C) Acquit the particular accused against whom the complaint is so withdrawn
(D) Convict all the accused

32. An application for bail under Section 438 Cr.P.C. can be filed before :
(A) Any Court
(B) First Class Magistrate Court/Metropolitan Court
(C) Trial Court
(D) High Court or Court of Session

33. In a trial before a Court of Session, Prosecution shall be conducted by :
(A) Magistrate (B) Public Prosecutor
(C) Amicus Curie (D) Advocate General

34. Private Complaint can be filed before the Court under Section ______ of Cr.P.C.
(A) 190 (B) 191
(C) 195 (D) 313

35. Examination of Complainant by the Magistrate taking cognizance of an offence is not required, if :
(A) He is a public servant (B) He is private complainant
(C) He is a doctor (D) A Court has made the complaint

36. Admissibility of documents procured by illegal means under Indian Evidence Act is:
(A) Admissible
(B) Not Admissible
(C) Admissible if relevant and its genuineness proved
(D) None of these

37. Primary Evidence under Sec.61 of Indian Evidence Act means :
(A) Certified copies of documents
(B) Photostat copies attested by the Gazetted Officer
(C) Original documents produced before the Court
(D) None of these

38. Unlicensed sale of food shall be punishable with:
(A) Imprisonment upto 6 months
(B) Imprisonment upto 6 months and fine upto Rs. 5 lakhs
(C) Fine upto Rs. 2 lakhs
(D) Imprisonment upto 1 year and fine upto Rs. 10 lakhs

39. Death caused due to consumption of any food purchased from a seller, is liable to be compensated with :
(A) Not less than Rs. 5 lakhs (B) Not less than Rs. 10 lakhs
(C) Not exceeding Rs. 3 lakhs (D) Rs. 7 lakhs

40. The maximum penalty to be imposed on a person who sells any food which is not in compliance with the provisions / regulations of Food Safety Act, is :
(A) Rs. 10 lakhs (B) Not Exceeding Rs.2 lakhs
(C) Not Exceeding Rs.5 lakhs (D) Rs.25,000

41. Energy yield per unit weight of food is known as :
(A) Calorific value (B) Energy density
(C) Both (A) and (B) (D) None of these

42. R.Q. of fats is less than carbohydrates because :
(A) Fats have lesser oxygen content (B) Carbohydrates have lesser oxygen content
(C) Fats have higher oxygen content (D) None of these

43. Specific Dynamic Action refers to :
(A) Energy required for physical activity
(B) Increased heat production following intake of food
(C) Extra energy for exercising
(D) Energy requirement by a person for dynamic activites

44. ________ is an essential amino acid.
(A) Aspartic acid (B) Glutamic acid
(C) Proline (D) Threonine

45. Which of the following has the lowest iodine number?
(A) Soybean oil (B) Cotton seed oil
(C) Beef fat (D) Corn oil

46. Scurvy can be cured by the administration of :
(A) Folic acid (B) Glutamic acid
(C) Fumaric acid (D) Ascorbic acid

47. Dietary fibre represents the following nutrient group :
(A) Lipids (B) Carbohydrates
(C) Proteins (D) None of these

48. The one which is not used as a clarifier :
(A) Phosphoric acid (B) Lead nitrate
(C) Phosphotungstic acid (D) Lead acetate

49. Ionisation technique not used in mass spectrometry :
(A) Fast atom bombardment (B) Field desorption
(C) Laser desorption (D) Radiation

50. Inhomogeneity of flow velocities and path lengths around packing particles in column chromatography leads to:
(A) Partition (B) Retention
(C) Eddy diffusion (D) None of these

51. The protective agent used in cryopreservation of bacterial cells :
(A) EDTA (B) DMSO
(C) SDS (D) NADP

52. Staining of specimens using uranyl acetate has been used in :
(A) Atomic force microscope (B) Confocal Scanning Laser Microscope
(C) Transmission Electron Microscope (D) Phase Contrast Microscope

53. Which of the following is a type of food intoxication?
(A) Botulism (B) Salmonellosis
(C) Cholera (D) Gastroenteritis

54. *Ashbya gossypii* is used commercially for the production of :
(A) L-glutamic acid (B) Invertase
(C) Cyanocobolamine (D) Riboflavin

55. Enrichment of lakes due to high concentration of organic nutrients :
(A) Humus formation (B) Biomagnification
(C) Eutrophication (D) Nitrosification

56. The sanitizer commonly used for treatment of drinking water :
(A) Sodium nitrate (B) Sodium hypochlorite
(C) Sodium sorbate (D) Sodium metabisulphite

57. Which of the following is a semi perishable food?
(A) Fish (B) Egg
(C) Milk (D) Potato

58. Temperature used in HTST pasteurization is :
(A) 161°F (B) 145°F
(C) 154°F (D) 175°F

59. Which of the following is not involved in the fermentation of Sauerkraut?
(A) *Leuconostoc mesenteroides* (B) *Lactobacillus plantarum*
(C) *Leuconostocdelbruekii* (D) *Streptococcus faecalis*

60. Enzyme used for the clarification of fruit juice:
(A) Invertase (B) Pectinase
(C) Protease (D) Lipase

61. Tapping and aroma are maturity indices of :
(A) Jack fruit (B) Water melon
(C) Tomato (D) Mango

62. Evaporative cooling system saturated with water is used in :
(A) Onion storage (B) Zero energy cool chamber
(C) Cold stores (D) Irradiation

63. "W" and "O" emulsions are used in:
(A) Storage of fruits and vegetables (B) Field spray of fruits and vegetables
(C) Waxing of fruits and vegetables (D) None of the above

64. The most destructive of all field rats is :
(A) *Mus booduga* (B) *Rattus rattus*
(C) *Rattus norvegicus* (D) *Bandicota bengalensis*

65. Aflatoxin is the mycotoxin produced by :
(A) Aspergillus flavus (B) Fusarium spp.
(C) Claviceps purpurea (D) Aspergillus clavatus

66. Khapra beetle is a serious pest of stored :
(A) Rice (B) Wheat
(C) Pulses (D) Fruits

67. Most widely used chronic poison in rodent control :
(A) Thallium sulphate (B) Barium carbonate
(C) Warfarin (D) Zinc phosphide

68. Callosobruchus chinensis is a storage pest of :
(A) Wheat (B) Rice
(C) Fruits (D) Pulses

69. Commercially the most viable mushroom world over is :
(A) Button mushroom (B) Oyster mushroom
(C) Paddy straw mushroom (D) Milky mushroom

70. The best disinfectant for the empty store is the use of :
(A) DDVP (B) Aluminium phosphide
(C) Malathion (D) Gamma-BHC

71. Temple Entry Proclamation in Travancore issued on :
(A) 12 Nov. 1936 (B) 24 Nov. 1936
(C) 12 Jan. 1936 (D) 24 Jan. 1936

72. Which of the following story was written by Lalithambika Antharjanam?
(A) Mudra (B) Thamarathoni
(C) Gosayi Paranja Katha (D) Marappavakal

73. Revolt of 1857 was started at :
(A) Delhi (B) Meerut
(C) Nepal (D) Kanpur

74. "Kaneerum Kinavum" was the autobiography of :
(A) E.V. Krishnapillai (B) G. Sankarakurup
(C) V.T. Bhattathirippadu (D) Changampuzha

75. Who was the founder of Samathva Samagam?
(A) Ayyan Kali (B) Sree Narayana Guru
(C) Dr.Palpu (D) Vaikunda Swamikal

76. Leader of Bardoli Sathyagraha:
(A) Nehru (B) Sardar Vallabhai Patel
(C) Gandhiji (D) Dr. Ambedkar

77. Who was the first General Secretary of Nair Service Society?
(A) C. Kesavan (B) K. Kelappan
(C) T.K. Madhavan (D) Mannathu Padmanabhan

78. Who was known as the father of Local self Government in India?
(A) Lord Rippon (B) Lord Litton
(C) Lord Minto (D) Lord Dalhousie

79. Who was the founder of Indian National Congress?
(A) Lord Duffrin (B) A.O. Hume
(C) Dadabhai Naoroji (D) Gandhiji

80. Who was known as "Kerala Gandhi"?
(A) A.K. Gopalan (B) M.C. Joseph
(C) K. Kelappan (D) P.K.Chathan Master

81. What is the next number in the series 6, 10, 9, 13, 12, _____?
(A) 15 (B) 6
(C) 16 (D) 11

82. Sum to infinity of the series 1/2 + 1/4 + 1/8 +.....?
(A) 1 (B) 1/4
(C) 2 (D) infinity

83. 2015 September 24 is Monday. After 61 days it will be :
(A) Wednesday (B) Thursday
(C) Tuesday (D) Saturday

84. Fill in the blanks :
Train :Staton : Ship : ________
(A) Sea (B) Harbour
(C) Backwater (D) Anchor

85. Ajith is in the East of Manu and he is also in the north of Akshay. If Raju is in the South of Akshay, then in which direction of Ajith is Raju?
(A) North (B) South
(C) South East (D) South West

86. Synonym of the word 'Nupitals' :
(A) Wedding (B) Death
(C) Birth (D) Disaster

87. Which is the odd one in the following?
(A) 63 (B) 28
(C) 124 (D) 215

88. If the surface area of a cube is 294 cm^2, what is the volume of the cube?
(A) 216 (B) 176
(C) 294 (D) 343

89. If the word 'INSPECTOR' is coded as 987654321, what is the code for 'INSPECTION'?
(A) 987654321 (B) 9876543928
(C) 9876543289 (D) 9876543288

90. If $x/5 = y/3$ then $x + 5 : y + 3 =$:
(A) 3 : 5 (B) 5 : 7
(C) 5 : 3 (D) 7 : 5

91. She accused me __________ poisoning her dog.
(A) of (B) for
(C) with (D) on

92. Pick out the plural form of "hero" :
(A) heros (B) hero
(C) heroes (D) heross

93. Germany is ________ European country.
(A) an (B) a
(C) the (D) no article required

94. Hema ________ one of the best students in the class.
(A) are
(B) has
(C) were
(D) is

95. The place where birds are kept :
(A) zoo
(B) aviary
(C) orchard
(D) aquarium

96. Choose the correctly spelt word :
(A) hypocrite
(B) hyppocrite
(C) hipocrite
(D) hippocrite

97. A Philatelist collects :
(A) coins
(B) clocks
(C) birds
(D) stamps

98. The antonym of "Confess" :
(A) admit
(B) deny
(C) contest
(D) neglect

99. Find out the passive form of the given sentence :
Mary's attitude surprised her.
(A) She were surprised by Mary's attitude
(B) Mary was surprised by her attitude
(C) She was surprised by Mary's attitude
(D)She had been surprised by Mary's attitude

100. Pick out the meaning of the given sentence :
He is high-handed.
(A) He is rich
(B) He behaves arrogantly
(C) He is in a superior position
(D) He is always pleasing

Kerala Food Safety Officer Exam, 2020 [Solved]

Total Questions: 100

Maximum marks: 100

Total time: 1 hr 15 min

1. Freeze drying takes place at
   (A) The triple point
   (B) Below the triple point
   (C) Above the triple point
   (D) At zero degree Celsius

2. Use of several methods like temperature (high or low), control of acidity, control of water activity for preservation of food is known as
   (A) Hurdle technology
   (B) Mixed technology
   (C) Stumbling technology
   (D) Multiple technology

3. Cause and effect diagram is also known as
   (A) Quality circles
   (B) Fish bone diagram
   (C) Five force diagram
   (D) Kaizen diagram

4. The process in which a specially designed hermetic centrifuge is used to separate bacteria and especially the spores formed by specific bacterias trains, from milk is known as
   (A) Sterilization
   (B) Pasteurisation
   (C) Aseptic packaging
   (D) Bactofugation

5. The most common bacterial cultures involved in acidic fermentation are
   (A) *Lactobacillus, Leuconostoc, Lactococcus* and *Streptococcus*
   (B) *Lactococcus, Biûdobacterium, Lactobacillus* and *Leuconostoc*
   (C) *Lactococcus, Rhizopus, Lactococcus* and *Streptococcus*
   (D) *Lactobacillus, Leuconostoc, Lactococcus* and *Aspergillus*

6. Which of the following statements are true?
   1. Foods high in sugar and other solutes dry more slowly.
   2. As drying progresses the concentration of solutes in water increases causing the drying rate to slow.
   3. Water that is most difficult to remove is that is chemically bound in the form of hydrates.
   4. Drying at high pressure occurs at lower temperature.
   (A) 1, 2,3,4
   (B) 1,2,3
   (C) 1,3,4
   (D) 1, 2,4

7. Foods processed using high-pressure technology, gamma irradiation, high electric field pulse and thermosonication are known as

(A) Minimally processed foods
(B) UHT processed foods
(C) Aseptically processed foods
(D) All of the above

8. Food items should be subjected to micro frequencies such that, the dielectric constant is and loss factor is ________

(A) Maximum, minimum
(B) Maximum, maximum
(C) Minimum, minimum
(D) Minimum, maximum

9. In which of the following ways does absorption of gamma radiation takes place?

(A) Photoelectric effect
(B) Compton effect
(C) Pair production
(D) All of the mentioned

10. Which among the following claims is prohibited?

(A) Unsubstantiated claims
(B) Claims of Veg./Non-veg.
(C) Claims of quality
(D) None of the mentioned

11. What is "carryover" principle?

(A) Additives added in the raw materials are not present in the final products
(B) Antioxidant added to oil is present in all oil based products made from it
(C) All of the above
(D) None of the above

12. Difference of Green Tea from Black Tea is that

(A) The oxidation process is omitted
(B) The tealeaves are steamedinapan before rolling to prevent oxidation by enzymes
(C) The oxidation process is omitted and the tea leaves are steamed in a pan before being rolled to prevent oxidation by enzymes
(D) None of the mentioned

13. When a deviation from critical limits happens what should be done?

(A) Documentation of corrective actions
(B) Stop the line and inform the supervisor
(C) Reassess the HACCP plan
(D) All of the above

14. Which type of packaging is appropriate for fruits?

(A) Ethylene absorbers
(B) Oxygen absorbers
(C) Carbon-di-oxide absorbers
(D) Nitrogen producing

15. Which of the following is true about death time curve method to sterilize canned food?

(A) It tells us the time and temperature to sterilize canned food
(B) It tells us about the heat penetration of the container
(C) It tells us about the heat conductivity of the container
(D) All of the mentioned

16. Which method is most energy efficient for making ghee?
(A) Desi method (B) Creamery butter method
(C) Direct cream method (D) Pre-stratification method

17. What will be the overrun, if 400 litre of mix produces 740 litre of ice cream?
(A) 60% (B) 85%
(C) 30% (D) 100%

18. What is the major defect that occurs in UHT milk during storage?
(A) Darkening of colour (B) Age gelation
(C) Cooked flavour (D) Absence of beneficial bacteria

19. During cheddar cheese manufacture, rennet split the kappa-casein at the junction of
(A) Phenylalanine-histidine (B) Methionine-lysine
(C) Histidine-lysine (D) Phenylalanine-methionine

20. UHT processed milk is aseptically packaged at
(A) 5 °C (B) 10°C
(C) 20°C (D) 40°C

21. The usual method of stunning cattle is by using
(A) Captive bolt pistol (B) Electrical stunning
(C) CO_2 an aesthesia (D) None of the above

22. Which Vitamin is not available in egg?
(A) Vitamin A (B) Vitamin B
(C) Vitamin C (D) Vitamin D

23. A meat borne bacterial infection
(A) Taeniasis (B) Toxoplasmosis
(C) Sarcocystis (D) Salmonellosis

24. A cured meat product
(A) Sausage (B) Bacon
(C) Keema (D) Cutlet

25. The method of preservation of egg using sodium silicate
(A) Thermal processing (B) Water glass method
(C) Lime sealing (D) Oil coating

26. The certified copies may be produced in proof of the contents of which document?
(A) All kind sof documents (B) Private documents
(C) Public documents (D) Government documents

27. 'Consumer' under the Food Safety and Standards Act, 2006 is the
    (A) Person who consumes food
    (B) Person and family who consume food
    (C) Person who purchases and receives the food
    (D) Person and families who purchases and receives food

28. The head office of the Food Safety and Standards Authority of India is at
    (A) Mumbai (B) Delhi
    (C) Kolkata (D) Kochi

29. The enactment of Information Technology Act, 2000 resulted in the introduction of which provision under Indian Evidence Act, 1872?
    (A) S.65A (B) S.64A
    (C) S.63A (D) S.62A

30. Who is responsible for the inspection of food business, drawing and sending samples for food analysis under Food Safety and Standards Act, 2006?
    (A) Commissioner of Food Safety (B) Food Analyst
    (C) Food Safety Officer (D) Live Stock Inspector

31. Which of the following is correct?
    (A) The accused cannot file written statements under S.233Cr.P.C. in support of his defence.
    (B) S.250Cr.P.C.empowers the magistrate to discharge an accused in a warrant case instituted otherwise than on a police report.
    (C) In a summary trial under S.235Cr.P.C.the maximum period of imprisonment that can be imposed is two years.
    (D) The bail bond executed for the appearance before the higher court under S. 437 Cr.P.C. shall be five years.

32. The magistrate can take cognizance of offence upon
    (A) Receiving information through telephone or e-mail
    (B) A police report
    (C) Information received from a police officer
    (D) All of the above

33. Under S.439Cr.P.C., which court has the power to release any person on bail and by a subsequent order cause him to be rearrested?
    (A) High Court (B) Session Court
    (C) Both High Court and Sessions Court (D) Magistrate Court and Sessions Court

34. The High Court may confer on any magistrate vested with the powers of a magistrate of the second class power to try summarily any offence which is punishable with imprisonment for a term not exceeding
    (A) 6 months (B) 3 months
    (C) 1 year (D) 7 years

35. Under S.374 Cr.P.C. who can file appeal to the Supreme Court?
(A) Any person convicted on atrial held by a High Court initsextra ordinary original criminal jurisdiction
(B) The prosecution which could not succeed in the trial in High Court
(C) Both A) and B)
(D) None of the above

36. Any person who manufactures for sale or distribute any article of substandard food for consumption is liable to the extend of
(A) 2.5 lakhs rupees and 6 months imprisonment
(B) 2.5 lakhs rupees only
(C) 5 lakhs of rupees and 6 months imprisonment
(D) 5 lakhs rupees

37. The Food Safety Appellate Tribunal shall consists of
(A) 5 members (B) 3 members
(C) 1 member (D) Any of the above

38. The defences which may be allowed in prosecution under the Food Safety and Standards Act is under
(A) S.78 (B) S.79
(C) S.81 (D) S.80

39. Where in a case the sample container received by the Food Analystis found to be in broken condition, he shall
(A) Inform the designated officer within seven days
(B) Inform the designated officer within reasonable period of time
(C) Inform the commissioner within seven days
(D) Inform the commissioner within reasonable period of time

40. The secondary evidence is defined under which provision of Indian Evidence Act?
(A) S.66 (B) S.44
(C) S.36 (D) S.63

41. In which of the following separation techniques the separation is based on the net charge of the molecule?
(A) Affinity chromatography (B) Ion exchange chromatography
(C) Molecular exclusion chromatography (D) Isopyenie centrifugation

42. An example for triose is
(A) Glucose (B) Ribulose
(C) Xylulose (D) Glyceraldehyde

43. The exoskeleton of insects (chitin) is composed of
(A) N-Acetylglucosamine
(B) N-Acetyl muramic acid
(C) N-Acetylgalactosamine
(D) Glucose-6-phosphate

44. Of the following, which amino acid is an imino acid?
(A) Histidine
(B) Glutamic acid
(C) Proline
(D) Tyrosine

45. The proteolytic enzyme trypsin, hydrolyses the peptide bonds in which
(A) Amino group is contributed either by lysine orarginine
(B) Carbonyl function is contributed either by lysine orarginine
(C) Carbonyl function is contributed either by phenylalanine or tyrosine
(D) Amino group is contributed either by phenylalanine or tyrosine

46. Which of the following is not an antioxidant?
(A) Vit.C
(B) Vit.E
(C) Carotenes
(D) Vit.B6

47. Iodine number of fatty acids denotes its
(A) Degree of unsaturation
(B) Chain length
(C) Molecular weight
(D) Solubility in water

48. Cold Sterilization means perseveration of food by
(A) Sterilizing at –179°C
(B) Radiation
(C) Sterilizing at 0°C
(D) Lyophylization

49. In humans the basal metabolic rate accounts for about______ percentage of the daily calorie expenditure.
(A) 60–75
(B) 40–55
(C) 25–40
(D) 80 –90

50. The Respiratory Quotient (RQ) is the ratio of
(A) O_2 consumed/CO_2 eliminated
(B) H_2O consumed/CO_2 eliminated
(C) CO_2 eliminated/O_2 consumed
(D) CO_2 eliminated/H_2O consumed

51. Biological Value of a protein is influenced by
(A) Amino acid composition
(B) Vitamin and mineral content
(C) Preparation (cooking)
(D) All the above

52. The absorption maxima λ_{max} of a compound is dependent on
(A) Structure of the compound
(B) pH of the solvent in which the compound exist
(C) The polarity of the solvent
(D) All the above

53. The purpose of guard column in HPLC systems is to
(A) Protect the peristaltic pump
(B) Protect the main column
(C) Protect the in jection port
(D) Protect the detector

54. All free radicals have_____in the irorbitals.
(A) Paired valence electron
(B) Unpaired valence electrons
(C) No valence electron
(D) None of the above

55. Of the following which is not an artificial sweetener?
(A) Saccharin
(B) Sodium cyclamate
(C) Butylated hydroxyanisole
(D) Acesulfame

56. Which is mordant in Grams staining?
(A) Crystal Violet
(B) Safranin
(C) Alcohol
(D) Iodine

57. The immersion oil used in microscopy will
(A) Decrease the numerical aperture
(B) Increase the refractive index
(C) Decrease the refractive index
(D) None of the above

58. Aflatoxins are
(A) Produced by certain fungi
(B) Cancer causing agent
(C) Causes immuno suppression
(D) All the above

59. Botulinum toxins are
(A) Neurotoxic
(B) Teratogen
(C) Carcinogenic
(D) Mutagen

60. MSA (Mannitol Salt Agar) is generally used for the detection of
(A) *E. Coli*
(B) *Staphylococcus aureus*
(C) *Bacillus sp.*
(D) *Aspergillus niger*

61. Enzyme used in fruit juice clarification is
(A) Protease
(B) Trypsin
(C) Cellulose
(D) Pectinase

62. Rotating Biological contactors are employed for
(A) Primary treatment of wastewater
(B) Secondary treatment of wastewater
(C) RBC isolation
(D) Solid waste management

63. This is not a method of enzyme immobilization
(A) Encapsulation
(B) Adsorption
(C) Nanomaterial immobilization
(D) PAGE

64. HACCP stands
(A) Health Analysis and Critical Control Point
(B) Hazard Analysis and Critical Care Point
(C) Hazard Analysis and Crucial Control Point
(D) Hazard Analysis and Critical Control Point

65. Which GM crop is approved in India?
(A) Bt Corn (B) Bt Brinjal
(C) Bt Cotton (D) GM Tomato

66. The trap which is used widely to kill rice field rats is
(A) Snap trap (B) Remote triggered trap
(C) Pot trap (D) Automatic trap

67. A dull hollow sound when tapped is the maturity index of______crop.
(A) Papaya (B) Pineapple
(C) Sapota (D) Watermelon

68. Bheemaisa high yielding variety of______mushroom.
(A) Paddy straw mushroom (B) Button mushroom
(C) Oyster mushroom (D) White milky mushroom

69. A chemical safely sprayed on bags of stored grains in godowns
(A) Carbosulfan (B) Malathion
(C) Dimethoate (D) Quinal phos

70. Which of the following is not an advantage of blanching?
(A) For precooling (B) To preserve colour
(C) To preserve flavor (D) To inactivate enzymes

71. Who among the following was the Anglo-Indian representative in the Indian Constituent Assembly?
(A) Morris Johns (B) Frank Anthony
(C) Sardar Vallabha Bhai Patel (D) K. M. Munshi

72. Which Article of the Indian Constitution deals with Right to Life?
(A) Art.–14 (B) Art.–19
(C) Art.–20 (D) Art.–21

73. Who among the following is returning officer for the election of President of India?
(A) Secretary General of Lok Sabha (B) Chief Election Commissioner
(C) Chief Justice of India (D) Prime Minister of India

74. What is the subject matter of Article 40 of Indian Constitution?
(A) Uniform Civil Code
(B) Prohibition
(C) Right to Education
(D) Panchayati Raj

75. By which Amendment Secularism in corporated in the Preamble of Indian Constitution?
(A) 24th
(B) 74th
(C) 42nd
(D) 44th

76. Which Article of Indian Constitution deals with Grama Sabha?
(A) Article 243
(B) Article 248
(C) Article 233
(D) None of the above

77. Which among the following are in the centre list of 7th Schedule of Indian Constitution?
(A) Markets and fairs
(B) Insurance
(C) Taxes on Profession
(D) Banking
(A) 1 and 2
(B) 1 and 3
(C) 2 and 4
(D) 3 and 4

78. In which year Balwant Rai Mehta Committee was appointed?
(A) 1947
(B) 1957
(C) 1967
(D) 1987

79. Identify the subject matter of the second chapter of the Indian Constitution.
(A) Citizenship
(B) Union and State
(C) Fundamental Rights
(D) Executive

80. Which among the following Act is related to Article 17?
(A) Nirbhaya Act, 2013
(B) Protection of Civil Rights Act in 1976
(C) Armed Forces (Special Powers) Act,1958
(D) Citizenship Amendment Act, 2019
(A) 1 and 2
(B) 2 only
(C) 3 only
(D) 3 and 4

81. Which among the following pairs of months will have the same calendar?
(A) April – November
(B) January – October
(C) July – October
(D) June – August

82. The difference between 75% of a number and 20% of the same number is 378.4. What is 40% of that number?
(A) 275.2
(B) 274
(C) 267.2
(D) 266

83. Neha walked 9 m in the East, then she turned to her right and walked 4 m. Again she turned to her left and moved 3m.Then she turned to her left and walked 9 m. How far is she and in which direction from the starting point?

(A) 13 m, South–West
(B) 13 m, North –East
(C) 15 m, North–East
(D) 15 m, South –West

84. If eye = ice, lips= rose and brows = black, what is coded as 'forehead'?

(A) Sindoor
(B) Flower
(C) Jasmine
(D) Frontier

85. A committee of 3 members is to be selected out of 3 men and 2 women. What is the probability that the committee has at least one woman?

(A) 1/10
(B) 9/20
(C) 9/20
(D) 1/20

86. Vaunt : Flaunt : : Disparate :?

(A) Similar
(B) Homogeneous
(C) Contrast
(D) Alike

87. What will be the next term in the following–DCXW, FEVU, HGTS,?

(A) AKPO
(B) ABYZ
(C) JIRQ
(D) LMRS

88. In how many different way scan the letters of the word 'PUNCTUAL' be arranged?

(A) 64
(B) 40320
(C) 960
(D) 20160

89. Find out the wrong term in the series.

2, 3, 4, 4, 6, 8, 9, 12,16

(A) 9
(B) 12
(C) 16
(D) 8

90. In a certain code if C = 3 and SCHOOL= 12, then LAMB = ?

(A) 28
(B) 12
(C) 7
(D) 8

91. My brother _______ the answer to the question.

(A) is know
(B) know
(C) knowing
(D) knows

92. I think I will buy these shirts._________me really well.

(A) They were fitting
(B) They fit
(C) They are fitting
(D) They have fit

93. Where ______ the book?

(A) did you keep
(B) did you kept
(C) kept you
(D) None of these

94. At five o'clock yesterday evening I______for the bus.

(A) were waiting (B) was waiting
(C) wait (D) waiting

95. Anne______ill for two weeks. She is still in hospital.

(A) was (B) had been
(C) is (D) has been

96. How did you come?______bus?

(A) in (B) on
(C) through (D) by

97. Choose the correct sentence from the following.

(A) I am not agree with what you say (B) Heisdoinga course in linguistics
(C) Children makes a lot of noise (D) He speak English well

98. Which of the following is the opposite of diligent?

(A) active (B) smart
(C) hard working (D) lazy

99. What is the one word substitute for one who is not sure about God's existence?

(A) Agnostic (B) Atheist
(C) Theist (D) None of these

100. What does the idiom kick the bucket mean?

(A) to die (B) to hit someone with a bucket
(C) to cry (D) None of these

ANSWERS

Kerala Food Safety Officer Exam, 2020

1. B	21. A	41. B	61. D	81. B
2. A	22. C	42. D	62. B	82. A
3. B	23. D	43. A	63. D	83. B
4. D	24. B	44. C	64. D	84. D
5. A	25. B	45. B	65. C	85. C
6. B	26. C	46. D	66. C	86. C
7. A	27. D	47. A	67. D	87. C
8. C	28. B	48. B	68. D	88. D
9. D	29. A	49. A	69. B	89. A
10. A	30. C	50. C	70. A	90. C
11. B	31. A	51. D	71. B	91. D
12. C	32. B	52. D	72. D	92. B
13. D	33. C	53. B	73. A	93. A
14. A	34. A	54. B	74. D	94. B
15. D	35. A	55. C	75. C	95. D
16. D	36. D	56. D	76. A	96. D
17. B	37. C	57. B	77. C	97. B
18. B	38. D	58. D	78. B	98. D
19. D	39. A	59. A	79. A	99. A
20. C	40. D	60. A	80. C	100. A

Manipur Food Safety Officer, 2014
[Unsolved]

Maximum Marks: 300

Total time: 3 hrs

Note: **Question from 1 to 150 are from Food Technology. Question from 151 to 200 are from general studies.**

1. Mold inhibitor used in bread is:
   (A) Sodium/Calcium propionate (B) Sodium chloride
   (C) Calcium carbonate (D) None of these
2. Who developed the process of canning:
   (A) Nicolas Appert (B) Louis Pasteur
   (C) Norman Borlaug (D) Walter Hesse
3. Nisin is used as:
   (A) Antimicrobial agent (B) Emulsifier
   (C) Stabilizer (D) Sweetener
4. Iodized salt contains iodine in the form of:
   (A) I_2 (B) KIO_3
   (C) KI (D) NaI
5. The first synthetic sweetening agent used was:
   (A) Saccharine (B) Cyclamates
   (C) Aspartame (D) Sucralose
6. Jam, jellies and preserves can be preserved by adding sugar at concentration of:
   (A) 65% (B) 70%
   (C) 40% (D) 30%
7. After drying moisture content in vegetables should be:
   (A) 6-8% (B) 8-10%
   (C) 10-15% (D) 15-20%
8. Agar-agar is used as:
   (A) Stabilizer and thickener (B) Antibiotic
   (C) Colour ingagent (D) Nutrient supplement
9. Frozen storage is generally operated at temperature of:
   (A) –0°C (B) –18°C
   (C) –50°C (D) –60°C

10. Toco pherol is an example of:
(A) Anticaking agent
(B) Antioxidant
(C) Flavouring agent
(D) None of these

11. Bitterness in colocasia is due to:
(A) Calcium oxalate
(B) Calcium chloride
(C) Potassium oxalate
(D) Calcium carbonate

12. In high temperature short time method of pasteurization, milk is heated at temperature:
(A) 72°C for 15 seconds
(B) 62°C for 15 seconds
(C) 72° C for 30 minutes
(D) 62°C for 30 minutes

13. Butylated Hydroxyanisole (BHA) is:
(A) Chelating agent
(B) Antioxidant
(C) Stablizer
(D) Emulsion

14. BIS Headquarters is situated in:
(A) Pune
(B) Chennai
(C) New Delhi
(D) Ajmer

15. Germination affects nutritive value of legumes by:
(A) Increase in vitamin C content
(B) Decrease in tryps in inhibitor activity
(C) Increase in enzyme activity
(D) All of these

16. Pineapple variety suitable for canning is:
(A) Queen
(B) Kew
(C) Mauritius
(D) Cayenne

17. Richest source of Riboflavin is :
(A) Papaya
(B) Mango
(C) Bael
(D) Karonda

18. Which of the following is non-Climacteric type of fruit?
(A) Pineapple
(B) Litchi
(C) Grape
(D) All of these

19. Emission of Ethylene during transportation of cut flowers causes a disorder called:
(A) Bud opening
(B) Sleepiness
(C) Bentneck
(D) Calyx splitting

20. Which is the precursor of Ethylene?
(A) Tryptophane
(B) Methionine
(C) ABA
(D) IAA

21. Cauliflower curds can be stored for a month at:
(A) 0°C with 85-90% RH (B) 15°C with 60-80% RH
(C) 15 °C with 60-65% RH (D) 20 °C with 50-70% RH

22. For curing, sweet potato are kept for 10 days at:
(A) 25°C and 85% RH (B) 40°C and 70% RH
(C) 80°C and 30% RH (D) 30°C and 80% RH

23. Tomato fruits for canning are harvested at:
(A) Mature green stage (B) Red ripe stage
(C) Immature green stage (D) Half-ripe/pink stage

24. Which chemical is used for controlling sprouting of onions in storage?
(A) Maleic Hydrazide (MH) (B) Ethylene (C_2H_4)
(C) GA (D) All of these

25. For Low Sugar content, potato tubers are stored at:
(A) 5°C (B) 10°C
(C) 15°C (D) 20°C

26. For longer storage of cucumber fruits, the temperature should be:
(A) 5°C (B) 10°C
(C) 20°C (D) 25°C

27. The limiting Amino acid in green vegetables is:
(A) Arginine (B) Lysine
(C) Methionine (D) Tryptophan

28. Which is the staple vegetable in Indian diet?
(A) Tomato (B) Cauliflower
(C) Potato (D) Chilli

29. Which bean is used for extraction of gum?
(A) Broad bean (B) Cluster bean
(C) French bean (D) Hyacinth bean

30. Chillies are rich source of:
(A) Vitamin A (B) Vitamin C
(C) Vitamin A and C (D) Vitamin E

31. Vegetables are subjected to drying after:
(A) Sulfuring (B) Sulphitation
(C) Blanching (D) None of these

32. Yellow coloured vegetables are rich source of:
(A) Vitamin A (B) Vitamin B
(C) Vitamin C (D) Vitamin D

33. Toddy from coconut is prepared by :
(A) Deep Frying (B) Fermentation
(C) Hydrogenation (D) Oxidation

34. According to FPO, the maximum limit of SO_2 allowed in squashes and cordials is:
(A) 350 ppm (B) 500 ppm
(C) 1000 ppm (D) 600 ppm

35. The toxicity of SO_2 increases at:
(A) Low temperature (B) High temperature
(C) Moderate temperature (D) No effect of temperature

36. Concentration of SO_2 in concentrated juice is:
(A) 500 ppm (B) 1000 ppm
(C) 1500 ppm (D) 350 ppm

37. Enzyme responsible for converting pectin into pectic acid is:
(A) Pectinase (B) Proto-peclinase
(C) Pectic Methyl Esterase (PME) (D) Poly Galucturonase

38. The term 'Climacteric' was first used by:
(A) Gane (1934) (B) Kidd and West (1927)
(C) Cruess (1912) (D) Bleekar (1929)

39. O_2 requirement for Apple storage in Controlled Atmosphere (CA) is:
(A) 2% (B) 3%
(C) 5% (D) 7%

40. Storage temperature for Asparagus is:
(A) 0-5°C (B) 5-7°C
(C) 7-11°C (D) 10-15°C

41. Vegetable which is not blanched before drying:
(A) Cauliflower (B) Palak
(C) Onion (D) Tomato

42. Moisture content in dried vegetable is:
(A) 2% (B) 3%
(C) 5% (D) 6%

43. Vitamin which is not found in Fruits and Vegetables:
(A) Vitamin A (B) Vitamin B_1
(C) Vitamin B_6 (D) Vitamin B_{12}

44. Best maturity index of orange is:
(A) TSS (B) Sugar%
(C) Acid% (D) Brix:acid ratio

45. Bacteria which is used to absorb ethylene from storage chamber is:
(A) *Agro bacterium* (B) *Mycobacterium*
(C) *Bacillus* (D) *Azotobacter*

46. Toughening effect on canned bean is due to:
(A) K (B) Ca
(C) S (D) None of these

47. Agriculture Produce (Grading and Marketing) Act (1937) is also:
(A) PFA Act (B) FPO Act
(C) Agmark Act (D) ISI Act

48. The term "three quarterful or full three quarter" is used to denote fruit maturity in:
(A) Banana (B) Mango
(C) Tomato (D) Pineapple

49. During controlled atmospheric storage composition of which of the following set of gases is controlled:
(A) $O_2 + N_2$ (B) $CO_2 + N_2$
(C) $C_2H_4 + N_2$ (D) $CO_2 + O_2$

50. At which pH fruits and vegetables are divided into acidic and non-acidic for thermal processing:
(A) 4.5 (B) 5.5
(C) 6.5 (D) 7.5

51. In pre-cooling, water is mostly removed by:
(A) Convection (B) Conduction
(C) Radiation (D) None of these

52. Albinism is an important physiological disorder of:
(A) Plum (B) Peach
(C) Strawberry (D) Cherry

53. Calliper grade is the maturity measurement for:
(A) Apple (B) Mango
(C) Banana (D) Pineapple

54. Formation of abscission layer is maturity index of:
(A) Tomato (B) Leafy vegetables
(C) Melons (D) Onion

55. What is the maturity index for Avocado?
(A) Sugar content (B) Acid content
(C) TSS (D) Oil content

56. Which of the following is biodegradable plastic?
(A) Poly propylene (B) LDPE
(C) Polythene (D) Polyhydroxy butyrate

57. As fruits mature, the specific gravity will:
(A) Increase (B) Decrease
(C) Remains constant (D) None of these

58. 'Solidity' is the maturity index for:
(A) Root vegetables (B) Seed vegetables
(C) Leafy vegetables (D) Cucurbits

59. Which of the following plant hormone is considered as ripen?
(A) Cytokinin (B) GA_3
(C) Ethylene (D) IAA

60. Maximum density of water is at a temperature of:
(A) 0°C (B) 4°C
(C) 4°C (D) –7°C

61. Guava fruit is botanically known as:
(A) Drupe (B) Sorosis
(C) Berry (D) Pome

62. In onion pink colour is due to:
(A) Anthocyanin (B) Carotene
(C) Xanthophyll (D) Quercitin

63. Secondary metabolites:
(A) are essential to microbe function
(B) are by-products of metabolism that are not important to microbe function
(C) are products that require additional processing before they can be packaged
(D) are harvested during the exponential phase of growth

64. Hen and Chicken disorder is associated with:
(A) Mango (B) Tomato
(C) Grapes (D) Guava

65. The membrane lipid hypothesis was given by:
(A) Kidd & West (B) James Harrison
(C) Raison & Lyons (D) Graham & Patterson

66. The point at which the dried products just become lumpy is known as?
(A) Danger Point (B) Saturated Point
(C) Critical Point (D) Safety Point

67. What is the percentage of sugars in Honey?
(A) 42% (B) 82%
(C) 65% (D) 62%

68. Fungus which mostly grown on grapes:
(A) *Geotrichum* (B) *Penicillium*
(C) *Botrytis* (D) *Colletotrichum*

69. Vitamin D is chemically known as:
(A) Retinol (B) Cobalamin
(C) Calciferol (D) Tocopherol

70. Lye peeling is done at a temperature of:
(A) 75°C (B) 84°C
(C) 93°C (D) 105°C

71. Which of the following is associated with 'browning' disorder?
(A) Apple (B) Cabbage
(C) Cauliflower (D) Citrus

72. What is the threshold level of ethylene in fruit and vegetables?
(A) 0.01 μL/L (B) 0.02 μL/L
(C) 0.03 μL/L (D) 0.04 μL/L

73. Which of the following is a rapid precooling method?
(A) Forced air cooling (B) Hydro Cooling
(C) Vacuum Cooling (D) Evaporative Cooling

74. In cucumber, chilling- injury symtoms occur at:
(A) < 7°C (B) 7°C
(C) 10°C (D) >10°C

75. Degreening is not applicable in:
(A) Banana (B) Guava
(C) Mango (D) Citrus

76. Under normal conditions Orchid can be stored upto 2 weeks at:
(A) 2-4°C (B) 5-7°C
(C) 7.5-10°C (D) >10°C

77. What is the operating principle behind oven drying for determining moisture content of foods?
(A) Colour change is measured
(B) Loss of weight represents loss of water
(C) Change in refractive index is measured
(D) Change in light absorbance is measured

78. Which of the following packages is an example of aseptic packaging?
(A) Tetra Pak drinking boxes
(B) Paper bag
(C) Milk carton
(D) Plastic bread bag

79. Which of the following ingredients in chocolate milk comes from seaweed?
(A) Carrageenan
(B) Cocoa
(C) Sucrose
(D) Glucose

80. Which microorganism is commonly associated with fecal contamination?
(A) *Clostridium botulinum*
(B) *Campylobacter jejuni*
(C) *Bacillus cereus*
(D) *Trichinella spiralis*

81. Which of the following analytical methods can be used to distinguish flavour compounds?
(A) Hydrometry
(B) Near infrared spectroscopy
(C) Polarimetry
(D) Gas chromatography

82. Which of the following microorganisms cannot tolerate oxygen?
(A) *Clostridium botulinum*
(B) *Staphylococcus aureus*
(C) *Penicillium roquefortii*
(D) *E. coli*

83. Which of the following methods is a quick test for sugar content during the early stages of the brewing process for beer?
(A) Hydrometry
(B) Babcock test
(C) Wet ashing
(D) Soxhlet extraction

84. Which of the following processing methods involves heating foods at high temperatures for short periods of time in order to reduce the risk of food poisoning?
(A) Blanching
(B) Ohmic heating
(C) Irradiation
(D) Pasteurization

85. Which of the following does not have antimicrobial activity?
(A) Chlorophyll
(B) Organic acids
(C) Spice extracts
(D) Hydrogen peroxide

86. What is the percent of acetic acid in commercially available vinegar?
(A) 2%
(B) 4%
(C) 6%
(D) 10%

87. Which of the following is not an intrinsic factor in food spoilage?
(A) pH
(B) Moisture
(C) Temperature
(D) Available nutrients

88. Lyophilization is synonymous with:
(A) Freeze-drying (B) Pasteurization
(C) Filteration (D) Spoilage

89. Antibiotics tend to be:
(A) Primary metabolites (B) Secondary metabolites
(C) Tertiary metabolites (D) Quaternary metabolites

90. Amino acids are used as food additives for which of the following reasons?
(A) As natural antibiotics (B) As natural growth inhibitors
(C) For nutritive purposes (D) As antioxidants

91. Grinding and mixing of foods such as sausage and hamburger:
(A) Increase the food surface area
(B) Alter cellular structure
(C) Distribute contaminating microorganisms throughtout the food
(D) All of the above

92. Louis Pasteur established the modern era of food microbiology in 1857 when he showed that microorganisms cause ______ spoilage:
(A) Beer (B) Wine
(C) Juice (D) Milk

93. Despite efforts to eliminate spoilage organisms during canning, sometimes canned foods are spoiled. This may be due to:
(A) Spoilage before canning
(B) Underprocessing during canning
(C) Leakage of contaminated water through can seams during cooling
(D) All of the above.

94. The effectiveness of many chemical preservatives depends primarily on the food:
(A) Temperature (B) pH.
(C) Water content (D) Acidity.

95. Which type of fermentation is used to produce yogurt?
(A) Mesophilic (B) Thermophilic
(C) Therapeutic (D) Yeast-lactic fermentations

96. Which of the following refers to the addition of microorganisms to the diet in order to provide health benefits beyond basic nutritive value?
(A) Antibiotics (B) Prebiotics
(C) Probiotics (D) All the above

97. Moisture content in intermediate moisture food (IMF) is:
(A) 10-20% (B) 20-25%
(C) 20-40% (D) 15-50%

98. Deep frying of potato chips lead to generation of carcinogen:
(A) Acrylamide (B) Acefamide
(C) Formamide (D) Antioxidants

99. Which of the amino acid is not essential in diet:
(A) Tyrosine (B) Tryptophan
(C) Phenylalanine (D) Lysine

100. Material suitable for micro-wave heating:
(A) EPP (B) LDPE
(C) PET (D) DAIP

101. Baking powder contains:
(A) NaCl (B) $NaHCO_3$
(C) Na-benzoate (D) NaI

102. FSSAI stands for:
(A) Food Safety and Standards Authority of India
(B) Food Security and Standards Authority of India
(C) Food Safety and Security Authority of India
(D) Food Safety and Standards Agency of India

103. Which one of the following is not a food preservative?
(A) Acetic acid (B) Propionic acid
(C) Butyric acid (D) Sorbic acid

104. Which out of the following is a non reducing sugar?
(A) Fructose (B) Glucose
(C) Mannose (D) Sucrose

105. In cooking oils, the antioxidant added to prevent rancidity is:
(A) Tocopherol (B) Ascorbic acid
(C) BHT (D) TBHQ

106. Most common toxicogenic spoilage in stored groundnuts is:
(A) *Aspergillus flavus* (B) *Aspergillus niger*
(C) *Aspergillus oryzae* (D) *Aspergillus albus*

107. Sauerkraut is the fermented product of:
(A) Cabbage (B) Turnip
(C) Raddish (D) Beetroot

108. Argemone oil is used to adultrate:
(A) Mustard oil (B) Milk
(C) Tea (D) Milk

109. "C" enamel cans are used for:
(A) High acidic food (B) Non-acidic foods
(C) Medium-acidic foods (D) Fat rich foods

110. AGMARK was promulgated in:
(A) 1937 (B) 1954
(C) 1935 (D) 2009

111. Cold test of fat is a measure of:
(A) Freezing point of oil
(B) Viscosity of oil at temperature just above its freezing point
(C) Resistance of oil to crystallization
(D) Total saturated fat

112. For manufacturing of pasta, wheat variety used is:
(A) Soft wheat (B) Hard wheat
(C) Durum wheat (D) White wheat

113. Which of the following is produced with the combination of apoenzyme and coenzyme?
(A) Holoenzyme (B) Enzyme substrate complex
(C) Prosthetic group (D) Enzyme product complex

114. The enzyme which hydrolyses starch to maltose is:
(A) Protease (B) Amylase
(C) Lactase (D) Maltase

115. Enzymes having slightly different molecules structure but performing identical activity are:
(A) Apoenzymes (B) Isoenzymes
(C) Holoenzymes (D) Coenzymes

116. Ribozyme is:
(A) RNA without phosphate (B) RNA with sugar
(C) RNA with enzyme activity (D) RNA with extra phosphate

117. Human insulin is being commercially produced from a transgenic species of:
(A) *Escherichia* (B) *Saccharomyces*
(C) *Rhizobium* (D) *Mycobacterium*

118. Example of a typical homopolysaccharide is:
(A) Lignin (B) Suberin
(C) Inulin (D) Starch

119. Which of the following is not a conjugated protein?
(A) Peptone (B) Phosphoprotein
(C) Lipoprotein (D) Chromoprotein

120. The "Repeating Unit" of glycogen is:
(A) Fructose (B) Mannose
(C) Glucose (D) Galactose

121. The catalytic efficiency of two different enzymes can be compared by the:
(A) Molecular size of the enzyme (B) The pH optimum value
(C) The Km value (D) Formation of the product

122. High value of BOD (Biochemical Oxygen Demand) shows:
(A) Water is normal (B) Water is highly polluted
(C) Water is less polluted (D) None of these

123. Which of the following is fermentation process?
(A) Batch process (B) Continuous process
(C) Both a and b (D) None of these

124. Who showed that *Sacchaaromyces cerevisiae* causes fermentation forming products such as beer and buttermilk?
(A) Louis Pasteur (B) Alexander Fleming
(C) Selman Waksman (D) Schatz

125. A bioreactor is:
(A) Hybridoma
(B) Culture containing radioactive isotopes
(C) Culture for synthesis of new chemicals
(D) Fermentation tank

126. Humulin is:
(A) Carbohydrate (B) Protein
(C) Fat (D) Antibiotics

127. Enzyme immobilisation is:
(A) Conversion of an active enzyme into inactive form
(B) Providing enzyme with protective covering
(C) Changing a soluble enzyme into insoluble state
(D) Changing pH so that enzyme is not able to carry out its function

128. Vinegar is obtained from molasses with the help of:
(A) *Rhizopus* (B) *Acetobacter*
(C) Yeast (D) Both b and c

129. Which of the following statements is incorrect regarding Gram negative bacteria:
(A) Cell wall has a thin peptidoglycan layer (B) Cell wall lipid content is very low
(C) Lipopolysaccharide layer is present (D) All of these
(Peptidoglycan is a polymer of sugars and amino acids that forms a mesh-like layer outside the plasma membrane of most bacteria, forming the cell wall)

130. Common food poisoning microbes are:
(A) *Clostridium* and *Salmonella* (B) *Clostridium* and *E.coli*
(C) *E.coli* and *Salmonella* (D) *Clostridium* and *Streptococcus*

131. Clostridium perfingens poisoning is associated with:
(A) Meat products (B) Vegetables
(C) Canned foods (D) Fish products

132. Salmonellosis involves:
(A) An enterotoxin and exotoxin (B) An enterotoxin and cytotoxin
(C) An exotoxin and cytotoxin (D) A cytotoxin only

133. The lipid with the lowest energy value for human nutrition is:
(A) Cardiolipin (B) Olestra
(C) Margarine (D) Olive oil

134. One serving of Cheddar cheese (28g) provides ______% of the RDA of calcium:
(A) 10 (B) 50
(C) 75 (D) 20

135. Which of the following is a Class II poduct?
(A) Frozen desert (B) Butter
(C) Fluid milk (D) Cheese

136. Class IV milk includes milk used to...
(A) Produce hard cheese and cream cheese (B) Fluid Milk
(C) Fluid cream and cottage cheese (D) Butter and any product in dried form

137. A food must contain less than _______ grams of fat per serving to be considered a low fat food:
(A) 8 (B) 6
(C) 3 (D) 7

138. _______ is a protein in milk that contains all the essential amino acids:
(A) Casein (B) Gluten
(C) a and b both (D) Whey protein

139. ______ is a defect in milk that is described as tasting papery:
(A) Bitter (B) Flat
(C) Oxidized (D) Salty

140. ________ is the general name for a class of bacteria that causes mastitis in dairy cattle:
(A) *Lactobacilus* (B) *E.coli*
(C) *Staphylococcus* (D) *Lactococcus*

141. Most UHT pasteurized milk has a shelf life of _____ days:
(A) 10 (B) 120
(C) 180 (D) 50

142. During malting, barley and other grains are broken down by:
(A) Heating to 95°C (B) Lagering
(C) Amylases (D) Yeasts

143. Milk fermentation to produce cheese is done initially by inoculating with:
(A) *Saccharomyces cerevisiae*
(B) *Streptococcus lactis and Lactobacillus ssp.*
(C) *Acetobacter and Gluconobacter*
(D) *Lactobacillus bulgaricus and Streptococcus thermophilus*

144. Nitrates maintain the red color of preserved meats and:
(A) Are among the most widely used preservatives
(B) Inhibit germination of botulism spores
(C) Maintain a high osmotic pressure to kill microorganisms
(D) Prevent mold

145. Salting, as a preservative:
(A) Retards growth of Staphylococcus aureus
(B) Plasmolyzes bacteria and fungi
(C) Is used to prevent growth of halophiles
(D) All of the above

146. In batch fermentation:
(A) Substrates are added to the system all at once and runs until product is harvested
(B) Nutrients are continuously fed into the reactor and the product is siphoned off during the run
(C) New batches of microorganisms are screened for increased yield
(D) Small-scale production is used to synthesize product

147. The technique first described to determine the incipient spoilage in meat was:
(A) Homogenate Extract Volume (HEV) (B) Agar Plate Count (APC)
(C) Extract Release Volume (ERV) (D) None of the above

148. Which of the following is responsible for a musty or earthy flavour?
(A) Actinomycetes
(B) Flavobacterium
(C) Both a and b
(D) Pseudomonas syncyanea

149. Molds causing spoilage of eggs include species of:
(A) *Cladosporium*
(B) *Mucor*
(C) *Thamnidium*
(D) All of these

150. Vacuum packaged meats are spoiled by:
(A) *B. thermosphacta*
(B) *Lactobacilli*
(C) Both *a* and *b*
(D) None of these

151. Which of the following pairs is not correctly matched?
(A) X-ray: Roentgen
(B) Radioactivity: Becquerel
(C) Microscope: Galileo
(D) Oxygen: Joseph Priestley

152. What is the correct sequence of Planets in terms of decreasing size?
(A) Saturn, Earth, Neptune, Mars
(B) Earth, Saturn, Mars, Neptune
(C) Earth, Mars, Saturn, Neptune
(D) Saturn, Neptune, Earth, Mars

153. Which of the following is incorrect about Nobel Prize 2014?
(A) The Prize in Physics was awarded for invention of efficient blue light emitting diodes
(B) The Prize in Medicine was given for discovery of cells constituting positioning system in brain
(C) Kailash Satyarthi became first Indian to receive Noble Peace Prize
(D) Malala Yousafjai became the youngest ever Noble Peace Prize winner

154. Which of the following is a Kharif crop?
(A) Tobacco
(B) Barley
(C) Potato
(D) Maize

155. Which of the following countries does not have Coastline?
(A) Zimbabwe
(B) Cambodia
(C) North Korea
(D) Finland

156. Name the first Vice President of India who was given Bharat Ratna:
(A) Sarvapalli Radhakrishnan
(B) Gyani Zail Singh
(C) Dr. Rajendra Prasad
(D) APJ Abdul Kalam

157. The maximum duration for which President of India's Office can remain vacant:
(A) 2 months
(B) 3 months
(C) 6 months
(D) It cannot remain vacant

158. Which of the following pair (National Park: State) is incorrect?

(A) Simlipal: Orissa (B) Nokrek: Meghalaya

(C) Tadoba: Maharashtra (D) Guindy: Karnataka

159. Which body part gets affected in Cirrhosis?

(A) Heart (B) Liver

(C) Kidney (D) Lungs

160. Which of the following teams did not play Semi Finals of inaugural edition of Hero Indian Super League?

(A) Kerala Blasters (B) Chennaiyin FC

(C) FC Goa (D) United North East

161. In Jainism 'Kaivalya' means:

(A) Perfect Knowledge (B) Meditation

(C) Nirvan (D) Ratna

162. Pulmonary artery originates from:

(A) Right ventricle (B) Right auricle

(C) Left auricle (D) Left ventricle

163. Which of the following means "by what authority"?

(A) Mandamus (B) Quo Warranto

(C) Certiorari (D) Habeas Corpus

164. Model Code of conduct comes into force during election from:

(A) Date of Notification

(B) Last date of filing nomination

(C) Date of announcement of election schedule by ECI

(D) Date of Nomination

165. Who was known as 'Little Corporal'?

(A) Bismark (B) Adolf Hitler

(C) Napolean Bonaparte (D) Lord Curzon

166. Which of the following states have only one representatives each in Lok Sabha?

(A) Nagaland, Mizoram (B) Goa, Nagaland

(C) Arunachal Pradesh, Tripura (D) Meghalaya, Mizoram

167. Beighton Cup is associated with:

(A) Badminton (B) Polo

(C) Kabaddi (D) Hockey

168. Average blood volume in a normal human being is:

(A) 5-6 litres (B) 3-4 litres

(C) 2-3 litres (D) 8-10 litres

169. Which of the following pairs is incorrect?

(A) Bora-Adriatic Sea (B) Mistral-Gulf of Lion

(C) Harmattan-Gulf of Guinea (D) Tocopherol

170. Which of the following pair (river: origin place) is incorrect?

(A) Chambal: Janapav (B) Son: Amarkantak

(C) Tapi: Multai (D) Godavari: Mahabaleshwar

171. What is the name of position in which Earth and Sun are nearest?

(A) Perihelion (B) Aphelion

(C) Apogee (D) Perigee

172. Who said that 'Education is the manifestation of perfection already in man'?

(A) Swami Vivekanand (B) Sri Aurobindo

(C) Ravindranath Tagore (D) Subhash Chandra Bose

173. INDICA was written by:

(A) Ban Bhatt (B) Kalidas

(C) Chanakya (D) Megasthenese

174. World's only floating National Park is located in:

(A) India (B) West Indies

(C) Malaysia (D) Australia

175. Jet Streams are:

(A) Wind System with a pronounced seasonal reverse in direction

(B) Winds blowing from subtropical High Pressure belts towards sub-polar low pressure belts

(C) Winds blowing from sub-polar low pressure belts towards subtropical High Pressure belts

(D) Narrow meandering bands of swift winds which blow in the mid latitudes near the tropopause and encircle the globe

176. What is the missing number in the series:
2,7,28,63,126,_____

(A) 215 (B) 245

(C) 276 (D) 296

177. A man starts walking from his house towards south. After walking 5 km, he turned to his left and walked 6 km. Then he walked further 5 km after turning left. Then he turned to his left and continued to walk for 9 km. How far is he from his house?

(A) 3 km (B) 4 km

(C) 5 km (D) 6 km

178. A man pointing to a lady said, "The son of her only brother is the brother of my wife". The lady is related to the man as:

(A) Mother-in-law (B) Grand Mother

(C) Mother's sister (D) Sister of Father-in-law

179. Which of the following country became first member of European Union to recognise the State of Palestine?

(A) Hungary (B) Sweden

(C) Poland (D) Iceland

180. The first border haat (market) facility on Indo-Bangladesh International border in Tripura was recently opened at:

(A) Sylhet-Chittagong border (B) Srinagar-Ramgarh border

(C) Khulna-Rajshahi border (D) Rangpur-Dhaka border

181. International 'Internet Day' is celebrated on:

(A) 27 August (B) 28 September

(C) 29 October (D) 30 November

182. Maya Rao who died recently was a renowned:

(A) Kathak dancer (B) Bihu dancer

(C) Odishi dancer (D) Kuchipudi dancer

183. The lifespan of Red Blood Cells (RBCs) is:

(A) 60 days (B) 120 days

(C) 180 days (D) 200 days

184. Biosensor is used to measure:

(A) Body pH (B) Blood Glucose level

(C) Haemoglobin (D) Salinity in urine

185. Which are primary colours?

(A) White, Black, Blue (B) Red, Yellow, Orange

(C) Red, White, Green (D) Red, Green, Blue

186. The percentage (%) of Carbon in atmosphere, by volume, is:

(A) 0.03 (B) 3

(C) 13 (D) 21

187. Which organization releases 'World Investment Report' every year?

(A) UNCTAD (B) WTO

(C) IMF (D) World Bank

188. Right to Property, according to Indian Constitution is a:
(A) Legal Right (B) Social Right
(C) Fundamental Right (D) Statutory Right

189. The book 'Planning and the Poor' was authored by:
(A) Gunnar Myrdal (B) Amartya Sen
(C) David Ricardo (D) B.S. Minhas

190. Which of the following pair (Country: Capital) is incorrect?
(A) Cambodia: Vientin (B) Philippines: Manila
(C) Syria: Damascus (D) Estonia: Tallin

191. Total number of High Courts in India is:
(A) 20 (B) 22
(C) 24 (D) 25

192. Which one of the following is the correct chronological order in which the Grand Slam Tennis Tournaments are held every year?
(A) US Open-French Open-Australian Open-Wimbledon
(B) Australian Open-French Open-Wimbledon-US Open
(C) French Open-Australian Open-US Open-Wimbledon
(D) Wimbledon-French Open-US Open-Australian Open

193. Which article of the Indian Constitution relates to "Right to Education"?
(A) Article 45 (B) Article 26A
(C) Article 21 (D) Article 15

194. When was Manipuri language added to 8th Schedule of Indian Constitution?
(A) 1992 (B) 1998
(C) 2001 (D) 2004

195. Which of the following pairs is not correctly matched in respect of Manipur?
(A) Nongeen: State bird (B) Pengba: State fish
(C) Sangai: State animal (D) Orchid: State flower

196. The components of Human Development Index are:
(A) Life Expectancy, Per Capita GDP and Sex Ratio
(B) Sex Ratio, Educational Attainment and Pure Drinking Water
(C) Life Expectancy, Per Capita GDP and Educational Attainment
(D) Per Capita GDP, Sex Ratio and Infrastructure

197. What is Potlei?

(A) A transparent and thin veil thrown over the head

(B) Ras costume of Sri Radhika and the Gopis

(C) Golden ring round the head

(D) An Embroidered brightly coloured silk skirt

198. 21st Commonwealth Games in 2022 will be hosted by:

(A) Australia (B) South Africa

(C) Cameroon (D) England

199. Irang, Maku and Tuivai are important tributaries of:

(A) Barak river (B) Imphal river

(C) Yu river (D) Chakpi river

200. Thabal Chongba is integral part of which festival?

(A) Yaoshang (B) Ningol Chakouba

(C) Heikru Hidongba (D) Cheiraoba

Food Analysis and Testing

1. Ion exchange chromatography is used for________
   a. Vitamin analysis
   b. Pesticide analysis
   c. Air & water pollution analysis
   d. Organic acid analysis
2. At present, the primary use for a mass spectrometer by the food analyst is as a
   a. Detector for GC
   b. Detector for HPLC
   c. Detector for paper chromatography
   d. Detector for NMR
3. Electrophoric mobility of molecule is defined as
   a. Migration of molecule per unit time
   b. Migration of molecule per unit area of membrane
   c. Migration of molecule per unit polarity of solute
   d. Migration of molecule per unit field strength
4. Beer's and Lamberts laws are principle law in the following
   a. Dialysis
   b. Spectrophotometry
   c. Polarimeter
   d. Bomb calorimeter
5. Why is it important to avoid air bubbles in the column during chromatography?
   a. The air in the bubbles might react with the compounds being separated
   b. Bubbles cause the samples to travel unevenly down the column and thus the components might not separate
   c. Bubbles may destroy the column
   d. Both b and c
6. Radioactivity of substance is determined by
   a. Isoelectric pH
   b. Conductivity method
   c. Isotopic method
   d. None of the above
7. Which of these effects results from slow injection of a large sample volume?
   a. Increased resolution
   b. Non-linear detector response
   c. Decreased resolution
   d. None of the above
8. Syringe pump, in HPLC, is a type of
   a. Reciprocating pump
   b. Gradient pump
   c. Positive displacement pump
   d. None of the above
9. Which of the following is an HPLC detector
   a. UV absorption detector
   b. Teflon Detector
   c. RI detector
   d. Both a and b
10. Which of the following is NOT the detector for GC
    a. FID
    b. RID
    c. ECD
    d. TCD

11. What does the selectivity factor describe?
    a. The proportional difference in widths of two chromatographic peaks
    b. The maximum number of different species which a column can separate simultaneously
    c. The relative separation achieved between two species
    d. Both a and b
12. Which of the following relationships between absorbance and %Transmittance is INCORRECT?
    a. A = 2 - log10 %T
    b. A = log10 100 / %T
    c. A = 1 - log10 1 / %T
    d. A = log10 1 / %T
13. Rutter technique is
    a. Horizontal chromatography
    b. Two dimensional chromatography
    c. Thin Layer Chromatography
    d. None of the above
14. In HPLC, isocratic elution occurs when solvent is __________ throughout entire separation process
    a. Kept constant
    b. Kept decreasing
    c. Kept increasing
    d. None of these
15. In preparative electrophoresis, thick slabs of buffer soaked into an appropriate medium is
    a. Horizontal
    b. Vertical
    c. Cross sectional
    d. None of these
16. __________ filter is recommended in HPLC for organic solvents
    a. Micorporons
    b. Cellulose acetate
    c. Pellicular
    d. Teflon
17. Gas Chromatography is used to analyse following substances
    a. Volatile
    b. Sugars
    c. Organic acid
    d. None of the above
18. The point at which three phases solid, liquid and gas coexists is________
    a. Critical point
    b. Triple point
    c. Freezing point
    d. Boiling point
19. In spectrophotometer, A compound with high molar absorptivity
    a. Have a higher limit of detection than a compound with low molar absorptivity
    b. Have a lower limit of detection than a compound with low molar absorptivity
    c. Have a constant limit of detection than a compound with low molar absorptivity
    d. None of the above
20. Texture profile analysis is determined by________
    a. Hakke's Viscometer
    b. Tintometer
    c. Texturometer
    d. Brookfield viscometer
21. Technique of separation of leaf pigment was first used by
    a. Russian Botanist
    b. Martin
    c. John Smith
    d. Fedrick

22. Incase of HPLC mobile phase is
a. He b. H_2
c. Organic solvent d. Air

23. Dialysis used to separate macromolecule from micro molecule
a. On the basis of size b. On the basis of molecular weight
c. On the basis of concentration d. Both a and b

24. Application of ion exchange chromatography
a. Toxilogy b. Air and water pollution analysis
c. Industrial hygiene d. All of the above

25. Relative movement of protein through polyacrylamide gel do not depend upon
a. Size b. Charge
c. Polarity d. Mol. Weight

26. Which of the following method can be used for hydrolysis of peptide for determination of total amino acid in milk
a. Acid hydrolysis b. Enzymic hydrolysis
c. Alkaline hydrolysis d. All of the above

27. Proteins show greatest absorbance at
a. 480nm b. 240nm
c. 360nm d. 280nm

28. Electropheric mobility of molecule is defined as
a. Migration of molecule per unit time
b. Migration of molecule per unit polarity of solute
c. Migration of molecule per unit field strength
d. Migration of molecule per unit area of membrane

29. Isotopic method of analysis is based on
a. Polarity of substance b. Conductivity of substance
c. Isoelectric pH of substance d. Radioactivity of substance

30. Volatile substances can be separated using
a. HPLC b. TLC
c. Gel electrophoresis d. GC

31. Which of the following supporting medium has advantage of transparency
a. Agar gel b. Silica
c. PAGE d. Cellulose acetate

32. A molecule when absorbs energy
a. Vibrates faster b. Vibrates with positive acceleration
c. Vibrates with greater amplitude d. None of the above

33. The energy associated with visible and ultaviolet regions are
a. 40-400 Kcal/mole b. 40-440 Kcal/mole
c. 30-350 Kcal/mole d. 40-140 Kcal/mole

34. Best %T of a solution that obeys Beer's law for most accurate reading
a. 39.5% b. 29.5%
c. 30.5% d. 39.7%

35. If the light through entire visible spectrum is absorbed in part, the object appears to be
a. White b. Black
c. Grey d. Opaque

36. Isoelectric focusing is a type of
a. Electrophoresis b. Ultrafiltration
c. Dialysis d. None of these

37. GPC means
a. Gas Phase Chromatography b. Gold phase Chromatography
c. Gel Permeation Chromatography d. Gas Permeation Chromatography

38. Why is it important to avoid air bubbles in the column during chromatography?
a. the air in the bubbles might react with the compounds being separated
b. bubbles may destroy the column
c. bubbles cause the samples to travel unevenly down the column and thus the components might not separate
d. Both b and c

39. A column chromatography procedure for the separation of a polar and a non-polar compound calls for sequential elution with the following two solvents: methylene chloride and hexanes Which solvent should be used first?
a. methylene chloride b. It does not matter which solvent is used first
c. Hexanes d. None of these

40. The point at which both liquid and gas phase coexist is
a. Critical point b. Triple point
c. Freezing point d. Boiling point

41. Which type of column has the greater efficiency and resolution
a. Packed b. Both have the same
c. Capillary d. None of the above

42. The response from a Flame Ionization Detector is
a. Affected by changes in mobile phase flow rate
b. Affected or not affected depending upon the sample
c. Not affected by changes in mobile phase flow rate
d. None of the above

43. Which of these effects results from slow injection of a large sample volume?
a. Increased resolution b. Decreased resolution
c. Non-linear detector response d. None of the above

44. Phenomenon occurring to ampholytes in a pH gradient influenced by an electric field is
a. Electrofocusing
b. Disc electrofocusing
c. Isoelectric focusing
d. Both a and b

45. Coulometric titrations are based on
a. Ohm's law
b. Coulson's law
c. Faraday's law
d. Cann's law

46. In preparative electrophoresis, thick slabs of buffer soaked into an appropriate medium is
a. Horizontal
b. Cross sectional
c. Vertical
d. None of These

47. Major component(s) of mass spectrometer is/are
a. Ion source
b. Detector
c. Analyzer
d. All of the above

48. At present, the primary use for a mass spectrometer by the food analyst is as a
a. Detector for HPLC
b. Detector for paper chromatography
c. Detector for GC
d. Detector for NMR

49. Which of the following is the basic unit(s) of NMR spectrometer
a. Magnet
b. Rf detector
c. Rf oscillator
d. All of above

50. _______ fields, all at right angles to each other are required for NMR
a. 2 fields
b. 4 fields
c. 3 fields
d. None of the above

51. Physical principle in thin layer chromatography is
a. Adsorption
b. Gel permeation
c. Partition
d. Ion exchange

52. Rf value is
a. Distance of solvent movement Distance of solute movement
b. Distance of solvent movement Standard reference of solvent movement
c. Distance of solute movement Distance of solvent movement
d. Distance of solute movement Standard reference of solute movement

53. HPLC stands for
a. High Performance Liquid Chromatography
b. High Pressure Liquid Chromatography
c. High Paper Liquid Chromatography
d. Both a and b

54. _____ filter is recommended in HPLC for organic solvents
a. Micorporons
b. Pellicular
c. Cellulose acetate
d. Teflon

55. Syringe pump, in HPLC, is a type of
a. Reciprocating pump
b. Gradient pump
c. Positive displacement pump
d. None of the above

56. In HPLC, isocratic elution occurs when solvent is __________ throughout entire separation process

a. Kept constant b. Kept increasing

c. Kept decreasing d. None of these

57. Particles type of HPLC column packaging is

a. None porous b. Macroporous

c. Circular d. Fully porous

58. Which of the following is an HPLC detector

a. UV absorption detector b. RI detector

c. Teflon Detector d. Both a and b

59. Which of the following is NOT the type of liquid chromatography

a. Liquid – Solid chromatography b. Gel permeation chromatography

c. Paired ion chromatography d. None of the above

60. Ligands are used in

a. High Performance Liquid Chromatography b. Gel Filtration

c. Ion Exchange chromatography d. Affinity chromatography

61. ______ is associated with the amount of flour produced per unitweight of wheat

a. Weight b. Hectolitre weight

c. Density d. Virtuosity

Hectolitre weight (or weight per unit volume) is the weight of 100 litres of wheat and is the simplest criteria of wheat quality. It gives us a rough index of flour yield.

62. Which of these regulators are not permitted for use in foods by FSSAI

a. Malic acid b. Citric acid

c. Succinic acid d. Lactic acid

63. If you are asked by FSO to indicate whether the sample is Khandsari Sugar (Sulphur Sugar) Khandsari sugar (desi), which method you will use

a. Sulphated ash estimation b. Conductivity method

c. LC-MS/MS d. ICP-MS

64. Analysis of the proline content of honey is a measure of its

a. Ripeness b. Shelf life stability

c. Added Sugar d. None of above

65. Test used to detect insect infestation in cereals and their products is

a. Peroxidase test b. Barfoed's test

c. Uric acid test d. Baudouin test

Bolder grains such as: Wheat/Maize/Barley/Whole pulses: 50 gm

Smaller grains such as: Rice/Split pulses/millets: 20gm

66. The extent to which an instrument replicates its result when measurements are taken repeatedly on the same unit is called;

a. Real bias b. Precision

c. Accuracy d. True value

67. The CAS registery number of a chemical is
    a. a rating of toxicity
    b. a unique identifying number for each chemical
    c. a rating of flammability
    d. None of the above
68. The quality standard for the laboratory accrediting body in India National Accreditation Board for testing and calibration NEW DELHI is;
    a. ISO 9001
    b. ISO 15189
    c. ISO 17011
    d. None of these
69. Which of the following test is a quick test for sugar content during the early stages of the brewing process for beer
    a. Hydrometry
    b. Babcock test
    c. Wet ashing
    d. Soxhlet extraction
70. A 3000 mg sodium diet has approximately how many meq of sodium?
    a. 69
    b. 77
    c. 117
    d. 130
71. Solometer (hydrometer) is used to test
    a. Brine solution
    b. Citric acid
    c. Juices
    d. All of these
72. Tintometer is used to find in liquid and solution
    a. Colour
    b. Texture
    c. Flavour
    d. All of these

ANSWER KEY

Q. No.	Ans.	Q. No.	Ans.	Q. No.	Ans.	Q. No.	Ans.	Q. No.	Ans.	Q. No.	Ans.
1	c	13	b	25	c	37	c	49	d	61.	b
2	a	14	a	26	d	38	c	50	c	62.	c
3	d	15	a	27	d	39	d	51	c	63.	b
4	d	16	d	28	c	40	d	52	c	64.	a
5	b	17	a	29	d	41	c	53	d	65.	c
6	a	18	b	30	d	42	c	54	c	66.	b
7	c	19	b	31	c	43	b	55	c	67.	b
8	c	20	c	32	b	44	c	56	a	68.	b
9	d	21	a	33	c	45	c	57	d	69.	a
10	b	22	a	34	d	46	a	58	d	70.	d
11	c	23	d	35	c	47	d	59	d	71.	a
12	d	24	d	36	a	48	c	60	d	72.	a)

Additional Notes

Awareness Initiatives Promoting Food Safety & Healthy Eating Practices

FSSAI (Food Safety and Standards Authority of India) has several awareness initiatives aimed at promoting food safety and healthy eating practices.

Eat Right India: This comprehensive program promotes healthy eating habits and safe food practices, encompassing initiatives like "Eat Right Mela" and "Eat Right Creativity Challenges," Zolvit says.

Clean Street Food: This initiative focuses on improving hygiene and sanitation standards in street food areas, including training for vendors and raising awareness about food safety regulations, FSSAI says.

Food Safety on Wheels: These mobile units conduct food safety testing and offer training and certification programs for food handlers and supervisors, particularly in small food businesses.

Reduce Sugar, Salt, and Trans-Fats: FSSAI campaigns like **"Aaj Se Thoda Kam"** and "Trans-Fat Free India@75" aim to reduce the intake of these harmful ingredients in food launched in 2018.

Food Fortification: FSSAI promotes the fortification of food with micronutrients to address deficiencies across the country, Eat Right India says.

Save Food, Share Food, Share Joy: This initiative promotes food donation and reduces food waste, connecting food-producing and collecting agencies.

Awareness Materials: FSSAI has created various awareness materials, including the Pink Book for home kitchens, DART Book for adulterant tests, and the Yellow Book for school children.

Project Dhoop: This initiative focuses on promoting noon assemblies in schools to address vitamin D deficiencies in children.

NetPro.FaN: FSSAI is establishing a Network of Professionals of Food & Nutrition in India (NetPro.FaN) to promote safe and healthy diets.

Food Safety Magic Box: This educational toolkit is designed for school students, teachers, and parents, and contains easy-to-use tests for detecting food adulteration through an interactive and engaging way for students to learn about food safety.

Food Safety Guidebook for Teachers/Students: The lesson plan booklet provides detailed information on how to conduct the different tests on food adulteration. These tests are mapped across the curriculum of upgrade value.

---

1. FoSTaC: Food Safety Training and Certification for Food Business Operators across the food value chain

FSSAI (Food Safety and Standards Authority of India) has made the following 2 trainings mandatory for Food Handlers

Food Safety Supervisor: For every 25 food handlers or less, there should be 1 Food Safety Supervisor [FSSAI] trained under the Food Safety Training and Certification [FoSTaC]. FSSA offer 2 types of FSSAI training:- 1. Advance Manufacturing, 2. Advance Catering

COVID-19 Pandemic: Training: Every Food handler needs to undergo this awareness training to understand the extra precautions to be taken during the COVID.

2. FSKAN (Food safety Knowledge Assimilation Network): About FSKAN: A system of network of organizations with the aim to facilitate a scientific co-operation framework by the co-ordination of activities, the exchange of information, the development and implementation of joint projects within the Food Authority's responsibility FSSAI has established Food Safety Knowledge Assimilation Network (FSKAN).

3. ITCFSAN: International Training Centre for Food Safety and Applied Nutrition (Ministry of Commerce and World Bank) in partnership with FSSAI imparting training programme in India

4. RUCO: Repurpose used cooking during frying, several properties of oil are altered, Total Polar Compounds(TPC) are formed on repeated frying. The toxicity of these compounds is associated with several diseases such as hypertension, atherosclerosis, Alzheimer's disease, liver diseases. Therefore, it is essential to monitor the quality of vegetable oils during frying. In order to safeguard consumer health, FSSAI has fixed a limit for Total Polar Compounds at 25 percent beyond which the vegetable oil shall not be used. From 1st July, 2018 onwards, all Food Business Operators (FBOs) are required to monitor the quality of oil during frying by complying with the said regulations. FSSAI is implementing an EEE Strategy (Education, Enforcement and Environment) - to divert Used Cooking Oil from the food value chain and curb current illegal practices. The EEE Strategy approach ensures good health and welfare for all 130-crore citizens, aiding energy security, climate change mitigation, and leading to environmentally sustainable development.

5. Dart Book Detect Adulteration with Rapid Test (DART) booklet is a compilation of common quick tests for detection of food adulterants at household by the citizens themselves so as to induce awareness among the consumers about food safety.

Orange book (FSSAI). 'The Orange Book' 'Safe and Nutritious Food at Workplace' is a nation-wide campaign to help people eat safe and eat right while at work. With the rising incidence of diet-related diseases. This initiative, therefore, educates people on safe and healthy diets.

6. Yellow Book: It guide to safe and nutritious food at school, that provides age appropriate content which can be adapted across school through state education ministry.

7. Pink book: The book has nine sections namely, buying food, storing food, preparing and cooking food, serving food, eating healthy food, managing leftover food, packaging food, maintaining hygiene & sanitation in the kitchen and managing waste. It provides useful tips, dos and don'ts, methods and practices that are recommended for Indian kitchens

8. GAMA (Grievances Against Misleading Advertisements): The Department of Consumer Affairs (DoCA) is one of the two Departments under the Ministry of Consumer Affairs, Food & Public Distribution. The mandate of the Department is consumer advocacy. In its endeavour to address the problem of misleading advertisements, the Department of Consumer Affairs has launched this portal for registering online complaints for Grievances Against Misleading Advertisements.

9. FoSCoRIS (Food Safety Compliance through Regular Inspections and Sampling) FSSAI is coming up with an online Food Safety Compliance through Regular Inspections and Sampling (FoSCoRIS) mobile app. The App will capture onsite inspection carried out by FSOs as per the inspection checklist.

FoSCoRIS will require a mobile/tablet with net connectivity. Many States/UTs already have their own Closed User Groups (CUGs) and provide hand held devices to Food Safety Officers for enforcement/surveillance© 2017 FSSAI - All Rights Reserved. Website Maintained by FSSAI.

10. FoSCOS (Food Safety Compliance System): Wef from 1st Nov. 2020 to replace existing food licensing and registration system. Users of ICRS are now required to visit https://foscos.fssai.gov.in

11. Food Safety Connect is the Food Safety and Standards Authority of India (FSSAI) initiative to enable citizens to share their concerns regarding food safety violations.